Stolen From Our Embrace

The Abduction of First Nations Children and
the Restoration of Aboriginal Communities

Suzanne Fournier and Ernie Crey

Photographs by David Neel

Douglas & McIntyre
Vancouver/Toronto

First paperback printing 1998

99 00 01 02 5 4 3 2

Douglas & McIntyre Ltd.
2323 Quebec Street, Suite 201
Vancouver, British Columbia
V5T 4S7

Canadian Cataloguing in Publication Data

Fournier, Suzanne, 1952–
  Stolen from our embrace

ISBN 1-55054-661-9

  1. Indians of North America—Cultural assimilation. 2. Off-reservation boarding schools. 3. Indians of North America—Biography. I. Crey, Ernie, 1949- II. Title.
E78B9F68 1997   971.1'00497   C97-910395-9

Editing by Barbara Pulling
Front cover design by Peggy Heath
Front cover illustration: *Ermineskin Residential School* by George Littlechild
Text design and composition by George Kirkpatrick
Photographs by David Neel
Printed and bound in Canada by Friesens
Printed on acid-free paper ∞

The publisher gratefully acknowledges the support of the Canada Council for the Arts and of the British Columbia Ministry of Tourism, Small Business and Culture. The publisher also acknowledges the financial support of the government of Canada through the Book Publishing Industry Development Program.

*For my family: my husband, Art, and
our children, Naomi and Zev.*

§∞ SUZANNE FOURNIER

*For my children, Saul, Naomi, Karrmen,
Aaron and Amber, and for my brothers and sisters.
Also for my friend Sarah.*

§∞ ERNIE CREY

CONTENTS

THE STORY OF TH'ÓWXEYA, MOSQUITO WOMAN

As told by Shoyshqelwhet, Gwendolyn Point

In the old days, the children were always told: when the sun starts to
go down, make sure you go home, because this old lady will come
with a great big basket on her back. She'll come and get you.
Th'ówxeya, they call her. Once, a long time ago, there were these
children playing out on the beach, dipping in and out of the water
all day. Finally they fell asleep on the sand, and when they woke up it
was almost dark. As the children sat and rubbed their tired eyes, they
could see the old lady walking towards them, and on her back was
the big basket they had heard about so many times. As quick as light-
ning, the old lady grabbed each child and put him in the basket on
her back.

The children sat huddled in the dark basket, and the littlest ones
began to whimper. Now, the first child she had picked up had been
playing with a clam shell on the beach and still had it in his hand.

He began to scrape the bottom of the basket with the sharp edge of the shell. It seemed to take forever, but at last there was a large hole in the bottom of the basket, and this child fell out.

The old lady heard the noise when the child dropped to the ground, and she called out, "*Kwómxwem?* What's that noise?" But she kept going, packing the children up the mountain. It wasn't long before another child dropped out. The old lady called out again, "*Kwómxwem Kwethá.* That noise again." One by one, four of the children dropped out of the basket.

Now, one of the kids that the old lady had picked up was a little boy with a hunched back. He was next, but he couldn't go through the hole because of his back. So he and the others who were piled on top of him had to stay in the old woman's basket.

Finally Th'ówxeya arrived at her home way up on the mountain. She took the children out of her basket and said, "*El'emímeth*, my grandchildren, you sit down there." This old lady always called the children she stole her grandchildren. Th'ówxeya picked up a big pole and some sticks and laid them in front of the children. She said, "You children are going to drum for me when I sing."

Then the old lady went out and got a branch with sticky pitch from a spruce tree and began to melt it over her fire. The oldest boy guessed why she was melting this pitch. He turned and whispered to the child next to him, "She puts the pitch on the children's eyes to glue them shut. So, when she comes, close your eyes real tight, and as soon as she lets you go, keep moving your eyelids. Then the pitch won't glue your eyelids together. Pass it on to the others." Th'ówxeya heard them. "*Chap xwe'í:t, a'am'ímeth?* What are you saying, grandchildren?" "Oh," said the biggest child, "I was just telling the children that when our grandmother starts dancing to make sure that they drum real hard with their sticks." "Ō, Ō, Ō, Ō, *a'am'ímeth*," said the old lady. "All right, my grandchildren."

Now Th'ów̱xeya had finished melting the pitch, and she came over to the children. The smaller ones forgot to keep moving their eyelids so that the pitch wouldn't glue them together. But a few of the older children remembered. Th'ów̱xeya called to them, "I'm going to dance now. When I get through I'm going to feed you kids." Now the biggest child knew Th'ów̱xeya was planning to cook the children over the fire and eat them. He saw the chance for the children to escape. He whispered to the one next to him, telling him to pass the word along. "When she dances in front of us, facing the bonfire, I'm going to shove her in the fire and I want you kids to help me." Th'ów̱xeya frowned. "*Chap yalh xwe'i:t, a'am'ímeth?* What are you talking about now, my grandchildren?" she asked. "Oh," the boy said, "I was just telling these children to make sure they sing and drum good when you start dancing." "Ō, Ō, Ō, Ō," she said. Th'ów̱xeya started to dance and sing. Just when she happened to be facing the fire, the oldest child shoved her right into the flames. The next two oldest helped him.

Well, of course, the old lady hollered when she was pushed into the fire. "*Lham thoxá a'a'mímeth, lham thóx:òx, a'am'ímeth!* Pull me out of the fire, my grandchildren!" she pleaded. "We are," said the oldest child, all the while pushing her further into the fire.

So the old lady started to burn, and instead of smoke coming out of the fire, mosquitoes came swarming out. And ever since, that's why mosquitoes sing in your ears, you know, because that old lady was singing when the children pushed her into the fire.

Now the children were free. They didn't know where they were going and they didn't know where they had come from, but they started out down the mountain, trying to find their way home. Although some of the little ones' eyes were still glued together, they followed the others the best they could. The children held on to one another as they crept through the dark brush. When the children heard a sound of "Whoooo, whooooo," they stopped, too scared to move. The oldest boy said, "Oh, maybe it's a sasquatch." They heard it again. The biggest boy said, "I'm going to climb that big cedar tree and see if I can find out what's making that noise." So he did.

Lights were flashing in the distance, and the boy knew that it was the people looking for the lost children with lanterns made from dried sockeye heads. Well, when the boy saw the lights, he began to holler. He hollered and hollered. Finally, the fathers hollered back, and the boy came down from the tree. So they waited there, and finally their fathers came. "*Ikw'eló*. Over here," the children called when they saw the lights.

When the children were home at last, they told their parents what had happened to them. Their parents got some melted bear grease and put it on the little ones' eyes. The grease softened the pitch and the children's eyelids came unglued. But that wasn't all that had to be done. The parents asked a special spiritual healer to come and work on all the children who had been stolen by the Th'ówx̱eya. The spiritual healer used his power to make sure the children wouldn't get sick from their experience.

The Sto:lo story of Th'ów<u>x</u>eya belonged to Dolly Felix. Born in
1897 to Sophie and James Johnson on a homestead at the mouth of
B.C.'s Harrison River, Dolly Felix was married in 1923 to Richard
Joe and moved to his home on the Chehalis reserve, where the
couple raised twelve children, sixty-two grandchildren and thirty-five
great-grandchildren. Dolly Felix worked for the Native Indian
Brotherhood, was an avid musician, and, all of her long life, kept alive
the Halq'emeylem language of her Sto:lo people by teaching it at
home and in schools. When she died in 1981, Dolly passed the
Th'ów<u>x</u>eya legend, which she had published in a small book for use
in an elementary school curriculum, to her granddaughter
Gwendolyn Point and the Felix Joe family.

We would like to thank Gwendolyn Point and the extended
family of Dolly Felix for permission to use the tale of Th'ów<u>x</u>eya,
Mosquito Woman.

INTRODUCTION

Suzanne Fournier

THE legend of Th'ówxeya is a traditional Sto:lo tale told by parents to frighten their children into coming home before dark. Mosquito Woman, the stalking sly thief of children, is every parent's nightmare. She is a *stl'alequem*, one of the supernatural beings who inhabit the dense rainforests and steep mountainsides of British Columbia's Fraser River Valley where the Sto:lo, People of the River, have lived since time immemorial. Similar cannibal figures exist in the cosmologies of First Nations all across North America.

"I remember my grandmother Dolly would tell all us kids, 'You older ones watch out for the little ones. When it gets to be dark, you go inside and don't leave the little ones behind, because Th'ówxeya, she will come and steal them away,'" says Sto:lo Education Manager Gwendolyn Point. As a child, Point shivered at the notion of a wild crone who could spirit away babies or her little brothers and sisters. Today, she sees the legend as a metaphor: the cannibal woman represents the predatory European society that swept into long-held First Nations territory to steal land, culture, souls and children. "Ever since the Europeans first came, our children were stolen from our embrace," says Point. "First the priests took our children away, to churches, schools, even back to Europe. Then the residential schools took three or four generations away; then the social workers took our children and put them in non-native foster homes."

Almost every First Nation in the Americas had prophecies of the coming of a new people in numbers so great they would threaten the very existence of the original peoples. When the strangers did arrive, they brought prosperity, but also alcohol, disease, poverty and famine. Some were greedy traders and soul-stealers, long black robes who would take children captive. The cannibal woman snatched children away for four, five, six generations: residential schools, tuberculosis hospitals, foster homes. The children were rocked helplessly back and forth in Th'ówxeya's dark basket.

But the story of Th'ówxeya also teaches resistance and self-reliance. Strong and wily children escaped her clutches. "The oldest boy could have run away in my grandmother's story and saved himself, but no, he wanted to save the other children," says Gwendolyn Point. "He told the other children not to allow Th'ówxeya to seal their eyes with pitch. He knew they were in terrible danger, that she would gobble them right up until there were no more aboriginal children left at all."

In the traditional tale, Th'ówxeya is finally vanquished when the children push her into the fire. As she burns, she is transformed from a fierce cannibal into a swarm of mosquitoes, small whining beings that bite and annoy but have no real power. "Social workers and churches will never swallow up our children again," says Point. "The priests and social workers who preyed on our parents, grandparents, our great-grandparents, have burst into pieces just like Th'ówxeya. Our children will triumph in the end. Some are still lost to us. They are still trying to find their way home, though they don't know where they came from or where they're going."

In the story, Th'ówxeya's escaped captives are taken to a spiritual healer when they return. "It has only been a few hundred years, four or five generations, since our children were stolen away, and now they're coming home: to the longhouse, to winter dances, to the sweat-lodges, to the big drum and the powwows—to heal," Point says. "We tell our children, you have to live in the modern world. Non-native people are not going to go away, but don't let them seal your eyes. You are different. You are Sto:lo. Look people in the eye and stand up straight when you are out in the world. But when you come home, cast down your eyes and show respect for your elders. And in the evening, when the mosquitoes are the thickest, when you can hear that whine of the Th'ówx̲eya singing, come back to your people because you never know, there can always be another Th'ówx̲eya out there. But remember, the children transformed Th'ówx̲eya into nothing but a cloud of mosquitoes. Mosquitoes we can handle."

As a journalist, I have worked with and written about aboriginal people for more than twenty years. In the late 1980s, while working on a series of newspaper stories on the "lost generation" of aboriginal children taken into state care, I interviewed Ernie Crey, then vice-president of the United Native Nations, an urban aboriginal organization. Ernie told me how, every day, aboriginal adolescents cast off from indifferent foster care or failed adoptions flocked into the UNN offices, seeking federal Indian status, their names, their birth families and their identities. It seemed there were enough missing aboriginal children to populate a small city. He told me how his own Sto:lo family had been split apart after the death of his father, when Ernie was twelve. Social workers had neither time to console his grieving mother nor money to provide her with a homemaker or counselling, resources that likely would have been available to a non-native woman in similar straits. Instead, workers stepped in to apprehend Ernie and five of his younger siblings, splitting them up into non-native foster homes scattered throughout the Fraser Valley. Ernie and his brothers and sisters would never reunite as a family or even be in the same room together again. I wrote about Ernie Crey's family, as had other journalists before me, but the devastation that resulted from the splintering of a Sto:lo family stayed with me. The flawed federal Indian policies that had led to the prolonged "Sixties' Scoop" were well known to me as an objective outsider; now I saw close up the damage done to the generations of people who narrowly escaped residential schools only to wind up in foster homes. I began to understand what Ernie meant by saying, "Mine is the first generation of aboriginal people to have the right before the law to parent our own children." In some instances the government of Canada may have meant well; in others it deliberately set out to fundamentally restructure aboriginal society. In either case, terrible harm was inflicted on the most helpless and vulnerable members of society. "The story of aboriginal children has never been told," Ernie said to me. It was a fascinating challenge. Together, we set out to tell the complex, many-faceted stories of what it has meant to grow up aboriginal since the advent of widespread European settlement in North America.

It has been a lengthy journey of learning and discovery for both of us. For me, it began in the community hall of the small Secwepemc community of Alkali Lake in February 1991. I had travelled to Williams Lake, in B.C.'s Cariboo region, to cover for the Vancouver *Province* the trial of Oblate Brother Glen Doughty, accused of sexually abusing several aboriginal boys in the 1960s and 1970s at St. Joseph's Indian Mission School. When Brother Doughty pleaded guilty, the trial was cancelled. But I was invited instead to attend a week-long healing workshop at Alkali Lake, a "Flying on Your Own" course led by Secwepemc pipe carrier Margaret Gilbert of the Sugarcane band. I knew about the well-documented journey of the people of Alkali Lake from alcoholism to sobriety, and I was interested in understanding how their workshops, which blended techniques from the contemporary human potential movement with traditional healing methods, had begun to uncover and heal the sexual and physical abuse that lay at the centre of aboriginal peoples' torment.

Phyllis Chelsea, then Alkali Lake's social services director, smiled at my plans to sit quietly at the back of the room and take notes about what transpired in proper journalistic fashion. "We've had judges, lawyers, police officers, media, Indian people from all over the world come here for our workshop," Chelsea assured me. "But you won't learn anything if you don't participate."

She was right. Thus began my immersion in a powerful healing workshop in which all the other participants were aboriginal except for a Catholic priest. My personal issues could not be isolated. The workshop stirred up all my own issues of identity: the denial of aboriginal ancestry in our family, as well as the sexual abuse, poverty and alcoholism that were part of my life when I was growing up. At least some of the responsibility for this I laid at the door of the Catholic Church. My father had attended a Quebec residential school run by Jesuit priests, which had left him with a lifelong love-hate relationship with the church. "Give me a boy before the age of eight and he is ours for life," my father used to quote the Jesuit priests as saying, and I felt sure that in that Jesuit school, or in the church where he was an altar boy, my father had been abused in ways that he could only allude to and never managed to fully resolve.

At Alkali Lake, sharing with aboriginal people from the north, the Prairies and all over B.C., I could feel not only the raw pain that people experienced but also the profound healing to which they had access, combining the cathartic process with the calming, strengthening spirituality found in the sweatlodge, in smudging with sage and at the start of each day in sharing stories with an eagle feather or talking stone in hand. In reporting the stories of First Nations peoples' lives, I've often been asked, and have wondered myself, how people can carry on in the face of such pain. Experiencing even a small part of the deep spiritual regeneration and comfort that exists in aboriginal communities has helped me to understand that—with the resources and restitution that are abundantly due to them—First Nations are infinitely capable of helping their own people to recover, and of restoring their communities to their historical power and strength.

All my life, my family has had a strong connection to the land, raised as we were in the rural foothills of Alberta without electricity or running water at a time when even the most modest homes in the town where we attended school were thoroughly modernized. Although we were poor in a material sense, it was something of which I was quite unaware until I went to school. Both my parents were intellectuals who read widely. I was raised with books and ideas; I can't ever remember not knowing how to read. We lived an idyllic life most of the year, running free along the river where our land lay. The land was my real home, where I went for comfort and to feel happy or safe. When we asked for things that our friends at school took for granted, like a telephone, a T.V. or teen-age fashions, my father would offer us a choice: we could have those things if we exchanged our land in the country for a town bungalow with a tiny strip of lawn. For us, it was no choice at all. Without our land, we felt we would die.

In high school, it was the Stoney Nakoda children from the nearby Morley reserve with whom my sister and I felt most comfortable; we preferred aboriginal children as friends. One of my sisters has lived much of her adult life in aboriginal communities; when she adopted a full-blooded Cree infant and then moved onto the Stoney Nakoda reserve at Morley, some family members expressed strong dismay. It was a subject none of us could discuss with our father, who often expressed disparaging views of "Indians," but all of us knew, deep down, that a significant part of his bloodline was aboriginal. As children, when we were asked, "Where do you get your dark eyes and hair?" we would respond that we were French-Canadian. I used to joke that I was the perfect Canadian: half-English and half-French, the two sides at war. Like many Canadians, I have also come to acknowledge that a significant part of my ancestry is aboriginal. My father's family resided in Quebec for seven generations. Like many Québécois, his family had intermarried with aboriginal people for generations, a fact he deliberately obscured for his own complex personal reasons. The parish south of the St. Lawrence River where he was born to parents who ran a small dairy farm was made up of "white" farmers interspersed—and intermarried—with Six Nations people: Mohawk, Huron, Onondaga. It had been that way since the seventeenth century.

When my eldest sister remarked recently that she always knew we were part Indian, another family member quickly corrected her: "Not Indian. Metis." Later I was told that my father had deliberately made a decision to consider himself white, that he "didn't believe in mixed blood." The old Quebec notion of *pure laine*, the so-called unsullied French ancestry, ruled my father's sensibility. In recent years, some family members have begun to acknowledge our aboriginal ancestry, although the instinct towards denial is still strong.

We also became intimately acquainted with the issues facing aboriginal adoptees as my young Cree niece, Anna, lived through the cultural dislocation, the rejection of her aboriginal ancestry and the rebellion that is common among First Nations children separated from their birth families. My sister and her family loyally supported Anna through her most difficult times, refusing to abandon her but painfully aware that Anna had her own path to travel. Even though she grew up most of her life around aboriginal people, for a time Anna tried to reject her Indianness. She has always been fascinated by aboriginal images, music and art, though. I cherish my memories of Anna as a child. I remember her on her fourth birthday, standing in a Yukon field of flaming fireweed in her bright red dress, her long dark hair neatly braided. When my sister came to live with me briefly when Anna was five, Anna absorbed my aboriginal art books and sat crouched with her ear to the stereo speaker for hours, letting the lyrics of Arawak musician David Campbell soak into her while she softly sang the words to "Pretty Brown."

Anna will always be a dearly loved member of our family, and in recent years my sister and I, with the help of Lizabeth Hall of the United Native Nations' family reunification program, have begun to search for Anna's Cree birth family. In the spring of 1997, Anna learned she is a member of the Kawacatoose First Nation, a large band of about two thousand Cree people in Saskatchewan's Fort Qu'Appelle Valley who are part of the Touchwood–File Hills Tribal Council. Anna said simply, full of emotion, "I feel that for the first time in my life I know who I am." Anna's birth father was artistic and musical, as is Anna, and her birth mother, who was very young when Anna was born, came from a family of twelve siblings. Anna also has an older brother. When she is ready, she will meet her Cree family, and she has asked her mother—my sister—and me to be with her. Last summer, Anna was married to a young Metis man, and she is learning to speak Cree.

Aboriginal communities demand—and have a right—to know who you are if you aspire to tell their stories. Ernie and I have been careful to go only where we were welcome and to try to observe aboriginal protocol. The rich diversity of First Nations made us mindful that we were not family but guests who often asked difficult and probing questions. I identified most strongly with the unique situation of Metis people, who feel at home in both aboriginal and white communities yet fully belong in neither. Metis therapist and filmmaker Shirley Turcotte has helped me to come to terms with, and fully accept, my aboriginal ancestry as the deepest expression of who I am, the part of my heritage with which I most identify.

In many ways, then, the writing of this book was also a healing journey. In travelling to aboriginal communities, staying with people who were welcoming and generous in the sharing of their stories and their experience, I had much to learn. From the Navajo people in New Mexico to the Secwepemc, Similkameen and Sto:lo people in B.C. and the Cree and Sioux in Manitoba, I received gifts of wisdom and acceptance. I felt a profound responsibility to relate to the world the stories and secrets that people had entrusted to me.

My relationship to the history of aboriginal children became most clear to me through my association with Ernie Crey and his nation, the Sto:lo. At the 1994 annual general meeting of the Sto:lo Tribal Council, held on the eve of the reunification of the entire Sto:lo Nation into one political entity, I was asked to be a "witness." "Witnesses" must respectfully pay attention and, if asked, relate what has occurred in an accurate, unbiased manner. I felt deeply honoured. I understood that the Sto:lo people who had come to know me while I conducted research on their fisheries and cultural heritage issues accepted me as I was—far from perfect, but possessing skills that would allow me in this transitional time to relate their story. With this book,

I believe my role is also to be a witness: to fairly, honestly relate what I have been told, to act as a bridge between people's life stories and the outside world.

When my spirits flagged at this demanding task in the years in which I travelled, worked as a reporter and raised my own family, I often turned to traditional healing for strength and support, whether it was a trip to visit friends and sweatlodges in Alkali Lake, a Sto:lo women's gathering, encouragement from Shirley Turcotte, or work with feminist shaman Naida Hyde in the Kootenays. There is always resistance to telling the truth about people's lives, and I experienced that emotionally and physically. Once, my arms seized up with an acute physical pain that did not respond to conventional treatment. I could not write; I could not open a car door or even carry a briefcase. Ernie took me to Sto:lo healer Bev Julian. We sat in Bev's small, homey kitchen in her house on the Matsqui reserve, and while Ernie and Bev's husband talked sports, Bev silently moved her hands around my body, not touching me or speaking, until I suddenly felt a powerful tug along my right arm, where the worst pain was. It felt as though Bev was using immense effort to pull something from my arm. When I was finally told to open my eyes, she explained: "It was wound around and around your arms very tight, strangling them, like a snake. It's gone now. You'll go home and have a very sound sleep, and when you wake up, the pain will be gone." Living in the twentieth century, I tend to be as skeptical as the next reporter, but Bev was right. I woke the next morning from a sound sleep, completely rested and free of pain.

In an aboriginal worldview, there can be those who resist with bad medicine the telling of the truth, particularly when it comes to painful issues such as the sexual abuse issues that Ernie and I explored in many aboriginal communities. As Ernie explained, there might be those who did not wish me well, or who wanted to prevent us from probing wounds we had been asked to open up and cleanse. Bev Julian refreshed my resolve to continue my journey.

In this book Ernie and I tell the story of aboriginal children from our blended perspectives as a journalist and an aboriginal activist. We shared insight and information, developed analysis and talked with many people over an intense six-year period. But initially it was through Ernie's tireless activism on social issues that I first became fascinated by the issues we explore in each chapter. I knew him as a credible, committed and persistent source, the vice-president and then president of the United Native Nations, who was often the first and loudest to raise his voice, calling for better housing; repatriation of women disenfranchised by marriage to non-Indian men, and of their children; more aboriginal foster homes; cultural competency for non-native social workers; labeling of alcoholic beverages to prevent Fetal Alcohol Syndrome; sexual abuse prevention and healing; and a national public inquiry on residential schools.

Ernie was always among the most fearless of aboriginal leaders to speak out for justice, and he stuck with his beliefs, even when they were unpopular with First Nations or government. He grieved for the aboriginal women who met death and degradation in Vancouver's Downtown Eastside, and for the youth who died violently. I also came to know him as a former foster child who took his painful personal experience and turned it into a campaign for the rights of aboriginal foster and adoptive children and their birth families. He wanted to set right the terrible wrongs that had so hurt his own family. These are the social issues still at the top of Ernie Crey's heart and mind, although he has become especially prominent in the past five years as a fierce, knowledgeable activist for aboriginal fishing rights.

Ernie and I chose to develop the themes of his life and the issues that were so close to our hearts into this book. Together we travelled to many First Nations communities, often with members of our respective families. Ernie and I brought different skills to the process, but since it is difficult to write a book by committee, I did the writing and much of the research. Together we drew out the often painful story of Ernie's family and wrote it down. We have chosen to respect the right to privacy of Ernie's siblings by changing their names, except for that of Bruce, who gave his consent. We are also well aware that we have only begun to tell the story of aboriginal children in *Stolen from Our Embrace*, for their story begins long before European contact, when the oral tradition preserved tribal and family history and children were reared through the modelling and practice of behaviour, done mostly by elders. We know this partly from ethnographic accounts but more reliably, since contact was relatively recent in British Columbia, from the living testimony of elders and adults who recall their elders' words.

In working on this book, we were struck by how consistently Canada's Indian policy, from its very inception, has sought to undermine the bond between aboriginal children and their families. European clerics accurately perceived that they were encountering a powerfully intact civilization in the New World, though they considered it pagan and inferior, and early on they focussed their attempts to indoctrinate aboriginal people on the children. On both coasts of what became Canada, the first Europeans seized aboriginal children, both as human trophies to transport back home and as recruits for forcible reeducation. Spanish friars took a boatload of Nuu-chah-nulth children to Mexico in the 1700s to produce a class of Indian priests who would return to convert their own people. When Spanish hegemony on the west coast collapsed, the Nuu-chah-nulth children were never returned; their fate remains unknown. Jesuits and other Catholic orders spirited aboriginal children off to Europe in similar attempts. This deliberate policy to separate and forcibly assimilate aboriginal children into the mainstream has pervaded every era of aboriginal history in Canada and profoundly injured of First Nations people both historically and today. Each era saw a new reason to take aboriginal children away from home, placing them in residential schools, foster care or non-aboriginal adoptive families. It is this story that Ernie and I want to tell. Our account is by no means exhaustive, and we encourage the interested reader to consult the Sources section at the end of the book, where we provide information on more detailed—and, where possible, first-hand—accounts of the experiences of aboriginal children.

Each chapter of *Stolen from Our Embrace* focusses on a particular aspect of the history of aboriginal children from the time of European contact. In the heart of each chapter, we have provided an opportunity for individuals to tell their own stories of their aboriginal childhoods. The book opens with the story of five generations in Ernie Crey's Sto:lo family. Theirs is a history that embodies the themes of our book. Ernie's family was as challenged and as blessed as any other aboriginal family of this era; their trials and their successes starkly reveal how gravely Canadian government policy and practice has failed First Nations children and their communities, and how First Nations across North America are reviving their own strengths in order to survive and flourish.

THE PERPETUAL STRANGER

Four Generations in My Sto:lo Family

Ernie Crey

THE shock of my ritual submersion in the Fraser River took my breath away. Waist-high in the water, I waded upstream against the swift glacial current, speaking my prayers of gratitude to the river for allowing me to cleanse in its embrace. I submerged four times, facing upstream. From my mouth burst forth the wailing sounds the Sto:lo call "quinning," the moaning infant sounds that for me represented my rebirth, a spiritual and cultural reconnection to my homeland. In my state of intense psychic distress, the icy waters no longer startled my skin.

As I plunged, I began to sing in a voice I didn't know existed. I was astonished until I understood that Sto:lo healer Gwendolyn Point hadn't been speaking metaphorically when she told me I was weary from carrying around an ancient spirit. He hadn't meant me any harm, she said; he had felt the need to watch over me until my own spirit revived. I began to cry like a "baby," as we Sto:lo call a new initiate into the longhouse. I wanted the old spirit I'd carried to know he could depart. I was in good hands. I let the river begin to wash away the burdens I'd carried my whole life, the blackness of despair and grief at the losses my family had endured.

After many years away, I had come home to Sto:lo territory to regain the wellspring of cultural knowledge and strength that had guided our ancestors since time immemorial. Gwendolyn and my other Sto:lo spiritual teachers did not view my loneliness, alienation and burnout as an individual crisis but as a sign that I was finally in touch with my longing to come home. I was honoured to receive their guidance. I knew the spiritual work they gave me would be arduous, though never beyond what I could endure.

As a child, I was forcibly removed from Sto:lo culture by social welfare authorities. Our family life was shattered after seven of my eight siblings and I were split apart into separate foster homes. We were never again to reunite as a family. My grandparents were proud, independent people who had lived through the deliberate dismantling of Sto:lo culture by priests who probed and pried into every corner of our lives. I had seen my father's spirit dimmed by the residential school where his culture was choked out of him, so that all his life he held his Halq'emeylem language and spiritual knowledge in check, depriving us, his children, of our most precious birthright.

Since my earliest days of adulthood, I'd preoccupied myself with political organizations, working for justice for aboriginal people. Burying myself in my work like many First Nations leaders, I sought to escape from my own pain. I tried conventional psychotherapy, which could not heal the aching cultural and emotional void inside me but did help to control my distress. My beautiful, bright children gave me joy, though my work kept me away from home for long hours. When I could no longer stand the suffering in aboriginal communities, I got angry. Non-native politicians got blistering broadsides from me about the welfare officials who were still abducting aboriginal children, including my own nieces and nephews, about the appalling living conditions on and off reserve, about the deaths and unsolved murders of aboriginal women and men, including my own brother.

It was not until I returned home to live and work among the Sto:lo in the summer of 1992 that a different kind of cultural and spiritual commitment was demanded of me. I wanted to reclaim my birthright for myself and my own children, but I could not cross that cultural boundary until I relinquished my despair, laid down other people's burdens and opened myself to renewal. I welcomed the icy embrace of the river that had sustained the Sto:lo—People of the River—for fifteen thousand years. It was the river, and the salmon, that had brought me back to work with my own Sto:lo Nation, as fisheries manager. We were not just another level of government, brown bureaucrats administering welfare on reserve; we were Sto:lo, working in every way to restore our nation's economic and spiritual self-sufficiency. I was invited into the longhouse of my Sto:lo forebears. After forty-three years, I had come home.

The Sto:lo are a large Coast Salish nation, now organized into twenty-five communities of 8,000 people, whose traditional territory extended from the ocean mouth of the Fraser River all along the valley to the Fraser Canyon. Four generations of my Sto:lo family lived through the maelstrom of social change that began in the late 1700s, when white people first entered the lush coastal rainforests of Coast Salish territory. The Salish were a trading nation, procuring ochre and obsidian from Oregon, mountain-goat horn from the N'laka'pamux and sage from the Secwepemc in exchange for our bounteous wealth of cedar, shellfish and five species of Pacific salmon. Traders from Asia brought curious coins and beads.

Our first clues to the European invasion were the whalers and traders who came from Spain and England. They gave us iron tools and trinkets along with an epidemic of disease. Our Upper Sto:lo tribes were decimated; population numbers fell from a pre-contact population of more than 25,000 to an all-time low of 8,046 people in all the tribes of the Fraser River by 1925, the year my mother was born.

Just two generations earlier, my great-grandparents had lived amid a thriving aboriginal populace, at the peak of the Fraser River civilizations. I'm reminded of what geographer Cole Harris has to say about those times in his book *The Resettlement of British Columbia*: "The Fraser was a huge source of food, and in the canyon, where fishing sites were abundant, and excellent, it probably supported as concentrated and dense a non-agricultural population as anywhere in the world."

In the midst of relative material wealth and ease, Sto:lo society evolved into a complex structure with a highly sophisticated government that we are now reviving after a century of imposed external rule. It was a harmonious, richly layered life, although not the idyllic era free of strife that has been conjured up. The Salish could be when necessary an aggressive people who took slaves from other tribes and used them as we pleased. We had our own rigidly observed caste system of high- and low-born people. Internal transgressions were swiftly and harshly punished. But a universal tenet that we shared with other First Nations all over the Americas was the reverence for and protection of children and elders.

Our Sto:lo life was stolen away. Our children were removed by priests, social workers and police to residential schools, foster care and jail. My own family was at the eye of the hurricane, and we are only now beginning to regain our bearings. All over North America, the experiences of other First Nations families parallel my family's trials and triumphs.

We would be dishonest if we said white people brought us nothing but bad. Some brought precious gifts. Nor is all change negative. We have moved on, and we cannot return to some false conception of a long-gone paradise. Nor do we want to. We are fortunate that we still possess within our First Nations links to a profound spiritual and cultural healing, from which other communities can learn. This is my story, and the story of my Sto:lo family.

My father was Ernie Crey, a Sto:lo born in 1905 at Katz Landing near Hope. The defining moment of his life came when he entered St. Mary's Residential School, which was perched on a high bluff overlooking the Fraser River in the town that became known as Mission, British Columbia. Until then, he had been raised as a boy of respectable birth and reliable prospects, in both the Sto:lo community and the non-native world. St. Mary's, founded in 1863, was the pride of the Catholic Oblate order that had established a "mission" to the Indians in the Fraser Valley. From their dormitory windows, Sto:lo children like my father would grieve for parents and home, pining for the life on the river they had left behind.

The school was such a powerfully negative experience for my father that as a parent he used it as a kind of threat to discipline us. If I didn't behave, he told me, I would be sent to a school where children had to rise at 5:00 a.m., say prayers on their knees for hours and eat thin gruel three times a day. Porridge, porridge and more porridge was his abiding memory of the school's fare, particularly galling to Sto:lo who thrived on the Fraser River's rich salmon and sturgeon resources. In my father's day, berries and wild game such as deer, duck, grouse and pheasant were still plentiful throughout the valley. His mother would preserve all manner of natural foods for the winter, and it must have caused my father special grief to know what he could have been eating if he had been home with his family.

My father was a fluent Halq'emeylem speaker, and he remembered having his knuckles rapped with a wooden stick or getting whipped for speaking either his language or the Chinook or N'laka'pamux languages, both of which he also spoke well as a child. He'd learned them while picking hops every year with his mother alongside aboriginal people from across B.C. and the northwestern U.S.

St. Mary's, like other Indian residential schools, was designed to strip aboriginal peoples of our culture. My father was at the school to grow up to be a little white man and to enter the white world. Children were warned not to listen to their parents and grandparents when they returned home for holidays. Some of the priests' words, enforced by the rod, must have stayed with my father. He refused to pass on his rich heritage in aboriginal languages to his children. He told us it was important to learn to read and write in English to get by in the world. We older children picked up the language anyway, because it was spoken all around us. But today, as an adult, I regret that I know too little of the Halq'emeylem language to pass on to my children.

My father had been raised in a loving, nurturing Sto:lo family where he knew first-hand the benefits of traditional parenting, and he was under no illusions when he came out of residential school that the treatment he and others had received was the way to raise children to be good parents. But like most residential school survivors, my father did not survive the direct assault on his self-esteem levelled by the priests and nuns who ran St. Mary's with an iron hand. As a fisherman, trapper and hunter, my father was proud to pass on to us these integral aspects of Sto:lo life. But the teachings he might have passed on about the heart and soul of Sto:lo life were withheld, as though his tongue was frozen. Some Sto:lo who went to St. Mary's said the priests stuck pins in the tongues of children who spoke their Indian language. If that, or any of the widespread sexual abuse now publicly disclosed from every era of the school's existence, happened to my father, he never spoke of it. The emotional, physical and cultural abuse, of course, was universal; my father escaped none of it.

The Church and federal Indian agents had begun to stamp out many practices from my grandparents' time: social interactions built around the potlatch, and the ceremonial/theological complex that included the winter dance ceremonial, the *sxwo:ywxey* dance, the first salmon ceremony and the series of teachings provided by our deity figures, Xexa:ls, the four powerful transformer siblings who were the three sons and one daughter of Black Bear and Red-Headed Woodpecker. Xexa:ls travelled among the people to tell us how to live. The Xwelitem, non-native newcomers in our territory, neither understood nor respected our traditions. They saw that the large gatherings throughout Salish territory took adults away from their employment in the fishery and the hops fields, which depended on their labour, and also took children away from their forced indoctrination at residential schools.

The colonial governments in Canada had begun to exercise control over aboriginal people long before the days of my grandparents. As early as 1830, the British passed laws designed to "protect" or "civilize" Indian people, laws that herded aboriginal people in eastern Canada onto artificial "reserves" of land. Then there was the Civilization Act of 1857, and by the time of Confederation in 1867, the Constitution Act gave the federal Parliament full legislative jurisdiction over "Indians and Land reserved for the Indians." Amendments to the Indian Act in successive years only served to tighten the grip of the government on our lands, our resources, our children: our very souls. All across Canada, traditional sacred and ceremonial practices were rendered criminal offences by white law. In Coast Salish territory, a legal ban against our spiritual practices, known to the Sto:lo as the anti-potlatch law, was imposed in 1884 and not lifted until 1951, when my father was forty-six and I was just two years old.

I can remember as a child standing with my father on the bank of the Fraser River near Hope, watching my sister take part in the canoe races for Indian women. He turned to me and said sadly that this was one of the few ways that Indian people were still permitted by law to congregate; political meetings were prohibited. The Catholic parish priest was a frequent visitor to our home, making sure we and other Sto:lo met his standard of good Christian homes, free of the contaminating Indian language and spiritual practice.

These European religious influences had been utterly alien to my family just one generation before. My father's mother, Mamie Pierre, was born in 1874 at Yale, B.C. She married Walter Crey, a European who had emigrated from Leipzig, Germany, and set up a dry goods store in Hope. Grandma Mamie was raised in the traditional Sto:lo manner. Until I was six, she would come to visit regularly, bringing food, small gifts and candy and speaking Halq'emeylem to me and my older brother. No English was heard during her visits.

My mother, Minnie Charlie, was born in 1925 on the Soowahlie reserve to Susan George of Squiala and George Batt, a man of mixed blood heritage. Minnie didn't have to endure the residential school experience but she spent some of her childhood in a hospital recuperating from tuberculosis. She did not leave the hospital until she was a young teen-ager. She met my father at a social gathering. They soon married, and my oldest brother, Gordon, was born when Minnie was nineteen. Her second baby, Dwayne, died when he was a few days old. I arrived in 1949, followed by Frances in 1952. I was five when the doctor arrived in the very early morning to take away the tiny body of our newest brother, David, who was just a few weeks old. Jane, Louisa, Bruce and Alice were born over the next four years.

Both happiness and terror colour my earliest memories. We lived in a tiny shack at the foot of Hope mountain, because my father was employed off the reserve in hard rock mining or logging in the area. Around the time I turned six, both of my parents began drinking alcohol to excess. My father's work buddies would come over and fall to hard drinking and scrapping. During one fight in our home, a number of men pinned my father to the floor. I remember grabbing a huge wine jug, one of the gallon-size jugs that liquor came in in those days, and hitting one of the men as hard as I could on the back of the head.

Just before I started school, we moved into the town of Hope. Despite the hard weekend drinking, my father always held down a job. In the summers, my mother would take Gordon and me to the hops fields. It was backbreaking labour for the adults, who picked hops all day in the hot sun, but it was great fun for us. We played with friends we hadn't seen all year, jumping into the hops sacks and playing hide-and-seek among the rows of vines and behind the pickers' shacks. We'd join the adults at coffee break or lunch hour. In the evenings, we'd sit around and listen to the women talk to each other in Halq'emeylem. We lived in little tarpaper shacks put up for us on the edge of the fields by the white farmers.

My maternal grandfather was known as a quiet conservative man who cut firewood for the paddlewheelers that still made their way up the Fraser River to Yale. The dry goods store owned by my father's father was the Hope Trading Company, the town's largest. Walter Crey had been on the local school board, and he was head of the merchants' association and a member of the Conservative Party. Well-educated in European schools, my paternal grandfather was also an accomplished pianist. My father had received a secure foundation in life in a home that brought together my grandfather's prosperity and European ways with my grandmother's Sto:lo cultural teachings. A generation later, it must have pained my father to see incipient instability and dysfunction in his own family. He prevailed upon my mother and announced they would both change their ways. Both of my parents quit drinking when I was about seven.

My childhood became much more stable and content. My father settled in to share with us some of his cultural knowledge. He would take my sister Frances and me wood-cutting and fishing for salmon in the Coquihalla River. Daddy was a patient man, ready to teach us all he knew. He possessed extensive botanical knowledge. In those days we didn't see a doctor; instead, my father would go into the woods and pick a plant. He had different kinds of teas that would cure headaches, stomach aches, cramps and other kinds of sickness. I can remember once when I was nine chopping kindling and having the axe strike deep into my left index finger. The wound was bandaged but did not heal. My father took me out in the woods near our home and picked a wide-leaved green plant from the forest floor. Its leaves had white stripes on each side. He grasped one of the leaves at the tip and neatly peeled it open along the white stripes, then wrapped it on my finger. He told me my wound would be healed in a day and a half, and it was.

At bedtime, my father sang traditional Halq'emeylem lullabies. He possessed all the songs meant to accompany traditional Sto:lo activities. When fishing, he had songs to will the salmon into the net and songs to the Sto:lo creators who put salmon into the Fraser River. He told how Xexa:ls had come up the river putting parts of the deer in different reaches of the river to create the five species of Fraser River salmon. Xexa:ls taught people how to live right, how to catch the fish he had put in the river and how to prepare and cook it. My father told me that the first spring salmon of the season had to be shared and its bones put back in the river. This special time with my father, almost a full five years for me, was a time of great security for our family. We children had a loving respect for our dad. I especially treasure the fact that I was able to know the man he really was.

But while my home life was happy, my school days were miserable. I attended a public school where I was made aware daily of the gap between my family's standard of living and that of my non-Indian classmates. The town of Hope was a working-class white community of loggers and miners mixed in with a few civil servants, social workers and police officers. At school I concentrated on surviving with some of my dignity intact; actually learning anything was secondary. At first I was bright and eager to learn, but my initial openness was not reciprocated by either the teachers or the other students. My relationship with teachers was combative. They expected me to do poorly academically. I received little encouragement or help. Neither the teachers nor the white parents were comfortable having me or the few older non-status Indian kids in the school. They made it plain they thought we should be on the reserve or in residential school. To them, Indians firmly occupied the lowest rung of the social ladder.

I learned not to expect smiles from teachers. I'd stick my hand up to answer a question, but I knew I wouldn't be called on. Teachers frequently showed their resentment at having me in the room by not including me in the lessons or in the social interaction between children in the classroom. I could expect to be treated curtly and summarily, without warmth or respect. The teachers appeared to share the view of Indians held by the priests and nuns in the residential school of my father's era, though in the public school those views were disguised under a thin veneer of civilized disinterest.

There were exceptions. I recall a teacher at Coquihalla Elementary School, a young man who seemed to make no distinction between me and the other children. Marvin Cope, who is now a retired principal, went out of his way to encourage me. He'd draw my attention to aboriginal role models in the fields of entertainment and athletics. He'd describe Will Rogers, the Indian journalist with his own radio program who almost ran for president of the United States, and American athlete Jim Thorpe. I was taken aback that a teacher would introduce into the classroom for my benefit alone this gallery of famous Indian people I knew nothing about. He made me feel that I, too, could be a high achiever. My improved self-esteem was reflected in the high marks I got in Marvin Cope's class.

And then my happy family life began to unwind. The death of my paternal grandfather stripped from my father whatever social status he had in the white community. From that point on, to the townspeople of Hope, my father would always be a halfbreed married to an Indian woman. Our family's economic fortunes went into considerable decline. By the time the fifth of my siblings was born, my father's health had deteriorated from a lifetime of hard physical labour. His spine had been broken during his time as a faller in the woods. Fortunately the accident had left his spinal cord intact, but he suffered intense back pain from then on. He also had a bad heart. Finally he was no longer able to work at all, and our family was forced to go on social assistance. One day, my brother Gordon and I returned from a fishing camp, walking the twenty miles from Seabird Island to Hope. As each step drew me nearer to home, my sense of foreboding grew until we reached our house. An ambulance bearing my father's body had just left. My mother wept silently, surrounded by frightened, sobbing children. It was the summer of 1961, and my father's death set in motion a string of events that would ultimately lead to the disintegration of my family.

Nothing in my mother's sheltered upbringing in a tuberculosis hospital—while recuperating from T.B., she had received very little formal education—had equipped her for life as a self-supporting single parent of six. My father had been her best and only lifelong friend, and his loss was devastating to her. She had a few people she could look to, including her beloved aunt, Rose Charlie of Cheam. But well before my father died, Rose had married Ed Sparrow, the patriarch of Musqueam, and had left the Cheam reserve to establish a new life for herself there. As the eldest child in the family, my mother would have been too proud and independent to appeal to her younger siblings for help. Without my father around, life in a white community became all the more confusing and threatening. My mother began drinking again. We all felt the tension. I can remember trying to bar the door to keep her from going out to get drunk. I started to act out in the community, stealing candy bars and soft drinks from the local stores, skipping school and, with my friends, making a general nuisance of myself.

A few months after my father's death, an R.C.M.P. cruiser pulled up in front of our home. I was taken to the local police station and placed in a cell that would be my home for the next week. No social worker or lawyer or courtworker visited me. I found out later that my brother Gordon had tried to visit and bring me food but was turned away. At the end of the week, I was brought before a judge. A number of people talked to the judge about me in a manner I couldn't understand. Gordon sat at the back of the courtroom. Finally, the judge told me that I was to be sent to someplace called Brannan Lake Industrial School on Vancouver Island. I was not allowed any contact with Gordon. I was led out of the courtroom and placed in the cell again. I was twelve years old.

I would not see Gordon or my mother for another four years. By that time, my younger sisters, my brother Bruce and baby Alice would all have been taken away. My family would never again live in the same home or even be in the same room together.

My mother had been judged by social workers, teachers and police officers as an inadequate parent well before the day I was asked to rise and stand in front of that judge. There was no one in the courtroom to represent my mother or me. Hiring a lawyer would have been unthinkable for my mother. The outcome of events was predetermined by legal, economic and social forces that Sto:lo families, including my own, had no chance of influencing or controlling.

It was 1961, the beginning of what became known as the "Sixties' Scoop." For the first time in Canada, provincial social workers were exercising the jurisdiction given to them by the federal government to go into Indian homes on and off reserve and make judgements about what constituted proper care, according to non-native, middle-class values. Their mandate was "child protection," which in practice meant the investigation of perceived neglect or abuse, then the apprehension of children and their placement in non-native foster homes. Poverty was the only reason many children were apprehended from otherwise caring aboriginal homes. For status Indians like my mother, there were none of the social services a white family in crisis might have received. For her, there were no homemakers, no preventive family counselling services, no funded day-care facilities. There was no respite at all from the day-to-day drudgery faced by an uneducated, widowed mother of six trying to survive on welfare.

My eldest two sisters, Frances and Jane, were placed in the care of an elderly fundamentalist Christian couple on Fairfield Island, near the town of Chilliwack. My brother Bruce and sister Louisa were fostered by a Christian family in Chilliwack, as was my sister Alice. They grew up within miles of each other but had no knowledge their siblings were so close by. Visits home were forbidden. Frances and Jane especially missed Gordon, the stable older brother who had looked after us all and tried desperately as a young teen-ager to keep the family together.

On my arrival at Brannan Lake I was "processed" in an office and then taken to an area of the institution where new inmates were showered, shorn and locked up. Each kid was given a pig-shave. My clothes were taken away to be replaced by a steel-blue institutional shirt and pants. Late in the evening of my first day, I was startled out of a fretful sleep by screams and the clanging of keys against the bars of the cell just a few feet from me. I couldn't make out exactly what was happening, but I found out in the morning that the kid in the cell next to mine had attempted suicide by slicing open his wrists with the metal top of an Old Dutch Cleanser container. I was to discover that self-mutilation and suicide attempts were common occurrences in that place.

Kids were forced to do hard physical labour at a nearby gravel pit, as well as more mundane chores such as sweeping and waxing floors. But the main "activity" at Brannan Lake was fighting. I was beaten up my first day in "intake," but after that I decided to establish my place in the pecking order by picking two fights in the most public areas of the institution. A guard broke up the first scrap I got into with a sharp blow to the back of my neck, and my opponent and I were thrown into the lock-up for several days. I swiftly learned that bullies were tolerated by the workers at Brannan Lake, so it was up to me to drop the most notorious bully or be left with the black eyes and welts most of the younger kids displayed. Officials used the violent hierarchy among boys to keep order. Rewards for the enforcers among the older boys included passes out of the school and small privileges such as cigarettes. The older boys also could count on school officials turning a blind eye when those boys preyed on smaller, younger boys for sexual favours.

Sexual abuse at Brannan Lake was common. Certain members of the staff preyed at will on all of us. To get a day trip out of the institution, a boy would have to be a "bum-boy" for certain male supervisors. Many of the older boys were street-hardened youth from big cities, used to trading sexual favours for money or privileges, and the staff willingly exploited them. It seemed as though there was no one safe to complain to.

As a relatively innocent twelve-year-old coming into this hellhole, I was deeply shocked and frequently terrorized. For stealing a few chocolate bars, I'd been thrown in with boys who had committed rape and murder and wouldn't think twice about doing it again. The reform school philosophy of hard knocks, of vigorous contact sports and tough discipline, didn't work at Brannan Lake. Tough kids left more hardened. It was what I imagined residential school had been like, from what my father had said.

Three months later, a social worker came to take me away from Brannan Lake. I desperately wanted to go home. I missed my mother and my brothers and sisters. But no one would answer my questions about my family, and I was told the ministry had other plans for me.

I arrived confused and afraid at my first foster home. It was a large German family who already had three other native foster children. In my presence, the woman of the house openly displayed her dislike of Indians. Aboriginal women were called "smoked meat" or "brown stuff." To me, coming from a well-regarded social stratum on both the white and aboriginal sides of my family, my foster mom seemed very common and coarse. It was mystifying to me how she could regard my people as scum without knowing anything about us. It's one thing to face racism at school, but to live with it in the face of a "mom" every day was crushing to my self-esteem. I had to learn to harden myself and block out any longing for comfort or nurturing.

As an older native foster child, I was swiftly put to work. The three younger native children weren't worked as hard, but they were treated just as rudely. None of us was shown affection. I was sent to school in ill-fitting secondhand clothes, especially humiliating since I already stood out as one of the few Indian kids there. It was clear to me that although this woman had been lionized in her home community as a Mother Theresa to Indian kids, she was in the foster-care business for the money. By this time, the early 1960s, the B.C. child welfare branch was taking aboriginal children into its care so quickly and in such huge numbers that anyone who was willing to take Indian children was deemed suitable. We were warehoused in homes that were by no stretch of the imagination suitable for any child, let alone a traumatized, culturally dislocated, grieving aboriginal child.

At fourteen, I was moved to another foster home in Chilliwack with a pleasant, middle-class family. The father valued achievement above all and soon made it clear that I was a disappointment to him, long before I'd been provided with enough stability to prove myself academically or in any other way. Pam Koczapska, the mother of the family, was a teacher and a well-respected woman in the Sto:lo community. I really came to love her, but she was unable to defend me when the father decided I had to go. Later, as an adult, he and I reconciled; I always remained close with Pam, but at the time the experience was very hurtful.

By then, I knew the basic lie of the foster "home," with its foster "mother" and "father" who supposedly loved me as their own child. If I made the most minor error, or a character trait of mine was judged wanting, I'd be out on my ear. I'd been cocky and defiant in my first foster home, hardened by their openly racist dislike of Indians in general and me in particular. But this second family had more power to hurt me, because I had come to care for them. After that, I was determined not to get close to anyone. I told the social workers I didn't want any more foster "homes." I told them just to give me a bed to sleep in.

But I continued to bounce around in non-native foster care. I was in the heart of Sto:lo territory, surrounded by villages in which my aunts, uncles and cousins lived, but I was the perpetual stranger. A palpable grief and longing seemed to dog my footsteps. I desperately wanted my own family back, but the social workers told me there was no one at home who wanted me. I tried to hide my loneliness and grief in long-distance running, running miles through villages like Rosedale, Tzeachten, Soowahlie and Cheam, my mother's home community. Powerful emotions welled up in me, but I felt helpless to stop in those Sto:lo homes. I'd run back, drained and exhausted, to the only sense of belonging I felt, however tenuous: my borrowed corner of the next white foster family's life.

Growing up as a government ward made me very cynical about the collaboration between the government and the evangelistic Christians who were "saving" Indian kids from their own families. Again I felt echoes of my father's residential school experience. We were kept from our families to hasten our assimilation into the white world. We were told our culture was inferior and doomed to extinction. My last foster family was an aged German-Canadian couple who practised relentless evangelism. I escaped as often as I could to my lonely upstairs room. I ended up in several different high schools but still managed to maintain a B average. Counsellors knew I was bright and could do better. But I was continually dogged by anxiety, worrying about my siblings and my mother. I was afraid I wouldn't be there to stop her from winding up dead in a ditch somewhere, from drinking.

Meanwhile, as I would later learn, my mother was frantically trying to find out what had happened to her children. She wrote letters to each of us individually. She and my brother Gordon, the only child left in her home, desperately searched for us. Gordon would take the bus to Fraser Valley communities, one by one, looking for Indian children, asking teachers and shopkeepers and visiting playgrounds to search for a sign of his brothers and sisters. He covered every street of Abbotsford on foot, because he believed at one point that we were in foster homes there.

None of Gordon's sleuthing met with success, although social workers could have helped him at any time. Our files were not sealed as they would have been if any of us had been adopted. But we were Indian kids in care. The social services ministry's ostensible goal to reunite families apparently applied only to white children. Social workers accepted letters my mother addressed to us, but these were placed in thick government files. None of those letters ever reached me or my siblings in our white foster homes.

The first time I saw those letters was many, many years later. I had dropped into a Fraser Valley social services office in my quest to re-establish my federal Indian status. (After my father's death, my mother had married a white man, which robbed her and her children of Indian status. Under Bill C-31, introduced in 1985, I knew I was enti-tled to get it back.) A sympathetic social worker in the office offered to show me my file from my days as a child in care. There were the let-ters my mother had sent me. They'd obviously been opened. In them, my mother poured out her fears and concerns for me and tried to reas-sure me that she still loved me, that I should never think she did not. She told me how much she missed me and thought of me. And in one letter, she had an ingenious plan. The social workers would not tell her exactly where I was, but she proposed that I meet her one Saturday at a tiny park in Abbotsford. My mother had died by this time, and I couldn't help but wonder how many times she had driven by that park, looking for me.

When I was fifteen, still in foster care, I figured out how to get a bus to Hope to see my mom and brother. By then I knew that all of the younger children had been taken away. When I stepped off the bus, there was Gordon. He was working as a janitor in the Greyhound depot. We hugged each other and tried to catch up on the past three years. Gordon told me that our mother had been searching for me and my siblings. We walked home after Gordon finished work and there was my mother. She was overcome with emotion, crying and laughing at the same time. She asked me questions about where I had been and exclaimed over my growth and the change in my appearance. She had gained control over her drinking; there seemed to be no reason why I couldn't remain in that cozy old log home with her. But I knew the police would come and get me if I did, and that would make it hard-er for her. I didn't tell her about my misery at Brannan Lake or in the foster homes; there was no point in hurting her any further.

I saw Gordon four or five more times while I was still a foster child. The thirty-two-mile distance between me and my brother and mother was a greater distance then, especially to people without money, than it is today. Gordon was especially dear to me. We'd been constant companions as children, and he'd saved my life three times. But the years we spent apart, in vastly different circumstances, divided us and eroded our special bond. Perhaps I resented that he had escaped foster care and had our beloved mom all to himself.

In the early 1970s, Gordon died in mysterious circumstances after a night of drinking. His body was dumped on the front lawn of my aunt's house. The police report said he had died of head injuries and exposure. True to form, the R.C.M.P. had little interest in the death of a young Indian male. Over the years, the circumstances of his death continued to plague me. When I had saved enough money, I tried to hire a prominent Kamloops lawyer, who later became a judge. I told him I believed Gordon had died of the severe head injuries someone had inflicted. The man gave a contemptuous laugh and told me no lawyer would bother looking into why a drunken Indian had died two years earlier. To my regret, I believed him.

Throughout my time in foster care, I beseeched social workers for news of my siblings. They responded with platitudes that my sisters and brothers were happy in good homes, far away. Based on my own experience, I viewed those statements as bald-faced lies. In fact, as it turned out, all my brothers and sisters lived within miles of me. One day Pam Koczapska called to tell me there were two little Indian girls named Frances and Jane attending the Chilliwack elementary school where she taught. I was sure they were my sisters. A strange but infinitely precious meeting was arranged.

The two little girls were dropped off at a prearranged spot at a playground. We were given an hour and told not to exchange information about where we lived. They were delighted to see me, even if they had no clear memory of what I looked like. Jane, nine and shy, left all the talking to Frances, who was a year older. She was full of questions. All

STOLEN FROM OUR EMBRACE

I could tell them was that all my mother's children except Gordon were gone and that my mother still loved them.

My former foster mom kept tabs on my sisters, and I was able to visit them later at a chicken farm in the Fraser Valley. She also found my brother Bruce, who was with my sister Louisa in a white Christian fundamentalist family. I went to visit them. The family sat me down in the living room and paraded out a nice young Indian boy, who was told to play the piano for me. Over the next eight years, until Bruce got out of care, I visited him and Louisa several times, but their foster parents were careful never to leave us alone. I didn't know what they were enduring until Bruce was an adult.

I had made no secret of my unhappiness in my current foster home, and finally a social worker took me to meet Frank, an engaging and handsome young man in his mid-thirties. Frank took me for a drive in his car and bought me an ice cream cone. He invited me to come and live in the group home where he worked, where he promised I'd have lots of freedom and few chores to do. He took me to see the home. There were five teen-aged boys living there, most of them non-native. I decided to move in. Shortly afterwards, Frank moved in too. He'd split up with his wife, and he appeared to have persuaded his superiors the group home experiment would work best with a resident supervisor.

I soon saw Frank's true motive for living with teen-aged boys. He openly pursued sexual relationships with them. "Watch out, Ernie, you're next for the blow job from Frank," was the joke. I'd hear boys tiptoeing down the hall to join Frank on the couch in the recreation room where he slept. He had a big collection of kiddie porn, which he left lying around. In one of the magazines, we found a picture of a boy we all knew, a child still in the care of the province of B.C., whom Frank had taken on a trip to San Francisco.

Frank was a skilled, intelligent pedophile, very exploitative. Boys weren't forced into sex, they were seduced. As foster children, they were starved for love, and very vulnerable. There was even competition to see who could win Frank's favours. I liked Frank. I had thought he was the first person to show a genuine interest in me, but it was only due to his sexual obsession. I experienced an enormous betrayal of trust, and I felt objectified. Frank even brought another social worker into the home to share the boys' sexual favours.

Looking back, I am angry and amazed that these two pedophiles could have preyed so openly on children in care in a government-financed group home. Mike, the young man who had been photographed for the porn magazine, bragged that Frank had arranged for him to have sex with two supervisors in the region. It seemed like a conspiracy to me. I made it my goal to develop a strategy to get out of there.

I was allowed to get a summer job on a Canadian Pacific railway gang. The next summer, I got my file as a government ward transferred to Kamloops and got a job as a bellhop in a hotel. I lived with a kind, elderly hotel janitor and his wife. I was earning real money. At the end of that summer, I called Frank and told him I didn't want to come back, but he said he wanted to meet with me in person. I realized he was afraid I'd expose his pedophilia, but I made it clear to him when we met that I only wanted to get on with my own life.

I started to attend high school in Kamloops, but only after Frank had convinced the principal that I was a bright, independent kid who deserved a chance. I did well, and the principal became fond of pointing me out as a model Indian foster child, something any kid could be if they'd just pull themselves up by their bootstraps. After I built up a rapport with a Kamloops social worker I trusted, I disclosed Frank's rampant pedophilia to her. No one ever contacted me. But years later, when I was the head of a provincial aboriginal organization, the same Kamloops social worker told me privately that police reports from the other boys as well as my disclosure to her had prompted an investigation. In 1984 Frank's fellow pedophile was convicted in provincial court on six counts involving four males aged thirteen to seventeen, some of whom were in his care. The offences included buggery, fellatio, fondling and masturbation. He was sentenced to four years in jail. Frank died in a mysterious accident, believed to be suicide. From time to time, I still come across some of the boys I knew from Frank's group home. One is a cocaine addict I've seen on Vancouver's downtown streets. I lost touch with Mike, the kiddie porn model, after he became a hustler and attempted suicide several times.

In 1969, the province of B.C. declared the age of majority to be nineteen. In June of that year, at the age of twenty, I was officially free of the Department of Social Welfare. The government was no longer my parent. But it wasn't for another decade, after my brothers and sisters were old enough to legally seek each other out, that I learned about the appalling treatment they had received at the hands of their foster parents. We began hesitantly, painfully talking as adults.

I did not suffer as severely as my siblings, escaping the worst of the physical and sexual abuse they endured. But my experiences in foster care left me just as scarred. I was fearful and guarded and could not trust people, something that has deeply affected my adult relationships.

I remember my first encounter with aboriginal politics: hearing the magnificent Shuswap orator George Manuel, president of the National Indian Brotherhood, speak at the Kamloops hotel where I was working. I was spellbound. He helped me to see the links between my own family's pain and the paternalism of a federal government that persisted in regarding all Indians as children and our children as their property. Manuel first spoke out loud for me what I instinctively knew, that as First Nations we had to wrest back control of our children if we were ever to return to being self-governing. When an opportunity came to work for the B.C. Association of Non-Status Indians, I leaped at the chance. I travelled all over the province to report on off-reserve living conditions. I found families living alongside railway tracks in abandoned shacks, squatting on Crown land and inhabiting the worst fleabag hotels. Non-status aboriginal people had been shut out of employment in ranching, mining and logging communities that openly loathed them. Nor were these disinherited families welcome back on the reserve. I realized the majority of aboriginal children were growing up off reserve, in mother-led families, without supports of any kind. They were the poorest of the poor in Canada and nobody gave a damn what happened to them, not the federal government, not the province and certainly not their beleaguered elected chiefs back home.

Later, I worked for the Company of Young Canadians in an isolated west-coast reserve, until the toll of suicides, alcoholism, poverty and unending human despair wore down even my boundless optimism. A physical and emotional breakdown taught me to use my resources more wisely. It also made me realize how lonely I was, that I had to let someone pierce my guard and open myself to the possibility of reciprocal love.

With my first wife, Bonnie, a schoolteacher, I moved to my next post as a social worker in the Shuswap village of Alkali Lake. At that time it was called "Alcohol Lake," a booze-soaked reserve of relentless misery. As two of the few sober people with a car, we were called upon every weekend to ferry the bloodied, drunken and beaten to the nearest emergency ward forty miles away. Once, an injured woman died, briefly, in our back seat. Roused back to life in the hospital, she described an out-of-body experience where she'd floated up in the air and watched us frantically racing towards help, with her lifeless form in the back of the car. That image, together with the sight of the hungry little faces of neglected children clustered around our back porch, has stayed in my mind to define the kind of social work I was able to do in that era, before the people of Alkali Lake, through their own heroic efforts, vanquished alcoholism and led First Nations all over North America on the path towards sobriety. I was honoured to return to Alkali Lake in the early 1990s for a powwow and community celebration, and delighted to see healthy, vibrant young girls with jingle dresses and braids flying in traditional dance, and young boys sporting coyote masks and elaborate feather bustles. A whole room full of healthy elders performed a slow honour dance. I could see that young adults affected by fetal alcohol syndrome were being well taken care of within their own village. The elders had their own memories: they teased me about the much slimmer young social worker who'd blown off steam by tearing around the dry Cariboo hills on a big motorbike.

STOLEN FROM OUR EMBRACE

To me, the journey of Alkali Lake, begun when a little girl named Ivy Chelsea refused to go home with a drunken mother, exemplifies the resolve and redemption of which our communities are capable.

My marriage to my first wife broke up in 1974. Although we had shared many profound experiences, including the birth of our son, Saul, I could not cast off my fear of abandonment. I tried to control her every move. I could not accept that anyone could love me and stay committed to me, because no one ever had.

When I remarried in 1977, and my second wife, Lorraine, and I subsequently had four children, I had to learn how to become a good parent. I had to be continually shown how to be a loving father, and constantly reminded to share the responsibilities of household chores and child care. I loved my children so fiercely that I feared everything would be taken away from me: I was hypervigilant about their safety and wanted their happiness so badly that it must have been quite oppressive. Still, despite my parental lapses, my children have all grown up to be independent, healthy beings.

My very public struggle to change the situation in which aboriginal families find themselves ironically came at a terrible cost to my own family life. After years of intense political activity as the vice-president and then acting president of the United Native Nations, including the failed battle to enshrine off-reserve aboriginal rights in the Canadian constitution, I felt drained and empty. I was appalled by the cynicism and financial wrongdoing of some urban First Nations politicans I saw around me. Then, after only a brief vacation with my family, I leaped with both feet into the fire of my first long hot summer as fisheries manager for the Sto:lo Nation. It was to cost me my second marriage, but it would lead ultimately to the cultural healing that would be my salvation.

During my years in urban aboriginal politics, I tried to keep an eye out for my siblings in the city. Over the years, I established the closest relationship with Bruce, while he in turn kept in touch with our sisters. The whole sad tale of my siblings' childhoods became known to me.

In the good Christian home in which Bruce grew up, he and Louisa were kept in the basement on Christmas Day while the foster family gathered upstairs for turkey dinner. Both Bruce and Louisa were subjected to bizarre, cruel punishments: they were locked in the closet, threatened with a large hunting knife when grades were poor, and had their heads stuck in the toilet bowl while it was flushed repeatedly. My brother and sister were told constantly that they were the spawn of the devil. Like most of the aboriginal children who grew up in care, they will battle self-esteem issues all their lives. Bruce, whose early job opportunities were compromised by an alcohol addiction, has now been sober for twelve years.

My sister Louisa is a strong woman, but in her early years as a mother, she was unable to cope on her own with two small children, and one of her children was apprehended. Her daughter stayed with her. My wife and I asked the ministry to place Louisa's small son, Jason, in our home until my sister was on her feet. Bruce, too, asked the ministry to be involved in planning for Jason's care. But on the eve of proposed changes to child welfare regulations, Jason was abruptly removed from the foster family and given up for adoption to a non-Indian family. His adoption was arranged with all the stealth and secrecy the B.C. Ministry of Social Services could muster, as if the minister of the day took special pleasure in thwarting the wishes of the Indian politician who had been such a thorn in his side. Louisa soon got on top of her alcohol problem and stayed steadily employed while Jason grew up hundreds of miles away in a white family. With support, Louisa could have parented Jason, but he was already gone, lost to Louisa as she had been lost to my mother. Within a few years, however, as soon as he was old enough to choose, Jason came home to Louisa and his extended family—with the support of his adoptive parents.

Frances and Jane had fared no better in their foster homes. Their fundamentalist Christian foster parents exerted strict "discipline" through whippings, psychological terror and heavy farm labour. The girls were told if they didn't submit to discipline they'd burn in hell along with all the other pagan Indians. As adults, my sisters told me with tears flowing down their faces about their foster father's favoured punishment. For any imagined infraction, he'd march the girls in the middle of the night down to the poultry barns to shovel out chicken shit until dawn. Both Frances and Jane carried deep shame throughout their lives about being Indian and a lot of anger towards white adults. After Frances began drinking heavily as a young mother, her baby daughter, Roberta, was apprehended by social workers, again without any notification of family members. The loss of a second generation of Crey children was well underway. It seemed like nothing could ever repair the abandonment and grief Frances felt, and her guilt for failing Roberta. In the late 1980s, she died of a heroin overdose.

As an adult, Jane told me of being sexually abused by her foster parents' son, who was never charged and is now a Christian missionary in Africa. In her late teens, Jane gave birth to a son who was adopted by the same parents and continues to live there. It hurts me to see my nieces and nephews repeat our history as foster kids in white, ultra-Christian homes. Jane now spends most of her time on Vancouver's meanest streets, on a methadone-maintenance program but receiving no psychiatric care or counselling to help her cope with the immense losses in her life.

My mother continued to drink after all her children were taken from her, and she later gave birth to two more children, Sally and Donald, both of whom wound up in the care of an aboriginal foster family. Both were abused. Donald, who suffers from minor intellectual impairments, is friendly and outgoing, though he will require assistance all his life. After Sally became drug-addicted herself, her two children were placed in the care of the new Sto:lo agency, Xolhmi:lh Child and Family Services. Our devastation about Sally's future was complete when she learned last year she is infected with AIDS.

The troubles my siblings and I have suffered can only truly be understood in a cultural context, not just as a series of traumatic life events but as a deep spiritual estrangement from the complex of Sto:lo beliefs. As Sto:lo, we believe that our ancestors continue to play a role in our daily lives. In our society, when you are ill or feeling discomfort, you are described as being "Indian sick," which means that spiritual forces are at work in your life. In order to understand these forces, you must return to spiritual teachers. The elders believe the voices and spirits that non-native medical experts might diagnose as a profound mental illness are in fact an expression of the cultural estrangement so many of us have suffered.

I had been able to survive by channelling my personal grief into anger and action, but in the autumn of 1993, everything seemed to come crashing down on me. I was consumed by an overwhelming feeling of fatigue and depression. Solace began only when I visited Sto:lo spiritual leader Gwendolyn Point. After examining me quietly, with her eyes closed and her hands moving over my body for several minutes, Gwendolyn told me a very old spirit had settled on me and was there to protect me. She told me this was a good thing. She advised me to hang cedar branches throughout our home. Undesirable influences would be caught in the boughs.

I was advised to embark on a course of spiritual healing, including immersions in cold water. The Sto:lo Nation's knowledgeable anthropologist, Gordon Mohs, arranged for me to go to the Nooksack reserve, accompanied by Yakweakioose Chief Frank Malloway, a spiritual leader known as Siyemchess. I was frightened about making the excursion, since I had had little direct experience with our cultural practice. But the two elders parked in front of a giant colour television in a small reserve bungalow turned out to be anything but frightening. Elders of the Indian Shaker church, they spoke with me quietly, then began to pray and move their hands over my body to sense where the sickness lay. After several minutes, my eyes began to stream and my chest to heave, and a clear mucus poured out of my nose. My long-confined pain and tension, like a band of blackness tightly wrapped around my chest, began to collapse and break up like ice floes in spring. I coughed and expelled mucus until I felt drained of all the negativity I'd carried around.

After my immersion in the glacial tributary of the Fraser River and the Nooksack men's workover, I felt a renewed optimism and a fresh wellspring of will to carry me through the work ahead, both in the aboriginal fishery and in my own spiritual development. My wife, Lorraine, agreed to undergo a similar experience with another Sto:lo spiritual leader, since, as my partner, she had absorbed unconsciously some of the blackness I carried with me. For a time our family life improved. But the demands of my job continued to put strains on our marriage, and in the spring of 1994 Lorraine and I separated. I am still closely involved in the lives of my children. Naomi, Karrmen and Aaron all have worked with the Sto:lo Nation at a sacred Sto:lo heritage site known as the Xa:ytem Longhouse Interpretive Centre. Aaron, now sixteen, works for the Sto:lo environmental youth corps and lives with me part of the year in my new home on the Soowahlie reserve, close to the banks of the Fraser River.

Through the Sto:lo spiritual practices, I know that the spirits of my parents, my grandparents and my ancestors are alive in this world. I call the spirits of my ancestors forth to invite them to a traditional Sto:lo burning to honour the dead, and I feel their presence with me, at the burning and in the smokehouse. When I walk in the ways my ancestors walked for tens of thousands of years, the pain of the last few decades seems to fall away. My parents, grandparents and ancestors walk beside me, concerned and involved in all the events of my life. This is not theoretical, but very real: it allows me the intimacy and unconditional love that was missing from the years I was culturally and spiritually separated from them. I've come to realize that they never left my side, even in my lonely days as a child kept away from anyone who knew me. I was blinded to their love.

For any Sto:lo or other aboriginal person who grows up in boarding schools, foster care, hospitals or jail, the traditional ways can heal. I feel this is the great hope for aboriginal children who have been devastated by their life experiences. By entering the belief system of their own First Nation, they can resume a spiritual relationship with their parents and grandparents that can comfort them and heal the emotional void they feel.

Despite a century of government interference, today the longhouse traditions of winter dances are flourishing among the Sto:lo. With my children, I go throughout the year to longhouses at Sumas for the dances that fill the long rainy winter months as they have since time immemorial. All important Sto:lo occasions, such as naming ceremonies and memorial services, are consecrated in the big house. Inside the huge cedar longhouse, smoke rises from two gigantic, constantly fed bonfires to smoke-holes fifty feet in the air. Drums rhythmically pound for dancers who are in a trancelike state. The Sto:lo dances are like no others. They are not a public First Nation ritual to be captured on videotape or performed for tourists. Neither the Syúwél winter dances nor the masked Sxwó:yxwey ceremonies have ever been photographed or filmed. My children know, as Sto:lo children have known for hundreds of generations before them, that the spiritual state of new dancers is so intense that young ones must stay well clear of them. There are always huge dinners served after a night's dancing, but what is really fed is the soul. My children know that the longhouse tradition is at the heart of their identity as Sto:lo. They may live contemporary lives in a suburban neighbourhood, but they are above all Sto:lo. They know that the door to the longhouse is always open to them.

In so many ways, the history of my family is the history of aboriginal children in Canada. We have lived through the worst of times: epidemics of disease brought by the first white traders; the black-robed Oblates who trekked into our territory and teamed up with the government to bring us residential schools; the cycle of disintegration that exposed us to all the ills of the modern world. I intend to make sure my family and my people will be around to experience the best of times, too, as First Nations all across North America work to restore and redefine our communities, economically, spiritually and culturally. What happened to me, to my family, to my community and to my First Nation has fuelled my work as an activist seeking economic justice, social cohesion and political power for all aboriginal people.

2

"KILLING THE INDIAN IN THE CHILD"

Four Centuries of Church-run Schools

EMILY RICE'S introduction to residential school will be etched on her soul for the rest of her life. Raised on a lush British Columbia Gulf Island replete with wild deer, gardens and orchards and surrounded by straits that ran silver with salmon and herring, Rice spoke little English at the age of eight when she was told the priest was coming to take her to boarding school. The nightmare began as soon as Emily and her sister Rose, then eleven years old, stepped on the small boat that would bear them away. "I clung to Rose until Father Jackson wrenched her out of my arms," Rice remembers. "I searched all over the boat for Rose. Finally I climbed up to the wheelhouse and opened the door and there was Father Jackson, on top of my sister. My sister's dress was pulled up and his pants were down. I was too little to know about sex; but I know now he was raping her. He cursed and came after me, picked up his big black Bible and slapped me across the face and on the top of the head. I started crying hysterically and he threw me out onto the deck. When we got to Kuper Island, my sister and I were separated. They wouldn't let me comfort her. Even today, all my sisters are strangers to me." (Father Jackson's name has been changed here since he has never been criminally charged, only named in a civil lawsuit.)

"Our Alcatraz," as survivors would later call the Kuper Island residential school, was just across the channel from the Vancouver Island town of Chemainus. The huge brick building, which towered over the island's only wharf, was operated from 1906 to 1978 by two Catholic orders, first the Montfort Fathers and then the Oblates of Mary Immaculate. (The school was built by the Canadian government in 1890, which hired Father Donckele from the Diocese of Victoria as principal. The Montforts took over in 1906.) The school's most notorious principal, who presided throughout the 1930s, was Father Kurtz, known in Straits Halq'emeylem as *a:yex*, the crab, for the cruel, pincerlike fingers he used to pull a boy's ear until it bled or to grope a girl's private parts until she wept with pain and fear.

By the time Emily Rice left Kuper Island in 1959, at the age of eleven, she had been repeatedly assaulted and sexually abused by Father Jackson and three other priests, one of whom plied her with alcohol before raping her. A nun, Sister Mary Margaret, known for peeping at the girls in the shower and grabbing their breasts, was infuriated when Emily resisted her advances. "She took a big stick with bark on it, and rammed it right inside my vagina," recalls Rice. "She told me to say I'd fallen on the stick and that she was just trying to get it out." The girl crawled into the infirmary the next day, too afraid to name the perpetrator. Nevertheless, when Emily returned to the dorm a few days later, the beatings by Sister Mary Margaret and the other nuns resumed without pause. In the years that followed, Emily would have to twice undergo reconstructive vaginal surgery, and she suffered permanent hearing loss. Father Jackson also wanted to make sure no one would talk. On the sisters' first trip home at Christmas, he suspended Rose by her feet over the side of the boat, threatening to release her into the freezing waves unless she promised to stay silent.

The stories of residential school survivors like Emily Rice began to slowly make their way into mainstream Canadian consciousness in the early 1980s. The schools' destruction of the lives of Indian children, in stark contrast to their supposed purpose of "saving" pagan youth from their parents' uncivilized fate, was known before that time to many Canadians who could have stopped it. The federal government—which by express legislation funded and guided the schools—amassed mountains of internal files over the years that documented not only the cruelties to which aboriginal children were subjected but also the shoddy education they received and the shockingly high rates of illness and death, often the direct result of federal shortfalls in funding and supervision. Despite this evidence, some sixty thousand files finally handed off to the Royal Commission on Aboriginal Peoples in 1993, the schools persisted as "internment camps for Indian children" for well over a century, ultimately affecting virtually every aboriginal community in Canada. The death toll, excessive discipline and overall educational failure of the schools—well-known to any Indian Affairs bureaucrat who possessed a critical mind or a conscience—also leaked out frequently into the public eye, through the news media of the day or in the House of Commons. Aboriginal parents sometimes contacted journalists or politicians when their pleas to have their children better-treated or returned home fell on deaf ears. In 1907, both the *Montreal Star* and *Saturday Night* reported on a medical inspection of the schools that found aboriginal children were dying in astonishing numbers. The magazine called the 24 per cent national death rate of aboriginal children in the schools (42 per cent counting the children who died at home, where many were sent when they became critically ill), "a situation disgraceful to the country," and concluded: "Even war seldom shows as large a percentage of fatalities as does the educational system we have imposed upon our Indian wards." But Indian Affairs' lawyer S. H. Blake Q.C. advised that since the department had done little to prevent the deaths it could "bring itself within unpleasant nearness to the charge of manslaughter" should it entertain the reforms being pressed for by some politicians. Indian Affairs quickly moved to silence the furore by promising improvements to the schools, but over the next half-century, any thoroughgoing examination discovered the same scandals locked within their walls. The

cumulative onslaught of criticism did little to deter Canada's complic-
ity with the churches in obscuring the schools' failures until well into
the 1960s.

Residential schooling reached its peak in 1931 with over eighty
schools across Canada. From the mid-1800s to the 1970s, up to a third
of all aboriginal children were confined to the schools, many for the
majority of their childhoods. The explicit mandate of the residential
schools, throughout the lengthy partnership between the Canadian
government and the churches who were responsible for operating
them, was described succinctly by one federal bureaucrat: "To obtain
entire possession of all Indian children after they attain to the age of
seven or eight years and keep them at the schools."

Nowhere in Canada was the instrument of the residential school
used more brutally and thoroughly than in British Columbia, where
despite relatively late settlement by Europeans, the schools endured
longer than anywhere else. The Anglican and United Churches, along
with several Roman Catholic orders, divided up the province, which
contained the largest population of aboriginal people in Canada, into
small religious fiefdoms. There, as they had elsewhere, clerics mounted
a concerted assault on the spiritual and cultural practices of the First
Nations by taking away their most vulnerable and precious resource,
their children.

The seeds of a national system of institutions for Indian children were
sown at the earliest contact between white Europeans and aboriginal
people in North America. In seventeenth-century New France, in
what are now the provinces of Ontario and Quebec, the first clerics
focussed their missionary zeal on the children. Their religious ideal was
to create a class of "civilized" young Indians who would return to
proselytize among their own people. In 1620, the Recollets, a
Franciscan order, opened the first boarding school for aboriginal boys,
but by 1629, the friars had given up and abandoned New France. The
Recollets were replaced by the Jesuits, the intellectual elite of
European religious orders, who were better-educated, more numerous

STOLEN FROM OUR EMBRACE

and eager to try their hand with the "savages" of the New World.

After decades of unrewarding toil with the downtrodden European underclasses, the Jesuits were entranced by the prospect of converting robust young aboriginal children into francized Christians who might, through intermarriage, improve the class of French settlers in the new country. The Jesuit mission's Father Superior Paul LeJeune observed in the early 1630s in the *Jesuit Relations*, an exhaustive diary—kept primarily by LeJeune—that was printed and forwarded to France and Rome, that the aboriginal people "are more intelligent than our ordinary peasants." Adult Indians were deemed unteachable, entrenched in their dying culture. As Father LeJeune remarked: "When we first came into these countries, as we hoped for scarcely anything from the old trees, we employed all our focus in cultivating the young plants."

When the practice of removing aboriginal children to France proved to be an abject failure—those children who did not die became neither miniature Frenchmen nor Christian proselytizers—the Jesuits moved to establish boarding schools in the new colony. They attempted at first to separate the children from their parents, so as not to be "annoyed and distracted by the fathers while instructing the children." But as their boarding schools stood empty, the priests tried siting schools closer to aboriginal villages. They soon found, however, as Father LeJeune reported, that the influence of the priests paled beside that of the children's families: "We could not retain the little Savages, if they be not removed from their native country, or if they have not some companions who help them to remain of their own free will ... when the savages were encamped near us, our [*sic*] children no longer belonged to us."

By 1668, the Ursuline order of nuns had arrived in Quebec from France and established a boarding school for aboriginal girls, but soon they too were discouraged at their progress. "Out of a hundred that have passed through our hands scarcely have we civilized one," admitted the Ursuline Mother de l'Incarnation. "We find docility and intelligence in them, but when we are least expecting it they climb over our enclosure and go to run the woods with their relatives, where they find more pleasure than in all the amenities of our French houses. Savage nature is made that way; they cannot be constrained and if they are they become melancholy, and their melancholy makes them sick. Besides, the Savages love their children extraordinarily and when they know that they are sad they will do everything to get them back."

It was their powerful cultural and spiritual traditions, founded on seemingly immutable bonds between children and extended families, that enabled aboriginal nations to hold their ground in these early encounters with Europeans. The initial period of contact represented a profound clash of cultures, and nowhere can that conflict be seen more starkly than in the radically opposed attitudes towards childhood.

Aboriginal children, regarded as the very future of their societies, were considered integral members of the family who learned by listening, watching and carrying out tasks suited to their age, sex and social standing. While diverse in language as well as cultural and spiritual practices, First Nations across North America shared a remarkable commonality in their approaches to child-rearing. Invariably they placed their children at the heart of a belief system closely aligned with the natural world. The economic and social survival of indigenous societies depended on the transmission of a vast amount of spiritual and practical knowledge from elders to the young, through an exclusively oral tradition.

By contrast, European society in the 1600s was evolving from a rigidly stratified feudal system, with monarchs at the apex and a powerful nobility sustained by the labour of a class of serfs, to "a new order in which trade and impersonal market-based relationships were becoming increasingly important," as author Margaret Conrad writes in her *History of the Canadian Peoples*. Political and financial alliances created competing nation-states in Europe, and the desire for overseas expansion was fuelled as much by population pressure and the need for trade and resources as by intellectual curiosity and religious zeal. The European cultural inverted pyramid, in direct contrast to aboriginal cultures, was based on "the profound oppression of women in society at large," Conrad points out. As women were devalued, so were children; they were the chattels of a patriarch. Child labour and the consignment of a vast number of children and their families to grinding poverty were not questioned. Even the children of European aristocrats were to be seen and not heard. Across all classes, Europeans believed children required strict discipline underscored by physical punishment.

Although European religious orders were concerned with converting the "pagans" right from the time of their arrival, direct intervention by colonial governments in the lives of aboriginal people did not begin in earnest until British hegemony was established in 1812. Until then, the various tribes had been needed as military allies by the French and the British, and both European powers recognized that meddling with the traditional Indian way of life would halt the valuable flow of furs. But just as the native peoples' military usefulness ebbed, so did their commercial value. By 1821, the two giant fur trade companies in Canada had merged and begun to directly employ their own people, including Europeans and an increasing number of Metis, who were able to range far and wide for furs, rendering aboriginal tribes no longer essential trade partners.

By the 1820s, the new government of early Canada found itself pressured by a flood of British homesteaders who demanded the Indians be somehow neutralized or removed from the land. This political and economic imperative was a direct motivation for the colonial government's support of religious-run boarding schools for Indian children. In 1830, jurisdiction over the management of Indian affairs, which the European newcomers by then had firmly appropriated, became civil rather than military. The government of Upper Canada perceived its new charges as burdensome responsibilities, a people in transition from a dying culture represented by the adults, "the old unimprovable ones," to the children, who were destined for complete assimilation. In 1846, the government resolved at a meeting in Orillia, Ontario, to fully commit itself to Indian residential schools. Thus the interests of church and state merged in a marriage of convenience that was to endure more than a century: the churches could harvest souls at government-funded schools while meeting the shared mandate to eradicate all that was Indian in the children. The "Indian problem" would cease to exist.

The major denominations had already carved up the country among themselves, with Catholics, Anglicans and Methodists launching schools for Indian children as far west as Manitoba and Alberta. In British Columbia, the earliest Indian boarding schools were established by rival Protestant and Catholic "missions," at Metlakatla in northern B.C. in 1857 and St. Mary's Mission in the Fraser Valley in 1861.

The churches soon received even more official support. With Confederation in 1867, the new national government was charged under the British North America Act with constitutional responsibility for Indian education. Limited experience had already indicated that day schools could not accomplish the government's goal of fully severing ties between aboriginal parent and child. In 1876, the federal Indian Act effectively rendered all aboriginal people children before the law, legal wards of the Crown. An Indian Affairs department was created in 1889, and Indian agents duly dispatched across the country. As the local hand controlling the government purse strings, the Indian agent could threaten to withhold money from increasingly destitute aboriginal parents if they did not send their children away to school; he could even throw them in jail.

Aboriginal leaders were not disinterested in educating their children for the emerging white man's world. They could see their destiny as a subjugated people if they did not adjust. Chief Paulus Claus of the Bay of Quinte Mohawks had told the government in 1846 that he viewed the supposed "great cause of Indian improvement" as "our only hope to prevent our race from perishing and to enable us to stand on the same ground as the white man." Other leaders, weary of being displaced and dispossessed of their land, also regarded the education of their young as inevitable, and even desirable. Treaties signed with aboriginal people, which covered virtually all of southern Ontario by the mid-1850s, even provided for schools on Indian land, funded by the government. But the apparently generous treaties were the harbinger of more sweeping provisions in the draconian Indian Act, which gave rise to the reserve system, under which aboriginal tribes would be rigidly confined to small tracts of mostly unproductive lands. Day schools near aboriginal children's homes were eliminated once it was determined they were unsuited to the primary raison d'être of Indian . education. Institutions far from the reserves could completely remove Indian children from their "evil surroundings" in favour of having them "kept constantly within the circle of civilized conditions," as Regina MP Nicholas Flood Davin urged in a report to the federal government in 1879.

For a model of institutional care for Indians, the fledgling Canadian government looked with interest to the south, where the United States was establishing a system of industrial boarding schools in the wake of a long and bloody conquest of American Indian tribes by the U.S. Army. The prototype of an Indian school there actually had its origins in a prison for "pacified" Indians commanded by Lt. Richard Henry Pratt. The U.S. government embraced Pratt's methods and endorsed the evolution of American Indian policy from its guiding principle "The only good Indian is a dead Indian" to Pratt's watchword: "Kill the Indian in him and save the man." Pratt established the Carlisle Indian School in Pennsylvania in 1878 with backing from the federal Bureau of Indian Affairs, which swiftly set up more "industrial" schools offering meagre academics augmented by agriculture and trades instruction for the boys and domestic training for the girls, sufficient to equip a servant class.

The American system was heartily recommended to the government of John A. Macdonald by backbencher Nicholas Flood Davin in the 1879 report. It was accepted that the Christian obligation to Indians could be discharged "only through the medium of children." The well-being of First Nations left bereft of their children was not addressed. Adults could not be rescued from "their present state of ignorance, superstition and helplessness," as they were "physically, mentally and morally . . . unfitted to bear such a complete metamorphosis." Pragmatically, Indian Affairs bureaucrats advised Macdonald, the schools were "a good investment" to prevent Indian children from becoming "an undesirable and often dangerous element in society."

By 1896, the Canadian government was funding forty-five church-run residential schools across Canada. Almost a quarter of these were located in British Columbia. In any given year, as many as 1,500 children from virtually every one of B.C.'s First Nations were interned in these schools. In addition to St. Mary's Mission, the Roman Catholic Church operated schools at Kuper Island, North Vancouver, Lower Post on the B.C.-Yukon border, Kamloops, Christie on northern Vancouver Island, Sechelt, Lejac in northern B.C., Cranbrook and Williams Lake. The Church of England, later the Anglican Church, operated three schools, the first in the model Indian village at Metlakatla, then St. George's at Lytton and one at Alert Bay, while the Methodist Church, later the United Church, ran schools in northwest B.C. at Port Simpson and Kitimat, Coqualeetza school in the Fraser Valley, and two schools in Nuu-chah-nulth territory on Vancouver Island: the Alberni Indian Residential School and another further north at Ahousaht.

In persuading Indian parents to send their children to these schools, authorities were assisted by a growing famine in Indian villages in western Canada. In this environment of hunger, amid recurring outbreaks of smallpox and influenza, the government withheld food rations from parents who resisted the removal of their children. Indian agents marched in lock step with the religious orders, preparing lists of children to be taken from the reserves and then organizing the fall round-up. Strapping young farm boys aided by R.C.M.P. officers herded the children onto buckboard trucks or trains like cattle.

Official policy called for children to be isolated not only from their family and homelands but also, once at school, from their friends and siblings. Isolation made children more vulnerable to the massive brainwashing that was undertaken to replace their "pagan superstitions" with Christianity, and their "free and easy mode of life" with relentless labour and routine. "There should be an object for the employment of every moment," an 1891 federal report urged. Girls were taught domestic duties such as sewing, laundry, cooking and cleaning, while boys were employed in agriculture, carpentry, shoemaking and black-smithing. Studies were confined to only half a day until well after the Second World War. Religion dominated every waking moment. Even recreation was controlled by European rules to teach "obedience to discipline." Expressions of aboriginal culture and individuality were harshly punished. As soon as children entered school, their traditional long hair was shorn or shaved off; they were assigned a number and an English name and warned not to let a word of their language pass their lips.

Aboriginal parents were not complacent once their children were installed in the schools, even though their letters were censored and their visits, even by the few who could afford to make them, were dis-couraged. As early as 1889, the people of St. Peter's Reserve in Manitoba complained officially to Indian Commissioner David Laird about the principal of Rupert's Land Industrial School near Selkirk, Manitoba. Young girls of eight or nine still bore bruises on their bod-ies several weeks after being strapped, they said. During an investiga-tion, the Anglican principal admitted he fed the children rancid butter and crept into the dormitories at night to kiss little girls, but he was reprimanded, not removed. Resistance among Indian parents mani-fested itself all across Canada and took many forms, from the with-holding of children despite threatened sanctions to petitions, visits and outright threats of violence. But despite these and other early signs of trouble, the Department of Indian Affairs continued to defend the boarding schools, declaring they were succeeding in "the emancipation of the Indian from his inherent superstition and gross ignorance."

Physical and sanitary conditions in schools all across the country were terrible. Children frequently fell ill due to poor food and over-crowded, airless dormitories. Many grieving parents finally saw their children only when they were sent home to die. When the new prin-cipal of the Alberni Indian Residential School on Vancouver Island complained in 1900 that his institution was "a den of consumption and other diseases," Indian Affairs replied only that "while the conditions at Alberni are admittedly bad, the records of some other schools are equally unenviable." Tuberculosis was the scourge of the boarding schools, bred in the draughty, overcrowded dormitories that housed malnourished children with little resistance to the highly contagious, often fatal lung disease. Schools began to report death rates of 11 per cent, as in the case of the Alberni principal, to 17 per cent at Saskatchewan's Crowstand school, to an average of 24 per cent in fifteen prairie schools. Of students at the Sarcee school outside Calgary between 1894 and 1908, 28 per cent died, mostly of tuberculosis. At the File Hills industrial school in Saskatchewan, 69 per cent of students died of tuberculosis during one decade at the turn of the century. A department medical inspector, Dr. P. H. Bryce, carried out a lengthy investigation of conditions in western residential schools, warning that the epidemic of disease threatened not only students but also the communities they infected at home. But few of Bryce's recommendations were ever heeded. Although Deputy Superintendent of Indian Affairs Duncan Campbell Scott was worried about the department's reputation, he concluded: "If the schools are to be conducted at all we must face the fact that a large number of the pupils will suffer from tuberculosis in some of its various forms."

At all periods of the schools' operation, it is certain that students died concealed deaths due to misadventure, abuse and neglect, which might be categorized—had the schools ever been held culpable—as criminal negligence, manslaughter and even murder.

At Kuper Island, where Emily Rice and hundreds of other children were confined, the Indian Affairs department's own files estimate that up to 40 per cent of the students died before they could return home. Rice's mother, now eighty-six, reported to an R.C.M.P. constable in 1996 that she had witnessed the secret burial of a baby born at the island school to a terrified young girl. Disease, brutal accidents, at least one alleged murder and failed escape attempts claimed the lives of others.

Students were so desperate to escape the school that they frequently drowned trying to flee on logs or in small boats. Even the earliest archives from the Kuper Island school reveal a litany of untimely deaths and vicious punishment. Published here for the first time are excerpts from the ominous "Conduct Book," a big black ledger in which priests recorded beside a child's name and number each offence and the punishment meted out.

In 1900, the little Coast Salish boy David Fallardeau was confined to bread and water for "entering an Indian house." On September 6, 1903, Thomas, No. 117, was whipped and locked up for "stealing apples." Albert, No. 77, tried to escape on September 21, 1897, only to be "arrested and given five strokes of the strap." In 1897, Charles, No. 62, got "a few slaps" for "disturbing the dorm," was forced to kneel down for an entire day for being "insolent," and when truant received "a public reprimand and lashes."

The Kuper Island priests reserved their most harsh punishments for aboriginal children who dared to express their cultural or spiritual identity. "Talking Indian" or "making Indian dances" was punished by "public whippings," "lashes" and forcible confinement for days. Hungry children who stole food were put on a bread and water diet. Still, the conduct ledger reveals that many children risked severe beatings to maintain their traditional ways. "January 21, 1912: In the evening an entertainment was given to the brothers. Brother Hyacinthe gave an exhibition of waltz and polka dances and got quite frightened by boys performing an Indian dance." Diaries and conduct ledgers from the same era indicate a defiant group of boys, led by Sammy Sam of the Penelakut band—the great-grandfather of a contemporary Vancouver Island elder of the same name—stole away to the woods or nearby villages for the Coast Salish winter bighouse ceremonies and were repeatedly whipped, confined and starved for a day or two for "practising Indian dances," "going to an Indian [long]house."

The ledgers record numerous escape attempts. A priest complained in 1897 of "an epidemic of truancy." On January 1, 1924, a priest recorded, "Tonight at 7:30 Eva Guerin, Clara Gabriel, Elferina Wesley and Eileen Henry (Touchley) deserted having passed out by the dining room window." January 2, 1924: "Father DeWiest and I leave at eight in search of them, we finally take the launch to the Gap and return at 4 a.m. Weather is cold and there is snow on the ground. Christopher Guerin deserted at 8 p.m. stole a canoe and is at the Gap." After enlisting an Indian man from the village to search all day and night, the priest reported that on January 4, he sent "Joe Jack with a warrant to arrest the fugitives." The next night, Christopher Guerin asked to go and see his mother. Permission was denied.

The priests also kept laborious diaries in which they recorded the illnesses and deaths of children as laconically as they might note those of cows or pigs. "Peter Samuel, age eight, sent home for being delicate, died at home." "George Baptist, No. 66, died of consumption of the bowels." "Caroline died after her clothes caught fire in the kitchen." From the diary for September 30, 1889: "Emily, no. 049, has, I am informed died at home from the effects of scrofulous abscesses inside the head. She was a very undesirable pupil, being deaf and taciturn, quasi-dumb."

"Dec. 31, 1920: Present: 26 boys 40 girls, total 66, 12 sick list, one helping father. Admitted 9 boys, 12 girls, total 21. Discharged 2, died 4. 3 horses, 6 cows, 1 heifer, 2 sows, 7 pigs, plenty in expectation."

Though the school was responsible for many if not all of these deaths, the priests appear to have blamed the children for being malingerers and their parents poor caregivers. "Considerable difficulty is experienced in keeping the sick pupils at the school, their parents living close to the school insist to nurse their own children. If opposition is made and the patients kept here, it happens frequently that they will cry-lament, refuse to take medicine and really try to get worse so as to carry their point and be allowed to go home. This is to be regretted as it is a well-known fact that Indians are poor nurses."

The archives contain many references to the heavy labour the children performed. "The conduct of the pupils has been exceedingly gratifying. The work of the farm boys consisted chiefly in cutting wood, feeding the stock and improving the surroundings. The shoemaker with his boys made 33 pairs of shoes and kept the old ones in repairs. In the sewing room the following articles were made, 12 jumpers, 29 pillow-slips, 28 caps, 22 chemises, 20 shirts, 11 aprons, one large mat, two small mats, one thick skirt, 10 washing aprons, two roller towels and two mats."

Although the Department of Indian Affairs admitted by the early 1920s "that fifty per cent of the children who passed through these schools did not live to benefit from the education which they had received therein," the residential school system expanded rapidly between 1910 and 1932, bolstered by amendments to the Indian Act making school attendance mandatory for at least ten months of the year for children older than six. Enforced by truant officers and police, attendance increased 110 per cent, from 3,904 students in 1912 to 8,213 in 1932. By 1930, almost 75 per cent of all Indian children in Canada between the ages of seven and fifteen attended residential school.

Not surprisingly, the residential schools were not successful academically. Indian Affairs' own statistics show that in 1930, 75 per cent of aboriginal students across Canada were stuck below Grade 3. Only three in a hundred ever went past Grade 6. By comparison, well over half the children in provincial public schools in 1930 were past Grade 3 and one-third were beyond Grade 6. "Let us be clear," declared Musqueam leader Wendy Grant-John in 1991 to the Royal Commission on Aboriginal Peoples' special hearing on residential schools. "These were not places of learning: they were nothing but internment camps for children."

The last residential school in Canada closed its doors in 1984. Today, as more and more survivors break their silence about the physical, sexual and emotional abuse they suffered, it is clear that the traumatic impact of the schools will endure for many more decades. "My hands are permanently injured from the beatings they inflicted on me," Musqueam Nation former chief George Guerin says of his years at the Kuper Island school. "Sister Marie Baptiste had a supply of sticks as long and thick as pool cues. When she heard me speak my language, she'd lift up her hands and bring the stick down on me. I've still got bumps and scars on my hands. I have to wear special gloves because the cold weather really hurts my hands. I tried very hard not to cry when I was being beaten and I can still just turn off my feelings. I still understand my language 150 per cent, but I cannot speak it. I've even seen a psychologist to find out why I can't voice those words any more.

"And I'm lucky. Many of the men my age, they either didn't make it, committed suicide or died violent deaths, or alcohol got them. And it wasn't just my generation. My grandmother, who's in her late nineties, to this day it's too painful for her to talk about what happened to her at the school."

Gilbert Johnson, now a forty-eight-year-old Gitksan father of three, emerged deaf and functionally illiterate after eight years at the Alberni Indian Residential School. "At the age of fourteen, I had a bleeding ulcer from the constant fear . . . It was like a concentration camp," says Johnson. "My main thought was, am I going to make it out alive?"

Johnson, who hunts and traps on his traditional lands near Kispiox, lost jobs when his illiteracy was discovered. "I could have been an engineer, earned big money if I'd gone back to school, but I can't go near any kind of school even now—it gives me the cold sweats," says Johnson. "The residential school finished me for learning for life."

Even those children who found ways to cope, or in some cases benefit from the school experience, were damaged by witnessing the abuse of others. Few children escaped with their cultural identity intact. And the impact on the communities left behind was severe. Displaced from their land, their villages sometimes literally depopulated of children, parents were vulnerable to the accelerated social and economic dissolution that affected virtually all reserves in Canada. Elders who had no one to receive their wisdom lost their reason for existence. Children returned home strangers who could trust no one; far from being "improved," they were demoralized, victimized and often unable to bond with their families or elders, so that their sad stories stayed locked within them. A Regina missionary noted that "many of the old people say that the worst element on the reserve is to be found among returned graduates who in a year or two, drift down sadly."

Graduates were also bedevilled by the rigid, authoritarian regime of the schools, which inevitably invaded their lives as adults. Some inflicted serious physical discipline on their own children, while others became overly lax and disorganized. The European clerics' ways of raising children—absolute obedience reinforced by shame, whipping and harsh denial—contaminated the traditional aboriginal childrearing traditions of modelling behaviour and never hitting a child.

In the past two decades, the grief and anger of residential school survivors have galvanized a drive for justice and restitution all across the country. Many of the initiatives currently underway were sparked by First Nations in British Columbia, where aboriginal people acting individually and collectively have launched a volley of attempts to secure redress through political and legal channels.

Residential school survivors who returned home from a miserable childhood of abuse and military-style discipline have found themselves still experiencing, decades later, symptoms of Post-Traumatic Stress Disorder not unlike those suffered by war veterans or police officers. Panic attacks, insomnia, uncontrollable anger, alcohol and drug use, sexual inadequacy or addiction, the inability to form intimate relationships, eating disorders: the list of symptoms is lengthy, but today it is more likely to form part of the legal documents filed in civil lawsuits than to describe an individual's silent torment. Survivors who sought solace in self-destructive acts discovered that eventually their memories had to be confronted, grieved and healed. There was no more powerful incentive to do so than the fact that many of them had become parents and grandparents who lived every day with the impact of their pain on the most precious ones, their children.

Once survivors were well embarked on their own healing journey, they soon realized that seeking an apology and restitution from the government of Canada and the churches was a healthy, empowering goal to pursue. Even more importantly, the survivors hoped financial compensation could help provide healing resources to ensure the cycle of pain and abuse would not be passed on to each successive aboriginal generation. At a men's talking circle held in the spring of 1996 in a downtown Vancouver hotel, Gitksan father Gilbert Johnson spoke eloquently about why he was willing to join in a civil lawsuit against the federal government and the United Church, and why he could finally share his long-buried horrors and tears with the other proud men. "This isn't easy for me to talk about; sexual abuse, being beaten so bad I was put in the hospital and wound up deaf, but all I have to do is look at my kids, and I know why I'm here," said Johnson. "I know why I'm going after the government and the church at my age: it's for my children, so they know no one can get away with hurting little children so bad, so they can have a good life and not carry on this pain of mine."

Willie Blackwater, a Gitksan father and millworker now attending college in Vancouver, was the first aboriginal person in Canada to win a medical claim for Post-Traumatic Stress Disorder as a result of his years in residential school. A survivor of the Alberni Indian Residential School, Blackwater saw his tormentor, former school supervisor Arthur Henry Plint, convicted in criminal court in Port Alberni in March 1995. Since then, Blackwater has launched a civil suit with twenty-three other aboriginal men against Plint, the United Church of Canada, the federal government and three former principals of the school: A. E. Caldwell, John Dennys and John Andrews.

Kispiox was my home village, where I was raised by my grandparents James and Mary Blackwater. They were my father's parents, but I called them Mom and Dad until the day they died. I had ten full years with my grandparents, the best years of my life, before I was taken by the DIA [federal Department of Indian Affairs] to residential school.

My grandparents gave me a true education, in the land, in survival, in values. They were really traditional people. My grandfather took me fishing, hunting and trapping with him, teaching me about the land

WILLIE BLACKWATER

and animals. My grandmother always had a big garden and picked berries, and they preserved everything for the winter.

My grandparents taught me and corrected me without ever raising their hand or voice to me. If I did something wrong, my grandfather would tell me a long story, and I had to figure out for myself its meaning and what it told me about what I had done. My grandmother had her own traditional spirituality but she also brought me to the United Church. She was always teaching. She'd cook wonderful things and tell me why it was so important to have respect for everything on earth that feeds us. From the time I was very young, she'd take me to all the feasts in the village, and carefully teach me the hereditary clan system of our people, how the chiefs got their titles and territories. My grandmother was a really important chief herself; her grandfather had been a big chief in the house of Delgamu'ukw.

When I first went to residential school, it was like tearing my heart out. My grandfather had died when I was about seven, and every time I came home my grandmother was pretty sick. I didn't want to burden her with what I was suffering at school. The day she passed away was the saddest day of my life. I was about eleven or twelve years old, at school, and my family brought me back for the funeral. When nobody could hear I talked to her. She was really the only one who loved me and I was living in the midst of this terror at school, far away. Nothing could save me from it now.

That school in Port Alberni was worse than I ever could have imagined. They took away our clothes, cut our hair and gave us a number. The abuse began as soon as I got there. It seemed like the perverts on the school staff knew how to pick the most vulnerable.

Arthur Henry Plint was the dorm supervisor for the younger boys, boys my age. My first week there he woke me up in the middle of the night. He told me to come into his office because there was an emergency phone call from my father. I got up immediately and went into the office. The phone was off the hook all right, but when he came in he hung it up and said there was no phone call, he just needed to talk to me. He said that he'd noticed me and taken a liking to me. He said boys like me could be treated special if they cooperated. I kept telling him that I wanted to go back to bed.

He had a door from the office right into his bedroom. He took me there and dropped his robe, and faced me, naked. I tried to run. He pushed me onto the bed and told me to shut up or I'd be in deep trouble. He told me to take my pyjamas off and started to masturbate me, then he put his mouth on my penis and made me do the same to him, until he ejaculated in my mouth. I started to get sick and tried to puke. He laughed and told me if I puked on his bed I'd get hurt.

When I left that first time he said to me, now when I wake you up I want you to come quietly or I'll hurt you pretty bad in front of everybody, and then everyone will know what I'm doing to you. The next time he got me in the night, about a month later, it was the same thing, fondling and everything, only this time he turned me over on my stomach and he penetrated me. It was so painful I tried to scream, but he grabbed a pillow and told me to bite on it. He said if anybody heard me cry out I'd be pretty sorry. After that Plint raped me anally about once a month for the next three years.

I finally got up my nerve to tell Mr. Butler what Plint was doing to me. [Mr. Butler's name has been changed since he has not been criminally charged; he is named in the lawsuit brought by Blackwater and others.] Butler gave me a severe strapping and called me a dirty lying Indian. A few days later, Plint kept me home from school. At that time, we were living at the residential school but being bussed into town to a public school. I was in Grade 5. After everybody left for school, Plint beat the hell out of me. He yelled, "This is nothing compared to what will happen to you if you ever tell anyone again." After that, I didn't tell anyone for another whole year.

The second year, in the fall, I told my teacher at the public school about the abuse. She phoned Mr. Butler. I was beaten badly by Butler and I got another severe beating from Plint. The third year, I finally got up the courage to tell my father. He phoned Mr. Butler, who told him the boys made up stories to stay away from school. I got another beating from Mr. Butler. He told me nobody was ever going to believe me. When Plint got hold of me, it was the worst beating I ever got. He held me by the neck, just choked me by the throat so my feet were dangling off the floor, and punched my head repeatedly. I lost consciousness and I woke up in the infirmary. I was in there two to three weeks.

Plint had his little clique of older students, too, like this guy named Gus, and he and Plint took turns raping me after my dad had called the school. I vowed I'd never tell anybody again. I lay there crying silently every night.

I did a lot of hard physical labour at that school, spent a lot of time in the kitchen as part of my ongoing punishment, most of the time for God knows what. I found a long kitchen knife and a sharpening stone. I hid them, and every chance I got I sharpened up that knife, until it was so sharp I could slice through a piece of paper in the air.

In June, just before I went home for the summer, I was determined I'd never have to go through that torture by Plint again. I told him one day, "I'm not feeling good, I want to stay home with you." He got a big silly grin on his face. I guess he figured he'd broken my spirit at last. He phoned the school and said I was sick. We did nothing in the morning, just hung around. At noon, he made a nice hot lunch, the most delicious lunch, not the slop I was used to eating.

Then he said, "Let's get down to business in my office." I played along with him. I got him to take his shirt off and then he unzipped his pants. He was lying back and I told him to close his eyes and I started to massage his neck and shoulders. Then I said, "Wait, I've got to take my pants off." I had the knife hidden down my pant leg into my boot. I got the long blade in position right at his throat and I said, "Wake up, asshole." I let the razor-sharp edge of the knife just graze his neck and I told him that I wanted to be the first guy on the list next year for the boarding-out program. I said, "I could kill you right now and I could kill you any damn day of the week. And if you come near me or hurt another kid like you did me, I'll kill you. I want out of here, asshole, and I'd better be on that list in the fall."

He lay there with his big pot belly and his bald head, half-naked with his pants down, scared and shaking. Like all bullies he was a coward. He never said a thing, and the next day I was gone for the summer. When I came back in the fall and got off the bus, there was no Plint grinning at us like he usually did. He was still at the school, but

STOLEN FROM OUR EMBRACE

he started keeping to himself and drinking a lot. And there was my name, on the top of the list for the boys who would be boarded out.

For the rest of my years at school, I boarded with Nuu-chah-nulth families who treated me like one of their own. I had friends, but I was terrified of getting close to anyone, especially girls. I got to Grade 12 but I quit before I graduated, because I didn't want to give the government the satisfaction of bragging about any more residential school graduates, after what had been done to me. I was eighteen, an adult, but I'd been a sex object, a toy, from the time that I was ten. It wasn't just Plint preying on young boys; there were other supervisors and older students.

I lived with a woman for four years, until our son was three, and then we separated. When we were together I had a lot of anger. I was like Jekyll and Hyde; I loved her and my son, but then the anger and violence would take over. I think about my son a lot and I really care for him. Someday maybe I'll be able to explain and apologize to him.

My aunt Charlotte took me in hand and got me a job at the sawmill in South Hazelton. She's the main reason I'm around. In 1994, I finally went to a treatment centre. I had a lot of pain locked up inside of me, from all the sexual abuse. By then I was with a woman I really cared for—Vivian Russell, a Gitksan woman from the Grouse clan, the daughter of a hereditary chief.

I was physically abusive and violent even with Vivian for the first three or four years. She quit drinking and then she told me she was pregnant. I kept drinking. On the night that our daughter Latishia was born, I tried to celebrate with booze, but I found I was so happy, I didn't want to drink any more.

The next morning, when I went to see Vivian and our newborn baby, I saw the miracle of a new life, a human being that I could love. I vowed to myself that I would never ever lose another child. Latishia's birth was the first stepping stone toward a new life for myself. I quit drinking. Latishia and Vivian gave me something to live for. Latishia is my great pride and joy. I am giving to her the strength and pride that my grandparents gave me, and I hope the cultural strength, too; all the things that the residential school and Plint tried to rob me of.

For decades I didn't talk about the sexual abuse. From the early age of thirteen I was addicted to drugs and alcohol. Before the birth of my daughter, I didn't care if I lived or died; I was just trying to obliterate the pain and the memories because I didn't see how I could deal with something so enormous on my own. I couldn't tell Vivian I'd been sexually abused until after I'd gone to treatment, and I'd known her for ten years.

Still, the pain I was carrying around seemed endless. I dreamt of my grandmother and remembered that she'd say, "Whenever you're in dire need of help, Willie, you can call on the Creator." She always told me, there is only one Creator, and nobody's got an exclusive pipeline to him. The Creator is there for everyone, white, red or brown. I began taking Latishia to the United Church. Because of Plint, I thought white people were evil, only out to hurt you. But the minister I met there convinced me that people in the church were different and did care deeply about what had happened to us as children. I didn't feel so alone.

I tried to go back to work at the mill after I'd settled down with my family. But my sexual abuse memories of Plint came flooding back. It was a disaster. My story had gotten out and some of the millworkers would tease me by getting behind me and pretending to rape me. If I was suddenly left alone with a white guy I'd get a panic attack and lose control of my bowels. I went through a lot of underwear. I became that terrorized little kid again, with no control.

Up north I could only see a therapist who flew in once a month, so I got the support of my band to go to school in Vancouver. In Vancouver I was referred to a psychiatrist, Dr. Charles Brasfield, who helped me and arranged for me to get a medical exam, because some of my problems were due to the physical damage from being repeatedly raped as a child.

I finally decided to take action because I felt the Canadian government and the church, who hired Plint, shouldn't get away with hurting so many thousands of vulnerable native kids. I contacted the

R.C.M.P. and gave them a statement. My home community of Gitsegukla supported me to go to court in Port Alberni. When I finally saw Plint in court, after thirty years of pain, my knuckles were white on the courtroom rail. I was trying to stop myself from jumping over the rail and choking the bastard. I wanted him to face all the men he abused, all of us he tortured when we were helpless children.

As we left the court, we told the reporters it wasn't over for Plint and the Alberni residential school because we were launching our own multimillion-dollar civil lawsuit against Plint, the school administrators, the United Church and the federal government. I feel we'll get justice in the end. It's been healing for me to speak out. I'm not the only one who was abused so bad, but I am the voice for those men who have the strength to join the lawsuit but not to talk about it publicly yet. Most of us want compensation for our children. We have the full support of the majority of our leaders, and hopefully in the near future we'll also have the support of mainstream society, once they realize the impact the residential schools have had on First Nations people. I believe we're only getting stronger.

It was March 20, 1995, when Willie Blackwater and a group of aboriginal men gathered in a crowded Port Alberni courtroom to face the man who had tormented them decades earlier. Though they were once small boys who had to perform oral sex before they could receive a letter from home, the First Nations men stood straight and proud.

Arthur Henry Plint, then seventy-seven, cursed his accusers as he walked into court under the glare of television lights, hitting out with his cane in a final act of contempt and violence. Inside, he pled guilty to sixteen counts of indecent assult of aboriginal boys aged six to thirteen, between 1948 and 1968. Three of the boys were forcibly sodomized, others forced to perform oral sex on Plint, often daily, for months and years. "I'll never get the stink of you out of my mouth," cried one man outside the courthouse.

Art Thompson, an acclaimed Nuu-chah-nulth artist who attended the Alberni school for nine years, addressed the sentencing hearing wearing a headband, a ceremonial robe with a thunderbird on the back, and the traditional black-painted face to ward off evil. "You're a constant reminder of cultural abuse. I want you to understand the anger and shame but, most of all, I want you to understand the dignity of these men," Thompson told Plint. As Thompson spoke resolutely, snow-white particles of eagle down, representing truth and purity, floated from his cape to the bright-red courtroom carpet.

Before sentencing Plint to eleven years in prison, B.C. Supreme Court Justice Douglas Hogarth said the former supervisor was a predator, "a sexual terrorist" allowed to prey unchecked. "As far as the victims are concerned, the Indian residential school system was nothing more than institutionalized pedophilia," said Justice Hogarth. "Generations of children were wrenched from their families and were brought up to be ashamed to be Indians."

All across Canada, First Nations survivors are speaking out to put the past behind them and to bring perpetrators to justice. Phil Fontaine, newly elected national chief of the Assembly of First Nations and former grand chief of the Assembly of Manitoba Chiefs, was the first high-profile aboriginal leader to publicly acknowledge his own abuse and its toxic effects. "The victim becomes the victimizer," Fontaine told a hushed audience at the first national conference on residential schools in Vancouver in January 1991. "I can never apologize enough to all the people I've harmed," he said, revealing he was sexually, physically and emotionally abused as a child during the ten years he attended two Catholic-run residential schools in Manitoba. "I have to heal as well," Fontaine said. "What I seek is forgiveness for the way I've lived. I need to be able to set my soul free."

Traditional healing, hand in hand with sobriety and conventional therapy, has helped to free the souls of many abused individuals. At the same time, action is underway in several complementary directions. Civil lawsuits have been launched, and there is continuing collective action to restore community strength. In the spring of 1996, the First

Nations Summit of B.C., representing the vast majority of elected leaders and community activists on the issue, gathered at the cedar longhouse of the Squamish Nation in North Vancouver to honour all the residential school survivors who had taken their perpetrators to court and to decide how to proceed.

Tl'azt'en Grand Chief Ed John, a lawyer and summit task force member, emphasized to the gathering that there is no one solution to suit all. "Each First Nation community must decide its own path," said John, looking around the vast hall full of chiefs in business suits with cellular phones, elders in long braids, health workers, non-native church officials and government bureaucrats. "Some of our people are calling for a national commission of inquiry. Others want financial compensation for their pain and suffering; they want to go to court. Still others just want to express their grief and pain and have it acknowledged. Some just want to know where their children and family members are buried. There is no one answer to the grief."

At the front of the longhouse stood an impressive array of almost two dozen men and women who had taken legal action against their abusers. There were Shuswap men, pioneers who ignited a national firestorm of criminal cases when they went to court in Williams Lake, B.C., to hear first the Oblate priest Rev. Harold McIntee, in 1989, and then the Oblate Brother Glen Doughty, in 1991, plead guilty to many counts of sexual and indecent assault. Nuu-chah-nulth, Nisga'a and Gitksan men who had taken Arthur Plint to court stood quietly while artist Art Thompson and Willie Blackwater spoke for them. The five women who had endured agonizing delays in the criminal case against Bishop Hubert O'Connor, the former principal of St. Joseph's Mission Residential School at Williams Lake, were honoured for their courage and patience.

Charlie Carlick stepped forward with an eagle feather in his hand to speak for the thirteen men who had ended "the silent scream of the North" when they stood in a Terrace courtroom just before Christmas, 1995, to see Catholic official Jerzy Maczynski sentenced to sixteen years in jail on twenty-eight counts of sexual abuse at the Lower Post

Indian residential school. Sharon Blakeborough, a Sto:lo sexual abuse counsellor, sang without accompaniment a song she wrote about her hellish years at the St. Mary's Mission school. The entire audience of more than a thousand people slowly circled the room to hug each of the residential school survivors in turn.

Many adults in the longhouse that day had believed that the men who terrorized them would never be brought to justice. The criminal cases were in large part due to the perseverance of key aboriginal communities, such as the Shuswap bands represented by the Cariboo Tribal Council. The Nuu-chah-nulth, fourteen communities along the west coast of Vancouver Island, had completed their own study in late 1995, based on interviews with more than one hundred former residential school students. Their preliminary findings, together with a growing number of allegations and convictions, finally shocked the authorities into action. In late 1995, B.C. First Nations representatives and the R.C.M.P. announced a joint task force to investigate residential school abuse.

Charlene Belleau, the dynamic Shuswap leader who helped bring about the first national residential school conference and provided key emotional and strategic support to several court cases, was appointed provincial coordinator of the task force. Police officers were given sensitivity training and sent out into the field to work directly with Belleau and her team of seven regional First Nations coordinators.

Hopes for the investigation were high, and it did help to bring some of the most notorious abusers to trial. Within six months, R.C.M.P. Staff Sgt. Doug Henderson announced that, after interviews with 150 survivors, the probe had yielded 90 firm suspects. Yet many of them, police said, were "elderly," deceased or impossible to locate. In keeping with a strict protocol initiated by First Nations, R.C.M.P. officers only interviewed victims who voluntarily stepped forward. By late 1996, the R.C.M.P. investigation had led to less than six actual convictions or guilty pleas in court, some involving offenders already found guilty in cases involving other complainants.

Neither Charlene Belleau nor Ed John are discouraged by the relatively low number of criminal convictions. Consciousness raising and healing are slowly proceeding, Belleau says, and for survivors to step forward in court takes great courage. To stipulate, as the task force did, that survivors must have some personal support, as well as access to the therapy and resources they need before speaking out also slows the process to a crawl, acknowledges John, "since many First Nations have very few resources, still, to help victims, especially in our isolated communities."

The task force was able to benefit in its work from painful lessons learned in the course of early investigations and criminal proceedings. In the late 1980s, R.C.M.P. Const. Bob Grinstead, conducting a police investigation into sexual abuse at the St. Joseph's school, found himself talking to sobbing adults revealing sexual abuse for the first time in thirty years. Although the constable gained the firm trust of Shuswap people for his sensitivity and professionalism, he recommended that in future police officers be given more training and that victims have access to counselling before being interviewed about buried sexual trauma. In an interview at the time of the March 1996 summit, Cyril Paul, a Shuswap man who was sexually abused at St. Joseph's, said, "My life fell apart after I went to court against Brother Doughty—I just couldn't handle the anger and pain. I started drinking again. It really hurt because my life was so damaged by him and then I saw him walk away with a year in a jail, which means only four months in a country club prison." Six months sober at the time of the summit, Paul, a logger and father of five, was getting back on his feet. Paul said he was pleased to be rebuilding his relationship with his children and expressed sorrow that some of his fellow residential school victims were not as fortunate. Simon Danes, a former paralegal with the Native Courtworkers, appeared in Port Alberni court to testify against Arthur Plint. A week after the trial, Danes was dead, by his own hand. Tragically, a little more than a year after the interview, Paul too would take his own life.

Nuu-chah-nulth leader Jarry Jack points out that many residential school survivors still don't trust police, because of their role in enforcing the Indian Act by dragging aboriginal children off to school. Sto:lo counsellor Charles Chapman adds that mistrust of police and confrontational, painful court proceedings, followed by relatively light sentences handed to perpetrators, have led many First Nations leaders to look for other routes to healing and justice. Chapman suggests that a national inquiry could travel to witnesses' home reserves to gently and respectfully receive testimony, while at the same time compelling the federal government and church officials to testify under oath and tender files.

In their search for justice, First Nations in B.C. have consulted other wronged communities, including Japanese-Canadian activists whose efforts resulted in an official federal apology and a $300-million redress payment in 1988. The Secwepemc community of Alkali Lake has retained Richard Rodgers, the lawyer who represented men sexually abused as children by the Christian Brothers at the Mount Cashel orphanage in Newfoundland. Rodgers is helping the community to prepare civil suits and is supporting them in their push for a public inquiry similar to the one that eventually led to the conviction of eight Christian Brothers.

The Royal Commission on Aboriginal Peoples, after five years and millions of dollars' worth of careful research, concluded in 1996 that a public inquiry into every aspect of residential schools should be established under the federal Public Inquiries Act, with a mandate to conduct public hearings across the country and to commission research. Remedies should include apologies, the commission concluded, as well as collective compensation "to enable Aboriginal communities to design and administer programs that assist the healing process and rebuild community life . . . as well as funding for the treatment of affected people and their families." Initially, the federal government seemed committed to its carefully crafted position of 1992, when then minister of Indian Affairs Tom Siddon refused demands by aboriginal leaders for a public inquiry and made it clear that there would be "no ministerial apology, no apology on behalf of Canadians," and that there were no plans for compensation. Siddon denied government liability and said the focus would remain on individual acts that violated the Criminal Code. Ron Irwin, Indian Affairs minister at the time the Royal Commission's report was released, snorted that the $58 million the commission cost would have been better spent on Indian housing and indicated that he had every intention of shelving the commission's recommendations.

In Saskatchewan, the federal government began in 1995 to quietly pay, without any formal acknowledgement of responsibility, out-of-court settlements to fifty former students of the government-run residential school on the Gordon reserve north of Regina. Although the size of the settlements is confidential, they are reported to range from $75,000 to $150,000 per person, totalling less than half the $35 million the sexual abuse victims were seeking. The secretive nature of the payout—in the absence of any apology—has angered aboriginal leaders further. Blaine Favel, chief of the Federation of Saskatchewan Indians in 1996, renewed a demand for a national inquiry. "There's a sense of injustice and that Indian Affairs is sweeping the issue under the table," said Favel.

In the absence of any federal commitment to a public inquiry, First Nations have had to be aggressive and innovative in seeking redress. Willie Blackwater, almost two dozen survivors and the estate of Simon Danes are pursuing their massive civil suit, which was launched on January 31, 1996. Emily Rice and her sister Rose Marie Mitchell, together with more than twenty other men and women, including four brothers sexually abused by the same Oblate brother, have moved to sue the Catholic Church, the Montfort Brothers, the Oblates, the Diocese of Victoria and the Sisters of St. Ann, as well as the federal government, for the staggering losses and injuries each sustained at the Kuper Island school.

Mediation has paved the way to at least one out-of-court settlement in B.C. and is being actively studied by other First Nations. In early 1997, Nisga'a brothers Dennis and Steven Nyce announced that after several months of negotiation through a professional mediator, they had reached a confidential financial settlement with the federal government and the Salvation Army. The Army apologized for its part in hiring the infamous pedophile William Gareth Douglas, who sexually abused every boy between the ages of six and eleven while he was preacher to the tiny B.C. reserve of Canyon City, known today as Gitwinsihlkw. The federal government, although it will pay part of the compensation to the Nyce brothers and their northern community, will do so "without prejudice"—or apology. As part of their own compensation package, the Nyce brothers have asked that their home community be given the resources it needs to start healing.

On June 26, 1997, after a federal election and Irwin's voluntary retirement as Indian Affairs minister, a slight thaw in the federal position was detectable, perhaps in response to the tragic coincidence of two events: the release of a report from a May 1997 inquiry into residential schools held by the Secwepemc village of Alkali Lake after demands for a national inquiry were rebuffed, and the suicide of Cyril Paul. Paul had told the inquiry, "I hurt a lot . . . I'm scared . . . I hope one day I will no longer need to hide my tears in the rain." Only two weeks later, the father of five put a rifle to his stomach and ended his life.

Cyril Paul's spirit, and the groundswell of anger and grief that filled the room, appeared to have finally reached the critical mass needed to break federal intransigence. John Watson, director-general of Indian Affairs' Pacific Region, acknowledged publicly that the primary goal of the residential schools was "assimilation"—the first such admission by any federal official—and added that calls for an inquiry were being "actively considered" by the federal cabinet. "We recognize the hurts of the past and our priority now is to build for a better future," Watson told reporters upon the release of the report by Tl'azt'en Grand Chief Ed John and former provincial court judge Cunliffe Barnett. John and Barnett, the commissioners who presided over the inquiry, were terse but angry in their report: "High government and church officials knew that Indian children were being neglected, abused and even killed" at residential schools, they said. The one hundred chiefs who heard John and Barnett deliver their report shed tears at the news of Cyril Paul's suicide, but beneath the sorrow lay a new resolve. "There must be a national public inquiry," said Robert Louie, a co-chair of the First Nations Summit. "There must be follow-up and there must be redress. Certainly the wounds have not healed and they can't heal until we get justice."

At the site of the old Kuper Island school, in October of 1996, the Coast Salish Penelakut people held a memorial service for all the children who had died there, and a healing ceremony for those who had survived. Several hundred former students from all parts of the province again took the small ferry to their Alcatraz. Many had not been back to the island for decades. Under a brilliant blue sky, people slowly filed around a long table laden with candles, flowers, photographs and lists of loved ones who never came home.

Led by Shaker church priest Eva George and her singing congregation, the entire gathering walked through the empty foundations of the old school down to the dock, for a service in memory of the children who drowned trying to escape. Each family who had lost a child carried a brilliant bouquet of carnations and dahlias, the scarlet, rose, green and gold colours of autumn. The flowers were flung into the ocean. Karen McCallum, a Surrey nurse who attended Kuper as a child, cradled her small baby, tears streaming down her face, as she recalled the drowning of her beloved older sisters Beverley and Carolyn Joseph. "We called them Bee and Cisco," said McCallum. "They never could swim, but they were so desperate to escape, they hid a small boat and tried to get across the channel at night. I was at school when they brought up Bee's body, all blue and still. Carolyn's body was never found, but I sense her spirit out there." It was thirty years since McCallum had been to Kuper Island, but she said the trip was crucial. "It's for my children that I want to release the pain I carried around, and I'm so happy knowing they'll never go through what I did."

At the ceremony's end, Penelakut Chief Randy James carried out a final symbolic act. Carefully backing a pickup truck down to the end of the dock, James and a crew of strong young men hoisted off the back of the truck the enormous concrete cornerstone of the old Kuper Island school, all that was left from the school's demolition in 1974. The massive stone crashed into the water, sending up a huge wave. Cheers broke out as the salt-water splashes mixed with tears, and the last vestige of the hated Kuper Island school sank without a trace to the bottom of the deep channel. "It feels good," said Chief James. "Today we did the right thing. I feel like I finally got those priests off my back and that prison out of my life. Now we're going to get on with our lives."

3

WOLVES IN SHEEP'S CLOTHING

The Child Welfare System

ALL aboriginal cultures teach that children are special gifts lent by the spirit world; if they are not loved and cherished, they may flee back to the realm from which they came. In traditional times, there was no greater dishonour than an extended family who could not look after its own young ones. In the rare circumstances where that was the case, the surrounding society always stepped in to share communal responsibility for raising the children.

Through its deliberate assault on the aboriginal family, the residential school system created the conditions that rendered First Nations vulnerable to the next wave of intervention: child abductions sanctioned by provincial child welfare laws. Residential schools incarcerated children for ten months of the year, but at least the children stayed in an aboriginal peer group; they always knew their First Nation of origin and who their parents were, and they knew that eventually they would be going home. In the foster and adoptive care system, aboriginal children typically vanished with scarcely a trace, the vast majority of them placed until they were adults in non-aboriginal homes where their cultural identity, their legal Indian status, their knowledge of their own First Nation and even their birth names were erased, often forever.

The transition began in the 1950s, when federal officials started using residential schools primarily as alternative parenting institutions rather than as educational facilities. The schools became a "general welfare resource for the care of children who, in the view of local Indian agents, were not being competently cared for by their parents," writes Andrew Armitage, director of the University of Victoria School of Social Work, in an article on the subject. The need to institutionalize former pupils' children, he notes, was in itself "a commentary on the effects of the residential schools, as these parents were now the second or third generation of former pupils."

In choosing "neglected" children to be sent away to boarding schools, Indian agents were already applying the culturally inappropriate judgements that would become commonplace in the child welfare era. Orphaned children were quickly scooped up, but so too were those cared for by an aged grandmother or by parents living in the impoverished conditions that were endemic on reserves by the early 1950s. Indian agents who identified children needing substitute care did, on occasion, seek help from extended family or relatives on reserve. This age-old First Nations tradition became known in the bureaucracy as "custom adoption." Ironically, it was the federal officials' use of residential schools and custom adoption that provoked disapproval from the burgeoning social work profession—and served to justify that profession's own removal of Indian children.

The immediate post–World War II years spawned a strong climate of social concern in Canada, and a new focus by members of the helping professions on individual and collective needs that had been postponed by the altruistic cause of defending world freedom. It took little insight to see that First Nations were among the most disadvantaged people in Canada. The Indian Act had set them up as legal wards confined to uneconomic tracts of land. By the late 1940s, four or five generations had returned from residential schools as poorly educated, angry, abused strangers who had no experience in parenting.

"They were aliens . . . who formed no bonds with their families," Spallumcheen leader Cinderina Williams wrote in a study submitted to the Royal Commission on Aboriginal Peoples in 1994. "Perhaps the greatest tragedy was . . . [by] not being brought up in a loving, caring, sharing, nurturing environment, they did not have these skills; as they are learned through observation, participation and interaction. Consequently when these children became parents, and most did at an early age, they had no parenting skills. They did not have the capability to show affection. They sired and bred children but were unable to relate to them on any level."

The Canadian Welfare Council and the Canadian Association of Social Workers argued in a 1947 brief to the Special Joint Committee of the Senate and the House of Commons that "Indian children who are neglected lack the protection afforded under social legislation available to white children in the community." They condemned the internment of any aboriginal child, neglected or not, in residential school, and charged that "the practice of adopting Indian children is loosely conceived and executed and is usually devoid of the careful legal and social protections available to white children." Ottawa listened. Amendments made in 1951 to Section 88 of the Indian Act stipulated that all laws of general application in force in a province should apply on reserves, unless they conflicted with treaties or federal laws. With these amendments, Ottawa effectively delegated the responsibility for aboriginal health, welfare and educational services to the provinces, although it remained financially responsible for status Indians. It took a few more years for social workers to act on these changes, however, while Ottawa negotiated separately with each province how much it would pay per capita for services delivered to Indians. In the end, inequity persisted not only between aboriginal child and white but also from province to province.

Once the provinces were in charge, and guaranteed payment for each Indian child they apprehended, the number of First Nations children made legal wards of the state quickly ballooned. Only 1 per cent of all children in care were native in 1959, but by the end of the 1960s, 30 to 40 per cent of all legal wards were aboriginal children, even though they formed less than 4 per cent of the national population.

Ottawa was only too pleased to hand off its responsibilities for Indian social services, just as it had delegated Indian education half a century earlier. Eager social work professionals needed employment, and reserves provided a ready-made industry. In the relative prosperity of the post-war period, it is likely that the federal government could have mustered the resources to substantially improve the lives of aboriginal Canadians. After a century of misguided federal policy, reserve life in Canada approximated a state of emergency: housing, sanitation, safe drinking water, schools, hospitals, clinics and social programs were urgently required. Instead, Ottawa decided to remove aboriginal children. Social services such as counselling, homemakers and child care were not available to intact aboriginal families from either the provinces or federal Health and Welfare. Only when aboriginal families were split apart and their children made legal wards—inducted into the mainstream—could aboriginal children count on attaining a standard of living even remotely approximating that enjoyed by other Canadian children.

University of Manitoba researchers Brad McKenzie and Pete Hudson concluded in a study published in 1992 that aboriginal children were taken away in hugely disproportionate numbers less for reasons of poverty, family dysfunction or rapid social change than to effect a continuation of the "colonial argument": that is, "the child welfare system was part of a deliberate assault on Native society designed to make changes in Native people." The white social worker, following hard on the heels of the missionary, the priest and the Indian agent, was convinced that the only hope for the salvation of the Indian people lay in the removal of their children. Adoptive families were encouraged to treat even a status Indian child as their own, freely erasing his or her birth name and tribe of origin, thus implicitly extinguishing the child's cultural birthright. In the foster care system, where native children typically bounced from home to home, a child's tribal identity usually became lost altogether.

The caseloads in social services agencies were so high that workers did not have time to properly screen homes, nor was monitoring of either foster or adoptive homes usually feasible. But most social workers, none of whom were aboriginal at that time, felt little harm could befall an aboriginal child rescued from poverty and placed with a nice, middle-class, white family. Yet behind the closed doors of their foster and adoptive homes, aboriginal children were even more isolated and vulnerable than they had been in residential school. Mary Longman, a Plains Cree artist, produced a series of paintings in the early 1990s to tell the story of her family of seven siblings, apprehended when the eldest was six and permanently separated into non-native foster and adoptive homes. In the home of her white adoptive parents, Longman was viciously beaten, sexually abused and treated as a servant. Her aboriginal culture was denigrated. After she was able as an adult to trace some of her siblings, they shared stories of foster care that were remarkably similar. Longman called her series of paintings *Wolves in Sheep's Clothing*. The first set of wolves were the social workers who failed to adequately screen the foster homes, Longman said. "The other wolves are families who adopt for the wrong reasons, be it money, extra hands for work, to impress their peers or for sexual pleasures."

Longman remembers vividly the day social workers descended on her little house on the reserve. A defiant six-year-old, she tried to help her mother and grandmother barricade the door. The painting titled *Separation* shows seven tiny weeping faces silhouetted in the back window of the social worker's car as it drives away. Longman never saw her grandmother again, and it would be eighteen years of a lengthy search before she and her mother were reunited.

Longman's paintings do not shrink from portraying the poverty and neglect faced by children of her generation in the post-residential school era. She painted her own desperate little face as a five-year-old, holding her wailing twin baby sisters in her arms. Left alone while the adults went to town, she had no food with which to comfort the crying babies.

In many cases, children were taken from parents whose only crime was poverty—and being aboriginal. Finding a grandmother caring for several small children in a home without a flush toilet, refrigerator or running water was enough to spur a worker to seize the children and take them into the care of the state. In rural areas, often the only difference between the parents whose children were stolen away and those who took in foster children for a little extra cash was the colour of their skin. A nuclear family model was rigidly imposed, even though it did not fit aboriginal cultural traditions. Placing children with another family on a remote reserve was not seen as a viable option when a child could be delivered by plane or bus to white foster parents in the big city. In any case, it was almost impossible for an Indian Affairs–built bungalow to qualify as a foster home. Few had running water, sewage hook-ups, electricity or insulated walls, let alone the middle-class standards demanded of foster homes: a separate bedroom for each child, sofas, rugs, two parents, Dad with a well-paying job and Mom at home.

Bridget Moran, who toiled as a B.C. government social worker in the worst days of child apprehensions from northern reserves, recalls those days with sadness and anger. One of the few civil servants to publicly challenge what was happening, Moran recalls that social workers "had no resources that might conceivably have helped to keep families together, and children in their natural homes." There were no family support workers, no treatment centres, no transition houses or programs to prevent sexual abuse or wife battering. "When we discovered a child at risk in his own home, we had no recourse but to move him into a foster home," says Moran in her book *A Little Rebellion*. "Over and over again we played Russian roulette with lives of the young. In the end, when we removed children from their own homes and put them in foster homes about which we knew next to nothing, no matter how we cloaked our actions in welfare jargon, we were putting those children at risk." After six years, Moran reluctantly concluded that "the welfare department which employed me was the biggest contributor to child abuse in the province."

Virtually every extended family in every aboriginal village across the country lost a child to "the welfare." Spallumcheen, a Shuswap community in central B.C.'s Okanagan Valley, lost almost an entire generation. A particularly zealous social worker named Edith Oram told an interviewer in 1989 that of thirty Spallumcheen children still living in foster homes in 1981, she could take credit for apprehending more than half of them while she was on duty between 1962 and 1966. Her successor, Mary Poggemoeller, apprehended fifty children in a one-year period alone. Poggemoeller, who was employed as a government social worker until 1970, recalled apprehending several whole families of children, sometimes as many as ten at one time. Many were placed with Mormon families living throughout southeastern B.C. and the northeastern United States.

One weekend, a social worker chartered a bus to apprehend thirty-eight children from the Spallumcheen reserve, recalls Ernie Klassen, the former district superintendent for Indian Affairs. "She was asking for thirty-eight separate foster homes in which to place these children," says Klassen, who remembers that by 1970 there were at least sixty Spallumcheen children in permanent care, and an unknown number who had already been adopted out. Spallumcheen became a quiet, dispirited town of adults and elders, with at times fewer than fourteen children left on reserve. Drinking and despair intensified rather than dissipated. "People were feeling completely helpless, useless and totally defeated," says Earl Shipmaker, who was a social worker in the community during the seventies. "They felt as though they had no control over themselves and that someone else, whites, was in charge." The Indian Affairs office in Vernon controlled Spallumcheen's chief and council; it "ran the meetings, set the agendas and made the decisions."

Apart from the difficulty of finding substitute care for typically large aboriginal families, a bizarre holdover from the residential school days dictated that native children could be better acculturated and assimilated if they grew up away from their brothers and sisters. The tradition of strong sibling ties, where an older aboriginal child took on lifelong responsibility for the protection of younger brothers and sisters, counted for little. Wayne Christian, a former Spallumcheen chief who is now director of the Round Lake Treatment Centre, was taken away as a child along with his nine younger siblings. They were split up and assigned to separate non-Indian homes. At seventeen, Christian returned to Spallumcheen. His mother had almost been destroyed by the removal of her children; although she had not been alcoholic before, she had turned to drinking as a release. A much younger brother of Wayne's who had been desperately unhappy in his foster home also came back to the community. "We tried to be a family, and I tried to connect my brother to what I found to be strong and good about our culture, but it was lost to him," Christian says. One morning Wayne found his beloved younger brother dead. He had shot himself in the head.

Patrick Johnston, a researcher for the Canadian Council on Social Development, has dubbed the accelerated removal of children beginning in 1959 the "Sixties' Scoop," but the wholesale abduction of aboriginal children has persisted long past that decade. By the late 1970s, one in four status Indian children could expect to be separated from his or her parents for all or part of childhood. If non-status and Metis children, on whom statistics were not maintained, are included, the statistics show that one in three, or in some provinces every other aboriginal child, spent part of his or her childhood as a legal ward of the state. In British Columbia, even today, one of every three legal wards is a First Nations child.

From the beginning, many aboriginal children were sent to the U.S. to be adopted. As late as the 1980s, the majority of those apprehended in Manitoba were shipped out of Canada by aggressive American adoption agencies. The trade in babies was primarily aboriginal; in 1981, for example, 55 per cent of the native children in Manitoba's care were sent out of the province for adoption, compared to only 7 per cent of Caucasian children. Manitoba judge Edwin Kimelman, called in to investigate, concluded that "cultural genocide has been taking place in a systematic routine manner. One gets an image of children stacked in foster homes as used cars are stacked on corner lots, just waiting for the right 'buyer' to stroll by."

The private adoption agencies, often religious, that scooped up Canadian Indian children for white Americans usually did little screening beyond ascertaining the applicant's ability to pay; typically five to ten thousand dollars changed hands during an aboriginal child's adoption. Although the situation has since been remedied, until 1982 there were no legal barriers to out-of-province or international adoptions or to social workers accepting financial "incentives" for finding adoptable children. There are no reports of money ever reaching the relinquishing family.

"Big, shiny American cars would come onto the reserve, followed by the social worker's car," says Maggie Blacksmith, now a Dakota Ojibway Child and Family Services social worker who herself lost a son to the Manitoba government. "When they left, there'd be a little Indian child sitting in the back of the American car, bawling their eyes out. The social worker always had a piece of paper saying it was legal. We know the social worker was paid but we'd have known right away if any parents got money, because we lived so closely together and we were all so poor, money would have been very conspicuous. If parents tried to keep their kids, the social worker called the Mountie."

Manitoba First Nations lost the greatest number, but aboriginal children from every province were sent to the U.S., particularly after the Indian Child Welfare Act of 1978 cut off the supply of adoptable aboriginal children there. First Nations writer and activist Lee Maracle, speaking after a 1995 Vancouver theatre performance on aboriginal adoption issues, charged: "Thousands of aboriginal children were scooped up in the fifties and sixties from Vancouver alone. A lot were sold south of the border, in Chicago, New York, Detroit, the Midwest. Some were used as slaves."

Aboriginal children were also seized from First Nations parents whose tribal territory traditionally ranged on both sides of the Canada-U.S. border. Daisy Hill, who was born on the Interior Salish Sliammon reserve near Powell River and is now a counsellor with the Hey'Way'Noqu Healing Circle for Addictions Society in Vancouver, lost her son Tommy as a toddler after she took him and his brother to the States as a young mother to visit relatives. There, Daisy was stricken with tuberculosis, which had flared up periodically ever since she contracted the disease in residential school. She was quarantined in an

American sanitarium, and her two small boys were placed in the temporary care of the Washington State social services department. When Daisy was well, the agency refused to return one of her sons. It was only after she had been reunited with her son twenty-five years later that she learned Tommy had been given to a white couple to adopt before she even left the hospital.

There were many non-native foster and adoptive parents who did their very best to nurture, heal and raise the First Nations children entrusted to their care. Tragically, the outcome of adoptions even by conscientious non-native parents was often disastrous, as the adoptee reached adolescence only to suffer the triply painful identity crisis of being adolescent, aboriginal and adopted. Canadian and American social service agencies now estimate that adolescence is the period when up to 85 per cent of transcultural adoptive relationships fail.

In a recent study, Christopher Bagley of the University of Calgary found that aboriginal adoptions are more likely to fail than even transcultural adoptions of children from countries outside Canada. Bagley's findings indicate that aboriginal children who stayed with their families, even if those parents had had another child removed, fared far better. The adoptive family's attempts at supplying aboriginal culture—museums, films or beading classes—were "too superficial" to bolster their adopted children's low self-esteem. Aboriginal adoptees had to suffer systemic racism in isolation, without enjoying any of the powerful spiritual or cultural benefits of being Indian.

All across Canada, homeless shelters, courtrooms, youth detention centres and prisons are full of aboriginal people who grew up in non-native substitute care. A 1990 survey of aboriginal prisoners in Prince Albert penitentiary found that over 95 per cent came from either a group home or a foster home. Jerry Adams, a Nisga'a social worker for Vancouver's Urban Native Youth Association, estimates that half to three-quarters of all the habituated native street kids that he works with "are graduates of the B.C. foster care system or runaways from adoptions that didn't work out. They're looking for the sense of identity and belonging with other aboriginal street kids down here that they never got in their non-native home. Maybe 80 per cent of the girls and more than half of the boys have been sexually abused in care, but even the ones from good homes are on the run." Concludes Adams, a former government social worker: "Foster kids tend to have children very young, and those children, too, wind up in foster care."

After four continuous decades of child abductions, there are enough lost and missing First Nations children, their fate a mystery to their home communities, to populate a small Canadian city. None of the private, public or religious adoption agencies that placed aboriginal children out of province or out of the country monitored the children, and few even kept records that would allow adoptees to retrace their roots or find their tribes. There are few government-funded programs in Canada to help adoptees discover who they are, and little repatriation assistance if they are fortunate enough to locate their First Nation of origin or their birth families. Aboriginal communities from B.C. to Nova Scotia are now in the process of trying to locate children sent abroad and to the U.S. After their program was publicized on American television, the Manitoba First Nations Repatriation Program received calls from "just about every state in the United States from Canadian Indians who were adopted down there as children," reports repatriation worker Shirlene Parisien.

Paddy Walkus, chief of the Gwa'Sala-'Nakwada'xw Council on northern Vancouver Island, has mounted a campaign to try to bring home his people's missing children, who were removed by the car- and busload throughout the 1960s and '70s. "We know they were scattered to all parts of the globe, to California, Oregon, New York, all over the States, Germany, England, Europe. I'm still trying to get my own niece returned from Australia, where she was taken by the doctor and his wife when they left this area," Walkus says. "Indian children were taken away like souvenirs by professionals who were supposed to be helping the whole family." In the 1980s, the Gwa'Sala-'Nakwada'xw band built its own receiving home for children and developed a protocol with police and social workers to prevent the removal of children from the reserve.

There is still no far-reaching federal statute in Canada comparable to the U.S. Indian Child Welfare Act, which stipulates the inalienable right of an Indian child to grow up within his or her tribe of origin. The act, though one of the most litigated Indian statutes in the U.S., has ensured that almost 85 per cent of all American Indian children are reared in Indian homes. To date, several British Columbia First Nations have signed tripartite agreements with the provincial and federal governments to give them jurisdiction and some funding to run their own child and family services. Under these agreements, joint planning is undertaken for all children in care, and adoptive homes are sought first within the child's extended family or tribe of origin. A few First Nations, including the Sto:lo, the Nuu-chah-nulth and the Squamish, have the delegated legal power to apprehend children in need of protection, as well as to certify their own foster homes on reserve and to decide on child placements. B.C.'s Nisga'a Nation, in the first modern treaty to have reached the agreement-in-principle stage, has accepted gradual delegation by the province of child and family services. Other First Nations engaged in the treaty process have served notice that they will seek full control of all social services, with delegation to the provinces of whatever residual responsibilities the nation cannot meet. In the interim, many have signed informal local protocols, at either the band or the tribal council level, with the province and R.C.M.P. requiring consultation before intervention. And the new Child, Family and Community Service Act introduced by the B.C. government in 1996 calls for aboriginal bands to be involved in the planning regarding any of their children in care. But despite these important steps, there is still a long to go. More than 52 per cent of all children taken into care in B.C. each year as a result of court orders are aboriginal, and a staggering 78 per cent of aboriginal children in permanent care in B.C. are still placed with non-native caregivers. Both aboriginal bands and activist groups have warned that they can't take over social services without adequate financing.

The mid-twentieth-century abduction of aboriginal children greatly compounded the spiritual and cultural losses suffered by First Nations peoples in the time since contact. As an elder sadly asked the

B.C. government at a 1992 hearing: "Where are our artisans, our weavers, fishermen, medicine people, dancers, shamans, sculptors and hunters? For thirty years, generations of our children, the very future of our communities, have been taken away from us. Will they come home as our leaders knowing the power and tradition of their people? Or will they come home broken and in pain, not knowing who they are, looking for the family that died of a broken heart?"

Joyce McBryde, born Joyce Aleck, is a First Nations school support worker at Florence Nightingale Elementary School in the inner-city Vancouver neighbourhood of Mount Pleasant. Her bright office is usually full of First Nations youngsters seeking her counsel and advice. As an infant, Joyce was taken from the care of her N'laka'pamux maternal grandmother, who was caring for several children in a tiny cabin high above the Fraser Canyon. After a harrowing stay in an abusive foster home, Joyce was placed with a loving non-native family, with whom she spent the rest of her childhood. But it was more than two decades before Joyce would find her way back to the large N'laka'pamux family who cherished her memory for all those years, but found it difficult to accept her once she returned.

This is Joyce's story, along with the voices of her maternal grandmother, Julia Frank, who died in 1996; her adoptive mother, Glady Tenning, and her birth mother, Faith Richardson.

Julia Frank:

Joyce's maternal grandmother was born Julia Michel in the N'laka'pamux Nation on April 1, 1911. A dignified, white-haired elder who still spoke with the trace of a British accent, a relic of her days at the Anglican Church's St. George's residential school in Lytton, Julia Frank spoke before her death in 1995 about how Joyce was stolen from her care.

When I left the residential school, the principal promised every girl who managed not to get married for two years after graduation either a cooking range, furniture or a sewing machine from Sears. He figured to keep us from falling back into our uncivilized ways, as he put it. When we went into Lytton he'd point to an Indian woman on the street drunk, or a woman with little children, and he'd say, "Is that what you want to become, after all we've given you?" I always knew I would marry John. But I wanted that cooking range bad, and as soon as I got it, we were married.

Over the years we had lots of kids. In those days, I had a big garden just above my cabin, and I looked after all the grandchildren while my daughter Winnie was in nursing school and Faith, Joyce's mom, she was in the hospital. That field nurse, Mrs. Dickinson, she used to come to check up on me almost every week, asking so many questions. She'd say the Indian agent sent her. I told her, "I have all the food we need. I gather food with the children." My brothers they'd bring me salmon and meat; I had all the older grandchildren to help me. I was never alone. But she kept threatening me. She'd take the babies, she had homes waiting for them in Merritt and Lytton.

Then one day I hear Mrs. Dickinson's car horn at the bottom of the mountain. I sent the older kids down to help her come up, and this time, she's got a social worker with her. I had a cold and I was lying in bed. But the babies were not crying, they were in their cribs, and I had the older kids to help me. This nurse she says, "You see you can't look after these kids. You're sick." I said, "I'm all right. You leave us alone." I didn't know while I was talking to the nurse in the bedroom, that social worker was taking Joyce. They leave, and all the kids are yelling, "Grandma, Grandma, they've got the baby." I couldn't stop them.

I never thought I'd see our baby again. I didn't know what you need to get a baby back from those white people, a lawyer or something. We had no money. That Mrs. Dickinson, she came back and told me some good people had Joyce. One day a few years after they took Joyce away, I saw a white lady in a hotel in Lillooet with a little Indian girl, telling the hotel operator that Joyce was adopted now. She looked okay, my

Joyce, and I thought this white lady she must be taking pretty good care of her.

You know, my grandmother used to talk about the first white people who came into N'laka'pamux territory. They were starving hungry, were eating rotting fish, and they even went into holes in the ground and ate rotten eggs. We fed them; we had dried fish, salted fish, smoked fish—we helped them survive. By the time I was a girl there were enough of the white people to have a town and the residential school. My parents said, "Well, they're going to stay, we've got to learn their ways." My children, my grandchildren, all got taken away to the residential schools. The Indian agent told my parents it was the law, they would go to jail if they didn't let us go to school. If we'd known they were going to take our children away, those white people, maybe we shouldn't have fed them and welcomed them here. That's how they paid us back.

Joyce McBryde:

I know that I am alive today because there are four women who love me. I don't have an aboriginal birth mother and a white adoptive mother. I have two mothers and I had two dear grandmothers. I know they love me and without the love of those four women, I wouldn't be here today.

After I found my birth family I wondered why I alone was taken away, not my brothers and sisters. Why did they let me go? Although it's not like they let me go, it's more like I was taken.

I always knew I was a native from the Lytton band and that I was adopted. My adoptive father, Ron McBryde, was a government worker in Lytton, B.C., who later became minister of northern affairs in Manitoba. My mother, Glady, stayed at home with us and took in foster children, then later became an employment counsellor. They had two birth children: Gary, who was older than me, and Greg, who's younger.

JOYCE MCBRYDE

My adoptive father was always busy. He did a lot for the northern aboriginal people, but on a personal level, it seemed there wasn't any intimacy. He just didn't have time for us. We presented a successful image of the happy family on all the election literature, but that wasn't always the reality. As I grew up I felt very distant from him. His natural children had much closer bonds with him. When he died, I looked outside and there were my mom and my two brothers grieving together. I felt a distance, as though I'd never have the same bonds with them that they had with each other.

Glady's affection for me and her support never changed. It was hard when I was a kid because I had a lot of racism at school and I know it hurt her too. My brothers were athletic and intelligent, they fit in. Because I was native, I was always picked on. In elementary school they'd call me dirty squaw and make all those silly noises we're supposed to make. I'd come home and cry and cry and cry. I'd go to sleep hoping I'd be sick so I wouldn't have to go to school.

I figured if I found my birth family then I'd belong somewhere, so in Grade 6 I ran away. My dad was furious. We tried family counselling, which was a disaster, but it did help my family understand how badly I wanted to find my birth family. I think my mother realized how unhappy I was, even though I was always passive and quiet and shy and well-behaved. We agreed that if I stayed with them we would look for my birth family when I was sixteen or when I graduated from high school. As a family, we had difficulty expressing our feelings and communicating with each other. There was lots of anger. There was no one to talk to about feeling disconnected from my aboriginal identity.

At sixteen, I became pregnant and chose to have an abortion, and my father was furious. After that, I didn't exist for him. It was as though I'd met his expectations for what an Indian woman would be like, and he didn't want anything more to do with me.

When I was eighteen, I decided to start looking for my birth family. I found my oldest brother, Terry, right away, because I called the band council looking for someone named Aleck and they told me to talk to the counsellor Terry Aleck up at the high school. It turned out that he knew a little girl named Joyce had been taken from his mother, so he realized I was his sister. I couldn't catch my breath for a few minutes. I had thought it would be a lot harder to find my family.

Terry told me nobody had forgotten me all those years. They had always wondered what happened to little Joyce. He told me I had four brothers, John, Rawleigh, Dwayne and him. My mother, Glady, had been told I had four brothers, but I also had a sister named Shari that I hadn't known about. Terry told me our mother was still alive and living in Lytton. So was her mother and sister and lots of uncles and relatives. Terry and I wrote back and forth for almost a year before I got up my courage to go to Lytton for the first time.

It was a culture shock. Right after I got there I was invited to a wedding reception. I wore a very nice outfit and I was totally overdressed. There were a lot of drunk people. I met so many people related to me that it was overwhelming. At first, I felt I was really very fortunate I didn't grow up on the reserve, and that if I had I would be either alcoholic or dead. It seemed as though my siblings were caught in that cycle.

At the same time, I wanted desperately to fit in. I had lots of energy and optimism, and I was determined to belong and have them accept me, without realizing all the changes and suffering and sharing they'd been through while I was away for twenty years. I returned to Lytton to live and I stayed there for four years.

I tried everything I could do to be the way I thought the rest of my family was. I became promiscuous, I drank too much and I got involved in an abusive relationship that was very bad for me. After I had lived like that for three years, I'd had enough. I left the man who'd abused me. I withdrew completely and I went to live in a trailer on the outskirts of town and I waited for my family to come to me. Then one Christmas I spent entirely by myself. No one from my family called me or came to see me. I decided it was time to move on in my life.

I came back to Vancouver and enrolled in the Native Education Centre. I try to go back to Lytton for community events or family gatherings when I'm told about them, which is not very often. When I go home, I give everybody my phone number and address and tell them to come by if they're in town, but no one ever does. I realized I had to develop my own reality, my own identity, separate from both families.

I've found my own sense of family with my husband Joel Dunstan, who comes from a big N'laka'pamux family. In December of 1996, Joel and I were married in our apartment, with only thirty people there. My two adopted brothers and Glady were great. From Lytton, only my mom and her husband came, and she was very, very quiet. A month later, we had a reception in Lytton, which my sister Shari organized, and it raised all those conflicting feelings in me, sadness, disappointment and wishing I belonged and people were different. My uncle showed up drunk to our dry reception. One brother dropped off his family and said he had to go shopping, and then never came back. Another brother came in grey sweatpants. My brother Dwayne, though, drummed us in with an honour song, and that was very special.

Now I feel secure and happy for my own reasons, not trying hard to belong to either family, just being who I am. On a daily basis, I still have to work at liking myself. I have a right to go home to Lytton if I want. I have a right to know my birth mother. I didn't choose to be brought up in a white middle-class home. I have two mothers who love me and I love both of them. But for the past two to three years I've felt a real distance from both of them. I feel like I'm betraying one or the other if I spend time with either. Christmas is still a very emotional time for me, especially now both my grandmothers are gone. But throughout it all I feel as if the Creator was looking after me when I took incredible risks to go back and live on a reserve in a community I knew nothing about. With the Creator looking after me, adoption has allowed me to live in two worlds.

Glady Tenning:

My husband was a probation officer. Most of his clients were native because we were surrounded by reserves. We became really involved with the native community. Native people around Lillooet were being really discriminated against by the white community and wanted to put out a newspaper of their own. I can remember people in the late 1960s who came into our home and said they had never been in a white home before.

My husband shared an office with a social worker, so we became aware that native children needed foster homes. I remember very clearly—it was a Saturday night—the telephone rang and it was the secretary my husband shared with the social worker. She said she had just had this hysterical phone call from this woman. She didn't know what to do with this little girl, she couldn't handle her. The secretary asked, "Can you take her?" I said of course we could take her. It was Joyce, and she was seventeen months old.

We were told that Joyce's mother had suffered a nervous breakdown after three extremely violent deaths in the family. When Joyce's mother went into the hospital the grandparents took the other children, but because the children were so close together in age, the grandparents felt they couldn't handle a baby. I know now that's not true, but that's what I was told. So Joyce was placed in a foster home in Lillooet, and she was there from the time she was ten months old until she was seventeen months old.

There was no question that she had been physically abused in that home. She had bruises all over her face and all over her legs. She cried for hours and hours, gasping for breath. She was really in trouble. She looked very frightened. She had hardly any hair. Her walking was very unsteady. She didn't say a whole lot. I can also remember that when they brought along whatever clothing she had, they also had medication for her to eat and medication for her to sleep. That went into the garbage the next day. I never had any trouble getting Joyce to eat. She didn't say anything about being hungry between meals, but she did go to the garbage a lot.

We have to remember it was twenty-seven years ago. The whole issue of abuse, sexual or physical, wasn't something that was talked about. What amazed me was the number of people I didn't even know in Lillooet who stopped me on the street and said, "Thank heavens you've taken this little girl." The social worker must have known about it. No charges were ever laid. No one ever said anything to the authorities. I was pretty naive in those days myself. If it happened today it would be investigated.

Clothes and medication were all she came to us with, no toys or

STOLEN FROM OUR EMBRACE

personal things. It took at least two months for Joyce to settle in, and then there were issues after that. At that point in my life I'd think nothing of giving a swat on the rear end, I'd do that to my own children. I can remember the first time I raised my hand to smack her. I was absolutely horrified at the look of terror in her eyes. She became absolutely stiff and actually screamed before I had even touched her. It was obvious something major had happened to her.

Joyce adjusted to our family and became more outgoing. She had no medical or physiological reason for not walking, it was all psychological: lack of love and attention, failure to thrive. When she settled down in our family, and realized we wouldn't ever hurt her, she became a normal, healthy, loving child who has always been a joy to us. We moved to Manitoba and finally adopted her when she was six.

I always thought that she would want to find out about her native family. When she did begin that process, I may have understood her need to do that, but I felt incredibly threatened. I went through, she'll never like me any more, she'll never want me any more, she'll never want to be my daughter any more. I felt, this is the end of our relationship. Of course, that's not how it worked out.

I can remember the first time I met her birth mom. I kept asking Joyce, "Are you sure your mom's ready for this?" and the question I was really asking was, "Am I ready for this?" Joyce's birth mother travelled all the way from Lytton to meet in Osoyoos at the house of my mother, Joyce's grandmother, which I thought was very brave of her. Joyce's birth mother, Faith, turned out to be a very tiny little woman, really an attractive woman. We looked at each other and gave each other a hug. I remember her saying, "Thank you." There weren't a lot of words, but she and I understood each other: it was, thank you for looking after this wonderful girl, and I too was thanking her. I realized finally how much pain and anguish and anger and guilt this woman must have experienced. I saw her as a person instead of judging her as a mother who would give up her child. It was actually incredibly courageous of both of us to meet.

My relationship with Joyce became much stronger, because even though I had all of these fears I still encouraged her and supported her and she needed that. If I had been defensive, our relationship could have suffered. When Joyce told me a month ago that in her estimation I did the right thing to adopt her, as far as I'm concerned that's validation itself. Whether anybody else thinks it's all right is basically irrelevant.

Faith Richardson:

My first husband, Nelson Henry, and I were separated just before Joyce was born, and he went off to Seattle to be with a white woman who owned a tavern. He was a rough, handsome man, very violent, but I loved him. On my wedding night, he ripped my wedding gown right off me because he was jealous that men thought I was pretty. I was left alone with four children and a baby after Joyce was born. We lived with my mother and I had to send the older boys off to St. George's residential school, just like everyone in my family, and both Nelson and me. I was there from 1946 to 1954. The principal would call us "heathens" and harped on how if we didn't work hard and pray we were going to end up like those drunk Indian women downtown with no husband. We were beaten pretty bad in my time, with a big leather strap or a ruler on the hands or the backside.

Even when Nelson was logging and making money, I'd have to pick berries to feed my kids. He drank, but I thought it was just natural, all Indians drank. In those days, there was no such thing as divorce. I got into drinking really heavy, too; it seems like I was beaten by Nelson for drinking and I was beaten for not drinking. He never used to pick on the kids, though. He didn't want another baby and, when he was drunk, he'd say he wasn't the father of my baby.

When he left us, I went into a deep depression. My mother was looking after my five kids and some of my sister's children too. When Joyce was six months old, I had what I guess they would call now a nervous breakdown and they put me in Riverview Hospital. They figured I was suicidal. When I was drinking, I did used to think about it. I worried about what was happening to my kids, but I was so doped up on drugs in there, I was like a zombie.

I used to love the old days, my grandmother who followed all the traditional ways, praying with fir boughs. I was brought up in a good home, my parents and grandparents kept big gardens with lots of fruit and vegetables; there was salmon to dry up in the canyon. Everyone shared. Our families were all intact, and everyone looked after everyone else. Then, in my generation, it all went haywire. At the residential schools, they told us we were no good, and then the alcohol made their predictions come true, I guess.

I wasn't there when Joyce was taken away. My mother wouldn't talk about it, but she said she never gave Joyce up. In those days, when they took our kids, they took them for good. Indians never got to go to court or anything. After I got out of the hospital, I was still hurting; my baby was gone, my husband was gone. Then I was put in jail for drinking and the social worker came to see me in jail, telling me to sign the papers for Joyce because she was in a good home, and a woman like me, I would never get her back. She told me they'd found Joyce's father in Seattle and he didn't want her either; I still don't know if that was true.

All those years, I wondered about Joyce. They wouldn't give me a name or address of where Joyce was staying; in fact they wouldn't give me the time of day. To them, I was just that drunken Indian woman in the street. I didn't have a right to be a mother, and my self-esteem was too low to fight back.

My boys went to live with their dad in Seattle for a few years, and then they all came back to me. Since I've been sober, and my kids are all older with their own kids, I've had to start all over again to try to have a relationship with them, because so much of our family life was just destroyed. All my kids turned out pretty skookum on top, although they've had their troubles.

When Terry told me that he had heard from Joyce, I was amazed. I didn't know if she'd ever come back. I didn't know what to say to her, or if I even had the right to be her mother ever again. It seemed like she'd been raised by her own mother pretty good. She was this wonderful girl, really smart and really ambitious, and I was really, really proud of her. It bothered me that other people, even her brothers and sister, were jealous of her. All I could say to Joyce's adopted mom was, "Thank you for taking such good care of my girl."

In the last couple of years, I've been taking life-skills courses. A lot of my life was so hard, so full of pain, it just went by in a blur, so I've got a lot to learn. I've been taking in foster children myself, with my husband Dave, because our tribal council now is starting to take control of our own children instead of just letting them wind up with the welfare or grow up in white homes. Last year, the band sent me down to Nevada with some other foster parents to the National Indian Child Welfare Association to learn more about taking good care of our children.

At the elegant old Heritage Hall on Vancouver's Main Street in October of 1995, a birthday party was in full swing. There were paper streamers, refreshments, even a clown in addition to the requisite crowd of partygoers. When the throng emerged outside onto the sidewalk and released, one by one, hundreds of white balloons, it seemed like any party. But each of the balloons had written on it the name of a loved one that someone was seeking, the name of an aboriginal child long stolen away, a sister or brother adopted out, a birth mother or grandparent someone desperately wanted to meet.

This was a celebration for the "people of the adoption circle," a tradition begun the previous year when a young aboriginal woman who had been adopted out as a child spent her birthday alone because the memories were too painful. "It just was not a day of celebration for her," recalls Lizabeth Hall, program manager for family reunification for the United Native Nations. "So we decided to get together every year on this day to celebrate our commonality, since all of us in the aboriginal community have someone who was taken away from us who we are searching for, or maybe we're looking for our own birth names, our cultural identities, our families by birth."

The gathering was part of the growing campaign by aboriginal activists to knit together families broken up over decades of legalized abduction. A giant cake, cut and served at the party, was emblazoned with names of missing aboriginal adoptees or of people at the party searching for their origins. Ernie Crey invited to the front anyone who wanted to tell their story, seek support or ask for advice.

A young man with a Kwakiutl button blanket around his shoulders and a wide carved silver bracelet on his arm was among the first to step forward. "Three months ago I didn't think I had a relative in the world; I had no clue where I was from," said Dennis Speck. "Now I have a community of five hundred people in Alert Bay, including more relatives than I can remember, my dad, sisters and brothers. I was given my Kwakiutl hereditary name, Goosti Uus Speck, at a big potlatch held in my honour. I feel like I'm walking on air."

Speck, a logger and deckhand who grew up as Dennis Cumberland in a non-native foster home in Fort St. James, B.C., was told as a kid that he had at least one aboriginal parent. As he reached his teen-age years, his desire to know who he really was grew stronger. He knew his birth name, Speck, and had been told it was a common Kwakiutl surname. Restless, he signed up on a fishing boat.

"One afternoon we stopped in this little abandoned Indian settlement on Village Island near Alert Bay, just a few crumbling houseposts and totem poles," recalled Speck. "The other guys soon went back to the boat but I was fascinated by this place. While I was walking around the house remains, I looked up and saw an old Indian woman beckoning to me. I just about jumped out of my skin that anyone could be living in this dump, but I started to follow her. It was getting on dusk and I lost sight of her in the trees. I told the guys on the boat and they laughed, they figured I'd lost it.

"It was years later that I found out I came from Alert Bay, and that there were a lot of people with that name. I found my father, living away from the village, and he told me my non-native mother left the reserve with me. He ran into her years later and she told him she'd been drinking a lot and I was apprehended. All those years he thought I was with her and had no way to find me. There was a lot of shyness and distance, but two weeks later he'd organized the potlatch. Finding my family kind of turned me around. My girlfriend had a baby last year and I didn't want anything to do with her or the kid. Now I have a new baby son, and he has a father who has Indian status, and a grand-pa, and a whole new life."

One night Speck told his father about the old woman he'd seen at the abandoned coastal village. "My dad looked at me really strangely. He said, 'No one lives at that old village. Your great-grandmother, my dad's mother, she lived there, and when the Indian Affairs relocated us from Village Island down to Alert Bay she refused to come. She lived there on her own but she's been dead for thirty years.'" Said Speck: "Chills ran down my spine. I believe I saw the spirit of my great-grandmother—before I even knew who I was—calling me home."

Not all reunifications between children fostered or adopted away and the families they left behind have led to happy endings. Five com-munities in B.C. who managed to trace seventy-five of their missing children failed to successfully repatriate even one of the young adults to the reserve. "Many went back and were living on the streets in Vancouver," notes Sharon McIvor, a staff lawyer with the Native Law Centre in Williams Lake, B.C., and a member of the Lower Nicola First Nation. "Many committed suicide either directly or indirectly by get-ting involved in drinking-related car accidents." Two teen-agers who had been adopted out, then found they couldn't reintegrate or adjust to reserve life, died holding hands as they stood in front of a train.

Even if adoptees do not attempt repatriation, they have a hard time making their way in the world. "I know a lot of adopted and fostered aboriginal women and I've got so I can recognize their look: very well-groomed, perfect hair and make-up, well-educated and trying desperately hard to be better than the Indians their adopted parents told them they would be like if they didn't achieve," says Plains Cree artist George Littlechild, who was himself a foster child from infancy and became a permanent ward of the Alberta government at the age of four.

Littlechild has participated in ongoing support groups for former adoptees and foster children. "With adopted or fostered aboriginal men, their anger comes out against society—it's not self-inflicted and it's not about trying to please—and a lot of them are in the jails and penitentiaries and mental hospitals across this country."

A crazy quilt of adoption and fostering rules and regulations from province to province has not made it any easier for aboriginal children to find out who they are. By law, the federal government is required to maintain an "A" list of adoptees who were born with aboriginal status. Provincial social workers must notify adoptive parents that the child in their care is entitled to Indian status, which brings with it significant financial and educational benefits at the age of majority. However, both policies have been honoured more in the breach than the observance, as repatriation workers have found. In 1981 then auditor-general Kenneth Dye strongly criticized the federal government for swelling its coffers with the proceeds from the unclaimed estates of status Indians instead of trying to find the adopted-out heirs to whom the money properly belonged. But Ottawa has done nothing to remedy that injustice. It is not unusual for information requests that jump through every bureaucratic hoop to take months or even years to process.

Lizabeth Hall points out that many adoptees start out with unrealistically high hopes and must learn a different set of cultural cues. She recalls one adoptee who returned bitterly disappointed after meeting his relatives. "He said there were no balloons, there was no big hurrah. I felt so sad that that was what he thought would happen," says Hall. Later, she was able to help him understand that the cousins who came to see him every day on the reserve but were too shy to talk were actually very glad to meet him, as was his reserved, quiet grandmother.

Hall, one of the few full-time aboriginal reunification workers in Canada, approaches each reunion carefully, advocating an exchange over time of letters, photographs and telephone calls before arranging a face-to-face meeting. "What you're doing is bringing together perfect strangers," she says. "And there's other dynamics too: the adoptees may have no knowledge about how aboriginal people behave together, how we socialize, why people are so quiet." Hall says most adoptees have "missed out on everything learned in our formative years, which you can't just pick up in adulthood overnight. They get called apples, red on the outside, white on the inside, or wannabe Indians. It's very hurtful."

Adoptees or former foster children may also have been taken as infants from a family and a community terribly fractured by pain and loss. "A lot of our families lost their children to social services and adoption because of poverty and alcoholism. They're in recovery or they have had no help in recovering from addictions or abuse," explains Hall. "It helps if adoptees know the history of First Nations communities, the government policies that caused dysfunction, and how aggressive the interventions were." Bands may resent sharing scarce resources or housing with adoptees who grew up in comparative privilege.

Other families and communities may have painful secrets. Aboriginal adoption therapists who understand the history and causes of conflict are urgently required, says Hall. "I have a client, a young woman who has discovered she was born from incest—her birth father is her mother's father. The whole birth family blamed her mother for having given birth to this baby who had come back as an adult to cause such pain." Hall says her client, an educated, stable professional woman who had approached the search for her roots with great enthusiasm, was devastated. "On the face of it she can talk openly about being a child of incest, but deep down she's suicidal. I hope and pray she'll recover, but now she not only has the cultural and spiritual loss, she has the grief of realizing her birth family probably never will be able to accept her."

Repatriation work is chronically underfunded. Hall notes that no aboriginal reunification program in any province of Canada has ever received federal funding. "It's amazing that the Canadian government still refuses to be held financially accountable for its own policy to separate thousands and thousands of aboriginal children from their families," she says. Working at the United Native Nations' family reunification program since 1989, Lizabeth Hall has seen her program struggle through drastic shortfalls and outright gaps in funding, leaving no extra money for consultants, lawyers or therapists. "And we're comparatively lucky—the B.C. government is the only province in Canada to give even one red cent to aboriginal family reunification," she says. Last year, Hall was finally able to hire an assistant, but she notes: "We still have only the resources to reach the tip of the iceberg—there is no funding, no planning and no network to help pick up the pieces of the federal government's failed assimilation policy, except what we as First Nations have been able to put together ourselves." She notes the Manitoba repatriation program has had to rely on intermittent funding from the Assembly of Manitoba Chiefs, augmented by its own fundraising efforts.

As adoptees' stories have filtered into the media over the last few years, there has been a strong emotional response from the public, and some changes have been made to the law in B.C. "But I don't see changes to federal law in the near future, or any source of federal funding for reunification," says Hall. A group of adoptees in Ontario who pressed for their government files to be opened were told by a bureaucrat that the federal government fears a lawsuit from aboriginal adults removed as children if it unseals its vaults. "What the aboriginal adoption movement needs is a revolt," says Hall. "And it will happen. I hear a lot of anger and determination in my work that one day is just going to ignite."

One small step towards adoption reform was taken by the B.C. government in November 4, 1996. Amendments to the 1957 Adoption Act now allow adoptees access to their birth records after the age of nineteen. The new legislation also permits a disclosure veto or a no-contact form to be filed by either birth parent or adoptee. Aboriginal adoptees, the largest single group of adult adoptees in B.C., were jubilant at the changes, but there were lingering concerns that the disclosure veto could serve to isolate adoptees from their First Nation of origin. "Collective aboriginal rights are also important," notes Hall. "We've had to compromise and find ways to respect everyone's rights, so that we can connect adoptees to their family and First Nation, but still respect a birth mother's no-contact request. We've had to work harder to do it, but I'm pleased we've been able to restore to First Nations some of their membership without intruding on the wishes of any individual."

In Plains Cree artist George Littlechild's portrait of Peggy Bull, the maternal great-grandmother he never knew, turquoise and fuschia follow the curve of his grandmother's cheekbones. Gold stars riot around her intelligent face, which is framed by long twin braids striped in mauve and aquamarine, and sparkling gold leaf embellishes her wide brow. Yet this celebrated artist once made a sketch of himself as a child, a little stick figure with mouth curving sharply down, eyes slits of pain, enclosed in a narrow, windowless room. "BLACK," he wrote above it, to describe both the absence of light in the room and the little hurt child who knew no family, no culture and no identity beyond a pained awareness that he was different from the Dutch-Canadian children in the private school to which his foster parents sent him.

Littlechild's research of his aboriginal ancestors unto the seventh generation, to the very roots of retrievable history, has put him in vital touch with his own past. Yet it was not until he was a young adult that he was able to find out his birth name and trace one by one his siblings and large extended family. Littlechild comes from Hobbema, in Alberta, 6,500 Cree people in four bands: Louis Bull, Samson, Montana and Ermineskin, the band to which his mother belonged.

Today, images of his ancestors fill Littlechild's glorious artwork. He has become an activist on adoption issues, speaking at aboriginal conferences and in the media and travelling to schools. *Wahkomankanak*, the Cree word for honouring ancestors, has become the inspiration for his art and his life. Theresa Wildcat, a respected Ermineskin elder, honoured Littlechild during one of his visits home. "You are no one if you do not know your roots," said Wildcat. "George grew up away from here and did not come back until he was a young man, but he did the right thing and found out who he was, who his people were." The affection and honours Littlechild receives when he returns home today are a long distance from his first arrival at the Hobbema bus station, full of trepidation about how his relatives would greet him. If he was disappointed at the quiet reception he received then, Littlechild has since come to understand that a less than effusive welcome did not mean he was not loved. George has been told by aunts, uncles and cousins that they would have stepped in to help had they known of the turmoil experienced by George's troubled mother, Rachel Littlechild, whose five children were apprehended by social workers in Edmonton.

The fourth foster mother found for George and his brother Jack by Alberta social services confined George to the basement, forced him to scavenge for food and beat him savagely, finally causing him to be removed at the advice of a doctor when he was only four. When he recovered, George was placed in the home of Winnie and Fred Olthuis, a kind Dutch-Canadian couple who lived in an Edmonton suburb, although his brother Jack was left behind with the woman who had beaten George.

Winnie Olthuis recalls that George was "very frightened and it took months for him to realize we would not punish him and that he was welcome to eat with us instead of snatching food off the table." Once George realized he was safe, he says, "I made up my mind that I could put my head down and be a good foster child. I became a survivor. I was ready to serve my sentence in a foster home until I could become an adult." The Olthuises sent George to a private school run by the Dutch-Canadian Christian Reformed Church, also attended by their own children. Winnie Olthuis finds it painful to hear that George was the butt of racist slurs and jokes. "One time he told me they had called him a stupid, ugly Indian. I told him to be proud of himself. I complained to the principal and I don't believe they ever again treated him badly. We had a church minister who used to work among the Indians, and he told us that the Indian people often lie about whether people are racist to them."

George's desire to find his birth family grew stronger as he entered his teens. At seventeen, he paid a visit to Alberta social services, the people who held all the answers he desperately was seeking: his name, who his parents were, whether his parents were alive, what First Nation he came from, if he had other siblings and where they were. The social worker who sat across the desk knew more about George from a cursory glance at his file than he had known all his life. None of that information was even his by law. But the scanty details the social worker grudgingly revealed were enough to change his world forever. He was told that his mother's maiden name was Rachel Littlechild, and that his father, James Ernest Price, was white; this news came as a bombshell to George, who had always assumed he was fully aboriginal. He was not told whether his parents were dead or alive, and the social worker responded to his thirst for information about his mother with indifference: "What do you want to know? She was a short, stout Indian woman with an attractive face who wore too much make-up and drank too much." He was told he had siblings: Jack, with whom George had had little contact since the abusive foster home, was now of legal age and beyond the government's grasp. The adoption records of another brother, Raymond, were sealed. Alberta social services refused to let him meet another sister, Marilyn, who was "a bad influence because she was in a juvenile detention home." They did offer to put George in touch with a younger sister, Shirley, who was living in a foster home in Saint Paul, not far from where George grew up.

On the night before he was to meet Shirley, an anxious George, waiting at a downtown Edmonton bus stop, asked a nearby woman the time. When she snapped at him, he took a closer look to see who had been so rude to him: "I noticed that she looked like me, and suddenly a voice said to me, 'George, that's your sister.' It was a literal voice that spoke to me. It said, 'Ask her if she was abandoned as a child.' I finally got the nerve to say, 'Excuse me, were you abandoned as a child?' She said, 'Yes,' as though I was really strange. I said, 'Is your name Marilyn Rose?' When she said it was, I said, 'I think I'm your brother.' We were very excited and a little hysterical, but so glad to connect with each other. It was like a miracle. Marilyn was the juvenile delinquent I wasn't supposed to meet, and yet I became very close to her. She was only sixteen and very beautiful, ethnic-looking, with dark eyes and hair."

A friend told George that the Littlechild surname belonged to people from the Ermineskin reserve at Hobbema, which gave George the first link to finding his large extended family and researching his Plains Cree ancestors, who had lived on the northern Alberta prairies since time immemorial. Rachel Littlechild, whose solemn little face George has discovered in photos of children at the Ermineskin Indian Residential School—"like children at Auschwitz," he says—died before her son George could find her. Rachel was the first and only Littlechild to slip away from her people, yet her children are lost forever to Ermineskin; they can never be fully repatriated even after a gap of less than one generation. James Price, the father whose own parents came from New Brunswick and whose genealogy George also meticulously researched back to the United Empire Loyalists, jumped to his death from the seventh floor of the Balmoral Hotel on Vancouver's skid road. In Edmonton Rachel too met her death as a lonely alcoholic who had lost her hope along with her children.

Mostly through his own tireless efforts, Littlechild has now found all his siblings, who include a successful administrator of aboriginal college programs and a young mother of three who was born with fetal alcohol syndrome but has managed to raise healthy children. "My sisters had the hardest time growing up; they were treated like slaves and inexcusably taken advantage of in foster care," says Littlechild. He also found and keeps in touch with his brother Raymond, who was adopted by a Metis family and now works as a manager for an aboriginal organization. Littlechild is still close to his sister Marilyn, who has three children, and to another half-sister, the daughter of his non-native father from a previous marriage.

Although George is warmly received in Hobbema, he is not a full-fledged member of his home Ermineskin band, despite the generations of his immediate family who have lived at Ermineskin since long before the advent of the Indian Act. Bands with few resources are often loathe to welcome home adoptees and foster children, as are relatively wealthy bands such as those at Hobbema who must share oil royalties with all band members. "I do feel at home in Hobbema, although I tried living there six months and I couldn't live there," says Littlechild. "Everyone spoke Cree, I couldn't speak Cree, I couldn't relate to it at the time because I was much younger. My city ways were deeply engrained. It took years for me to get people to respect me."

Littlechild has been generous with his time in speaking to adult aboriginal adoptees—and to children in elementary and secondary schools—not only about how and why he creates art but also about his healing journey back to his ancestral roots. "I think the art comes from a very special place. To me, the dominant society tried to strip our culture, to rob our souls, but what they didn't realize is the soul cannot be robbed unless we allow it. There is always innate genetic material that couldn't be damaged; it's passed down and remains deep within us. That's why as a group of people we've survived. I was driven to do my art by who I am; that could never be taken away."

Littlechild's reconnection with his cultural background has given his life, and his art, vigour and purpose. Some of his strongest supporters are fellow adoptees and foster children who can understand his experience. "Now I've forgiven my parents and I'm free," Littlechild says. "Now I have my ancestors to sustain me. I feel they are with me. They're my friends. I'm telling my story for foster children, for the adult survivors. There are so many. And I want to tell the government to stop, stop doing this. It's up to you to stop doing this and up to us as First Nations to make sure it never happens again."

4

"INFINITE COMFORT AND TIME"

Healing Survivors of Sexual Abuse

HORRIFIC television footage from Davis Inlet, Labrador, in early 1993 served as a dramatic wake-up call to Canadians about the hopeless lives endured by so many aboriginal children in the nation's North. The sight of seventeen Innu children huddled in a shack, high from sniffing gasoline fumes and crying out that they wanted to die, was impossible to ignore.

Viewers may have been shocked by the self-destructiveness of gasoline addiction, but it soon became apparent the children's despair had an underlying cause. As hordes of media personnel descended on their remote community, the children said they could see no other way to escape the torture of the sexual abuse they were enduring than to die.

The adults of Davis Inlet, demoralized, dispossessed of their traditional land base and their spirituality, sexually victimized themselves in church-run schools, were preying without mercy on their own children. Canadians learned that virtually no Innu child in Davis Inlet reached adolescence sexually unmolested. Many had been violently raped by drunken adults, mostly their own relatives, and assaulted by older children crazed on gas fumes.

After some bureaucratic scrambling, the Canadian government paid to fly the children out of Davis Inlet to the Poundmaker's Lodge and Treatment Centre near Edmonton, in a bid to "cure" their addiction to solvents and gasoline. Although the treatment also attempted to address the children's lengthy history of sexual abuse and incest, most of them returned to their self-destructive behaviour once they got back home. By the following December, not even a year later, the children were once again prowling the streets. "Everybody knows everybody here," Katie Rich, then chief of Davis Inlet, told reporters. "At least sixteen of the seventeen are back sniffing gas."

This tragic episode graphically illustrates how pervasive and deep-rooted the pain of sexual abuse is for First Nations people. "Sexual abuse is a frightening reality of First Nations communities across this land," writes Shuswap author and playwright Vera Manuel in a report prepared for the National Native Association of Treatment Directors. "The devastation it continues to leave is immeasurable . . . for the victims, their families and their communities." A 1990 survey at native treatment centres across Canada found a staggering 80 to 95 per cent rate of sexual abuse among their clients. Manuel's report notes that directors of these centres, barraged by sexual abuse disclosures over the last two decades, have come to see alcohol and drug addiction merely as symptoms, with sexual abuse as the underlying cause. "Ultimately, alcohol and drugs are used as a means to escape the trauma and emotional aftermath sexual abuse has inflicted and the vicious cycle that follows," writes Manuel. "Many native communities that have sobered up have discovered that once the drinking stops, other issues will emerge—and the most common issue emerging in our communities today is sexual abuse." For Manuel, the eldest daughter of tireless aboriginal rights fighter George Manuel, the formula for building powerful, self-sufficient communities is that healing from sexual abuse must come first.

The burden of evidence indicates that more forcible sexual assault has been perpetrated on aboriginal children than on the young people of almost any other nation, except during times of war. The sexual victimization that began as a smoldering ember in the early days of European contact flared to a full blaze during the residential school era. It continued unchecked in the foster-care system, then returned full circle to engulf aboriginal families at home. Without resources on reserves to combat sexual abuse, victimization began to extinguish the hope, self-esteem and well-being of generations of aboriginal children.

Sexual abuse was not unknown historically in aboriginal societies. But the consensus among First Nations in B.C., as reported by an aboriginal panel that travelled around the province in 1992 reviewing social legislation, is that traditional sanctions, laws and the clanship system among disparate First Nations did much to eliminate or control it. Because the laws "were motivated by internalized acceptance rather than external coercion," authors Eva Jacob of the Kwakiutl Nation and Haida elder Lavina Lightbown conclude in the panel's report, "they were much more binding on each individual." The report deplored the "contemporary escalation of the sexual abuse of children." By any measure, aboriginal communities have been infected with child sexual abuse as virulently and persistently as the introduced diseases of smallpox or flu.

Child sexual abuse is a very serious problem in mainstream Canada. In 1984, Professor Robin Badgeley, who had been commissioned by the Canadian government to assess the dimensions of child sexual abuse, concluded that one in four girls and one in seven boys had been the victims of unwanted sexual acts. Today, those figures are seen as conservative. A 1992 survey conducted by the Institute for Social Research at York University in Toronto found that 43 per cent of women respondents had been sexually abused at least once in childhood; 17 per cent were survivors of incest. The sexual abuse of males in particular is seen as having been vastly underreported; from recent disclosures in Canada about sports coaches, choirmasters, teachers and older male children, it appears one in four boys is sexually molested, many more than previously suspected. Indeed, it appears that too few children can expect to grow up safe from sexual abuse in mainstream North America. Statistics Canada noted in 1992 that fully 40 per cent of all sexual assaults committed in this country are on children under eleven years of age. The pre-eminent American psychiatrist Dr. Roland Summit calls child sexual abuse in North America a "normative experience."

Yet there is no question that aboriginal people have suffered sexual abuse in even greater numbers. Of the few communities to conduct systematic research among their members, both Canim Lake in B.C. and Hollow Water in Manitoba found that a remarkable 75 to 85 per cent of people reported they had endured unwanted sexual contact as a child. And almost 35 per cent of respondents to the 1991 Statistics Canada *Aboriginal Peoples' Survey* named sexual abuse as the most serious problem in their community, as worrisome as alcohol and drug addiction or unemployment. Behind the statistics lies the daily horror of sexual abuse, the shame and sorrow of children sexually victimized by the only people they may ever love or trust.

Contact with Europeans marked the introduction of sexual abuse that was outside the control of aboriginal society. As historian Bruce Trigger notes, Samuel Champlain, the governor of New France in the early 1600s, warned aboriginal tribes they would injure relations with the French if they did not continue to surrender "very nice little boys" to the religious schools; later he pressed for "twenty little Hurons" in exchange for twenty Frenchmen, an exchange in which the Iroquois showed no interest. In 1628, a group of desperately hungry Montagnais, who had rebuffed Champlain's avid interest in their young women, were forced to allow three girls aged eleven to fifteen to stay briefly with the French in exchange for food. Champlain began openly consorting sexually with at least one of the three girls, whom he chose to rename Faith, Hope and Charity. Faith eventually escaped, but Champlain refused to let the other girls return home—even offering to buy them outright—until the chiefs' council conveyed serious threats through the local Indian agent, Nicolas Marsolet, who Champlain then accused of harbouring his own carnal interests in the girls.

The first incursions by missionaries into aboriginal territories in northwest B.C. and the Yukon provide evidence of unchecked pedophilia. A Catholic order, the Oblates of Mary Immaculate, dispatched Father Emile Petitot, a gifted linguist, anthropologist and artist, to Fort Providence in 1862 to establish a mission. Almost immediately, Petitot began to sexually victimize a young aboriginal boy in his employ. Oblate Bishop Grandin responded by transferring Petitot to the other side of Great Slave Lake, but Petitot was not deterred; one of his first acts as director of the Fort Resolution mission was to boldly ask Grandin to send the young boy to him. The bishop refused, saying he did not want to indulge Petitot's "fatal attraction to a child." But when he learned Petitot had defied him by having the young boy brought to Fort Resolution, the bishop did nothing further.

For almost two decades, the church hierarchy tacitly allowed Petitot to sexually exploit Indian boys while publicly excoriating him for his pedophilia. "When Bishop Faraud or the Oblate Superior General Father Fabre intervened, Petitot would utter the most sincere confession, beg forgiveness, and promise never to succumb to his sexual instincts again," notes Robert Choquette, a University of Ottawa professor who delved through the Oblate archives while writing a book on the Catholic order. "Given the priest's mastery of Indian languages, his zeal and his indefatigable labours, his superiors chose to believe him, and nothing changed." Petitot remained a priest and a practising pedophile in the North for eighteen years. It was not until he developed a raging dementia that the Oblates finally removed him.

A few decades later, the unspoken church policy of tolerating pedophiles was in full swing. "The failure of the church organizations to take action to weed out sexual exploiters, and to prevent the entry of others, leaves the missionaries open to severe censure," says University of Saskatchewan historian J. R. Miller in *Shingwauk's Vision*, his 1996 book on residential schools. "Too often missionary efforts at prevention and correction of deviants on their staffs were limited to moving them out of a posting when their actions made their proclivities notorious."

Abuse of all kinds was the hallmark of the typical aboriginal child's residential school experience, and the sexual abuse many suffered would leave scars that were particularly damaging. Opetchesaht leader Danny Watts, former co-chair of the B.C. First Nations Summit, recalls the toxic blend of confused sexuality and religious evangelism that was "shoved down his throat" when he was a frightened child at the Alberni Indian Residential School. "I was so godawful lonely when I first got to that place that I was pretty gullible when this supervisor started to befriend me," Watts, now fifty-two, told the 1992–94 Nuu-chah-nulth Indian Residential School Study. "I became very religious, to mask all of the horrid experiences and living conditions in the school. I could recite the Bible, tell you all the books and dates of the Bible, at that very early age. He was the one that taught me that. He was a good boxer, and a good soccer player, and he seemed to really have a good rapport with the boys. Until one day, he invited me up to his room. Because of the fact I liked him, I went with him.

"Of course he began by praying to the Lord. Then he proceeded to take my pants off, and then his own pants, and he would have an erection, and he'd lay behind me. And simulate sex, and have a climax. It was bad enough that this man was doing this to an eleven-year-old boy. What made it even worse was he used to make me kneel and ask for forgiveness. We'd do this bullshit about, oh Lord we've sinned, and please forgive us. What did I do? I was just a young boy being manipulated by this old man."

Watts recalls that Sunday afternoon, after a morning of pious prayer in the chapel, was a popular time for pedophiles to pick out favourite boys for sex acts. "You always had to be careful. On a Sunday afternoon, you stayed as far away from the building as possible, so that you wouldn't be picked for this." Watts sought out the worst jobs, often hiding in the animal barns. "I would clean the inside of that pig pen to such a state that I would sit inside of it and just sort of contemplate. Then I wouldn't have to be a part of what was going on at the school."

Watts describes the spiritual and sexual abuse as "violence to your soul, to have this Christianity shit pushed down your throat day in and day out, to have to pray before you eat and pray before you go to bed. And pray after some guy is trying to shove his prick up your ass."

The residential schools did virtually nothing to foster healthy sexual development among the aboriginal children consigned to their care. Instead, all kinds of behaviour was sexualized. Sto:lo grandmother Mary Chapman recalls the shaming punishments meted out by the Sisters of St. Ann when she was a student in the 1940s and '50s at Kuper Island residential school. "When girls were caught doing something like stealing food or talking Halq'emeylem, the nuns would make them stand in a long line in front of the whole school, then lift their skirts right up. They had to stand there in front of everybody, naked, with their genitals exposed." Another sexualized punishment favoured by the nuns was a group whipping, Chapman recalls. "The nuns would strip the girls naked from the waist down and force them to lie face down on their beds. Then all the rest of us were told to parade by the girls and hit them as hard as we could on their bottoms. The nuns would just stand there and watch."

The fact that the people meting out this abuse were the de facto "parents" or figures of authority for lonely, vulnerable aboriginal children only served to compound the damage. Children subjected to this kind of treatment came to believe they were only sexual objects, a devastating blow to their self-esteem expressed later in their lives through compulsive sexual behaviour, promiscuity, sex addiction, prostitution and an inability to found relationships on love rather than lust. Over several generations, residential schools created young adults who were walking time bombs, waiting to explode once they returned home to their communities.

The Sixties' Scoop gave rise to a new epidemic of sexual abuse. While many aboriginal adults who grew up in substitute care believe they were fortunate to escape the sexual abuse they might have suffered at home, far more report they were treated as domestic and sexual slaves in homes of foster parents. Social workers in Vancouver's Downtown Eastside acknowledge that of the aboriginal adolescents who have become street-habituated, the vast majority are graduates of government foster care. Some professionals estimate that about 85 per cent of these former foster kids have been sexually abused, and some say they've never spoken to a foster child who has not been sexually victimized in some way. In "Boystown," the young male prostitutes' territory in downtown Vancouver, more than 70 per cent of the "hookers" are aboriginal boys fleeing sexual abuse at home and the strong aversion to homosexuality in aborignal communities.

Mary, a Cree community health nurse from Norway House, Manitoba, spoke at a 1993 aboriginal women's healing conference in Vancouver about the abuse she had received at the hands of a foster father, a white Methodist minister who was a pillar of the community in Mary's remote northern Manitoba village. Mary's biological parents were neglectful only when they were drinking, but the minister was granted permission to take Mary into his home after the young girl had spent several weekends seeking refuge with the community health nurse. Shortly afterwards, the minister moved his entire family—and Mary—to Manitoulin Island in northern Ontario.

By the time Mary reached puberty, she was being routinely tormented by the minister, who displayed an obsessive interest not only in her religious faith but in her body. "He drilled holes into the bathroom and my bedroom walls so he could peep at me, to make sure I didn't touch myself," recalled Mary. "I realized that it was him who was masturbating while he watched me, but he was obsessed that I was evil. Then he began to touch me, and make me touch him, and finally engage in sex with him at every opportunity. After he'd ejaculate on me, he'd curse and wail and ask God to forgive him, and call me a dirty, heathen temptress . . . I'd try to hide my underwear and stained sheets until I could wash them in secret because I knew what happened was my fault. I'd made him abuse me because of who I was."

Today, Mary has two daughters and an infant son. Yet despite her training as a health professional and many years of her own healing, the minister's hateful abuse still recurs in unsettling ways in her life. "I am so terrified of anything happening to my own girls that I can't relax around anyone, including my own husband," Mary said. "Once when I was way up north, I spoke to the baby-sitter, who said she'd found a slight discharge on my daughter's panties. Instantly I booked a plane and flew back home, all the way cursing myself for suspecting my very own husband of abusing her. It turned out she had a slight infection. I know rationally that my husband would never abuse our children, but the abuse in my own childhood has just made it so difficult for me to trust even the man that I love."

After several generations of invasive, inappropriate contact between substitute caregivers and aboriginal children, incest began to invade aboriginal homes in epidemic proportions. Violent sexuality was acted out primarily within the family or affinity group; aboriginal offenders seldom committed sexual offences against strangers. The prevalence of sexual abuse at home challenged many a strong young person who might otherwise have stayed to rebuild his or her community. That was true for Lillian Howard, who at forty-five is a respected leader of her Nuu-chah-nulth Nation on Vancouver Island. As a young woman, Howard was desperate to get away from her own people.

Howard was raised in a traditional manner by great-grandparents who taught her their language and values. But as a student at Christie Indian residential school near Tofino, she experienced physical and sexual abuse by nuns and priests, as well as the sexually predatory ways of already victimized older students. When she first returned to live at Mowachacht at the age of sixteen, her home life was again stable and loving, except on weekends when her parents drank. Then Howard and her siblings became vulnerable to the predators of the community. "Little boys weren't any safer than girls," she recalls. "There was a gang of older boys back from boarding school who brought their habits home. I remember them grabbing a boy of ten or eleven and tying him to a tree and sodomizing him."

An older cousin sexually molested Howard and her sisters; later they would find out that the young man had been an offender since he was fourteen, with hundreds of victims from within his own extended family and community. "Incest became common in our communities because the abuse took the form of angry men lashing out at the people they loved, trying to take back their power by victimizing their loved ones as they had been victimized," Howard says.

Howard became almost suicidal after an incident in which she tried to stop her grandfather from raping his own daughter, Howard's aunt. Ambrose Howard, orphaned as a boy and tragically abandoned in Christie residential school for virtually his whole childhood, turned instead on Lillian and violated her.

Howard's recovery was long and painful. The rape by her grandfather paralyzed her into silence, and she felt she had to leave Mowachacht to recover her will to live. She moved to Vancouver, where her depression translated itself into anger and, eventually, into a lengthy career of political activism with the Union of B.C. Indian Chiefs. Later, while working for aboriginal bands in northern B.C., Howard began to face her slowly emerging memories of abuse at residential school and at home. Therapy and support from other aboriginal leaders helped her to decide to return home after almost twenty years. "After I came home, my grandfather was lying alone, dying, with none of his family near him. Several of his children had died violent deaths, including a suicide. I told him how angry I was that he had raped me. He wept and asked my forgiveness, and said he loved me. I told him I loved him as my grandfather, not as the man the Christian church had created, and not for what he had done to me. I don't know if I could forgive him his violent rapes. I felt sorry for him that he hadn't had the benefit of traditional teachings as I did, that each person deserves respect, that our children are sacred."

Sharon Blakeborough, a bright, energetic Sto:lo woman from the Chawathil community near Hope, has a calendar dauntingly crammed with meetings, conferences and events. After graduating in 1992 from Vancouver's Hey-Way-Noqu Healing Circle for Addictions Society, Sharon became a sexual abuse therapist for the Sto:lo Nation. Then she began to work directly with survivors of residential school sexual abuse, travelling all over southwestern B.C. as the Lower Mainland coordinator for the provincial Residential School Project, a joint project of B.C.'s First Nations Summit and the R.C.M.P.

STOLEN FROM OUR EMBRACE

SHARON BLAKEBOROUGH

As a child, Sharon was hurt by virtually every person she tried to trust in her family and her community. Her will to survive and her spirit have inspired her own ongoing healing and enabled her to reach out to others. At women's gatherings and aboriginal conferences, Sharon's strong, beautiful singing voice soars out. With a warm smile and hug, she shares her humour and joy in life.

They say that the Great Spirit only hands you as much as you can handle. For a while there I thought, Holy smokes, does he think I'm a superhuman person? It seemed in that first two-year period when I started dealing with my own abuse like I was fighting with the whole world to tell my story. It seemed like I was on a battlefield. Once it came out of me I wanted to tell the whole world, we've got to stop sexual abuse. I know what it done to me as a child growing up. I was never a child.

Because I grew up with sexual abuse and neglect and the chaos of adult relationships around me, I thought it was okay to live like that. Many, many children do disclose abuse to me. I have to let them know it is wrong and they do have a right to be protected, that they are infinitely precious little people. I know what they're living through and I may be the first person in their life to tell them they don't have to live like that.

I remember the little girl that I was, alone and crying with no one to comfort or protect her, abusers all around her—all the male relatives, my father, my stepfather's father, all the old men who prowled at drinking parties, my first husband who sat me on his lap when I was nine years old to tell me I belonged to him.

There was never a safe person for me. There was never a safe place. Everywhere we'd go the abusers would always be around. And the horrifying things I seen as a child, the open sex, the noise they made. I seen male genitals when I was probably five right through to my teen years. It was disgusting. I used to see three of them in bed together. There was nothing sacred about love and marriage. There were no values. It was nothing like the traditional days, because the residential school, the poverty, the alcohol had all done their job to take away from us everything we held sacred.

When everybody was drinking, some of the children used to go and sneak upstairs, to our hiding place. But they'd still come up. One old grandfather in particular, he was terrible, he molested so many kids. We used to sleep with our bathing suits on because it would be harder to get a bathing suit off or for him to get his disgusting hands underneath.

I can remember being so angry, and hating, that I used to take it out on cats and dogs, and my poor little dollies. At Christmastime somebody would bring over a whole bunch of toys. I used to just rip them apart. I'd try to squeeze the life out of the kitties. I had so much anger. That's the part that really hurts me, because that anger carried through with me right till I had children and into my children's years where I really physically abused them. I'm still working on my shame over that. I think that I was so powerless, and my mother and sisters were so powerless, that we didn't have a chance to stop the abuse; it was just handed down as a behaviour pattern we had to accept, and pass on ourselves.

I was sexually abused by my brother, at home, even in residential school; when I was desperate for food, he'd take advantage of me. He committed suicide about twenty years ago, that is, he got drunk and was hit by a train. I could never trust him. Even when I was really young, my body was always watchful, telling me to watch out, don't trust anyone. No one deserved my trust. I couldn't trust the women, the men, even the kids. No wonder it's hard for me to trust anyone today.

Sometimes I have this dream: There's a little girl child sitting on a log, crying. You ask her, "What's wrong, dear, why are you crying?" She just sits there and cries, as if she hadn't heard what you said, so you ask her, "Are you hurting somewhere?" but the little girl child still doesn't hear you, so you pick her up and put her on your lap and begin to tell her, "It's okay, girl child, you're okay now, please stop crying and tell me where you hurt, so I can help you make it better." If only that was a reality, if that could only have ever happened to me. But no one came, so I started to block it all out.

There was so much incest in our family, there was so much abuse; there's only a few of us who are talking about it. If I say something, most people just walk away. They don't want to hear about it. I believe my mother was probably also molested, but it was her decision whether to talk about it, and she never did. I know that when my father came home, it was rape, if he wanted her. I myself have come to the conclusion that not one of us were born because our mother wanted us, but because she was raped by our dad.

My grandfather was an Italian, Joseph Marino. He was born in Revelstoke. My grandmother was from the Peters reserve. Her name was Martha, and she was a really beautiful woman. They had three girls, Laura, my mom and Theresa. I don't know if Grandmother went to residential school, but my mother did. On my father's side, it's a large, large family. His name was James Charles Peters. His mother was an angry, angry person and the father was really physically abusive. At residential school, and probably on the reserve, Dad was very badly sexually abused, to the point where he started offending and he never stopped.

I never could stand my father touching me as a child, even putting a hand on my shoulder. It was filthy, gross, my skin would crawl. He did things so horrible to me that I felt that way towards my own dad. I believe the abuse started when I was at a pre-verbal stage.

I grew up on a reserve called Katz. At the time, I would say it was remote even though the town of Hope was only six miles away, because the only way there was by boat or rail. There were seven of us, two brothers and five girls. I was the second youngest. From what I remember and what people have told me, we were very poor, ragged, starving, with just a one-room shack by the river to live in.

I can only imagine the horror that happened when Dad came home drunk. I heard that he used to beat my oldest brother senseless, and when my mom tried to say anything then she would be beaten. He would even pull a knife or gun to her, so that she became so deathly afraid of him.

I'm sure my mother did love me, but I don't think she was capable of showing it. The residential school did that to her. I can never ever remember being cuddled or loved. I never ever heard the words, I love you. Although I had lots of brothers and sisters, and half-siblings too, it seems like there was never anyone for me to play with. Children in an incestuous, abusive family like ours, they grow up in emotional isolation from each other, even though they have parallel experiences.

My mom finally got the courage to leave my dad when I was three and a half. She got together with Hoppy, who was to be my stepfather for the next thirteen and a half years. Again the vicious cycle of abuse began.

We lived with his parents for a while. His mother was my dad's aunt. She was cold and unfeeling and hated us. To her we were no good, just like our mother. Then there was Hoppy's father, who was really bad. This was to be my first conscious memory of abuse, one that I put away and never told anyone. He had this clear plastic box with change in it and he told me, come here and sit on my lap and I'll give you this money. So I did because he was being so nice to me. But after that first time I knew that what he was doing was so wrong and that I was never to trust him ever again. I was afraid to go to bed and afraid to go to sleep. I had a bed under the stairs. I can remember being so scared when Mom and Hoppy would go away for a couple of days. I'd stay outside or hide under the stairs or in the old woodshed because I was so afraid of the old man.

The Sister Superior at St. Mary's Mission residential school just seemed to hate me. When she looked at you, you'd just cringe in fear. She's why I stopped telling people that I was being abused, because when I told her she would just turn on me and say, "Stop being such a crybaby and stop making up stories." I once asked the Sister Superior an ordinary question, like, "Who is God?" and she turned around, swung with the full force of her arm and just smacked me as hard as she could on the head. That terrible, tall, black-gowned Sister Superior still comes back to me in my nightmares.

Two months of the year were spent at home. We'd go to a berry camp in the States. But it was frightening, too, because of all the alcohol. Half of the time I never knew where my mom was. I remember being left alone even when I was really little, like one awful night when I was molested by an older cousin who had started to rape me when someone suddenly came to the door.

I know I was so sexually aggressive as a child because it was taught to me. Then it became a pattern. At Hope, a lot of our play was sexualized because we were all exposed to open sexuality and molestation, at school and at home. Both the boys and the girls were being abused by priests, and not just priests—some of the nuns preyed on both girls and boys. The abused ones would turn around and act that out on other kids. If only someone could have taught us how to protect ourselves or helped us understand the horrible life we were living by then. We were just seeking love and comfort, and we didn't know what was appropriate or not.

You know, the priests and nuns were like our parents, and I really believe it's from there that the incestuous patterns began. Already before us, there'd been two or three generations who'd been taught at residential school that it was okay for adults to go after children sexually. And these were priests, and nuns! Although they were on us all the time about our behaviour, they never seemed to interrupt or punish the sex play.

By 1963 they finally built a brand-new school. Life was a little nicer then. The school started a drum and bugle band which I joined. We got to be pretty good and we actually played all over, which was great because we got to go to different places. I was so proud of myself. I played the one valued bugle, and I was the best. I love music; it's always been my strength and my salvation.

After the berry camps in summer, we started going fishing in Yale. These were to be the scariest times. We would travel to Yale in a very old car, and my mom and Hoppy were so drunk, I'm lucky to be alive today. They would catch and sell the fish sometimes by 11:00 a.m., then right down to the pub they would go with us kids. We would be waiting outside the pub all day and until closing time at night. No food except chips and pop they'd send out sometimes; we were cold, and always dirty. Then we had to drive that winding narrow highway through the Fraser Canyon with my parents who by then didn't even know their names.

It was a combination of both, residential schools and alcohol, that robbed us of our childhood. The residential schools, to me, they took our parents. Our grandparents had no choice but to send their kids.

They would go to jail if they didn't get their children in school. The horrendous abuse, physical, sexual, spiritual—we were practically slaves. Our parents had learned absolutely nothing about parenting. When we were taken away, they had nothing left but alcohol.

I had a very addictive relationship to John, my first husband, the father of my first child. He paid attention to me and groomed me from a very young age. When I was nine, he told me he was going to marry me. I first dated him when I was fifteen. He always had many, many women. When he finally got me, he put me out in the country in a shack so I wouldn't be in town where men could look at me. He was very possessive. John didn't want the first child we had together. He said, abort it or give it up for adoption. But I kept my son and I'm so glad that I did.

John pretty much left me alone with the baby. I couldn't afford food or diapers most of the time. There was no inside plumbing in this tiny shack, and I'd have to go and pick up sticks to burn so I could keep warm. John had at least eight kids and was a full-time father to none of them. My mother was close by but she was drinking all the time and calling me down for winding up in that mess, alone with a baby. There wasn't a day went by that I didn't cross that old green bridge near my cabin and want to die. I came so close to lifting my son and plunging over the side. After one night when John hit me, when I was pregnant with our second child, I left him for good. I finally decided, from this day forward I will never let a man hit me again. And to this day I have kept that promise to myself.

Now I was a real single parent, and an alcoholic. It was very tough. I always felt so unloved, so used and abused myself. I did see a therapist about my abusive behaviour toward my children, because I loved them and I didn't want to lose them. I had this uncontrollable anger. I just hit and hit and kicked and kicked. I would punch my son. Once when I was feeding Lisa in a high chair, I told her to eat and she wouldn't, so I smacked her right off the chair onto the floor.

I never learned any parenting skills, not at residential school, not with the childhood I had. Finally I did lose my children to social services, and the result was that I was drunk for a whole year, just totally drunk. I was told if I didn't straighten up, go to school, I'd never get them back. That woke me up. I was thirty-four years old when I began recovery from alcoholism. Then I started living through my daughter. Everything that I wanted as a kid I gave to her. I burdened her with material things, but I still couldn't show her that I loved her.

My healing from all the abuse, sexual, physical, emotional, didn't really start until a very low point in my life. I got married in 1983 to my second husband, Stan, a non-native, stable, loving man. A month after we were married, a foster child was raped in my own home. Stan stood by me completely. He was so supportive; he cared about what I needed.

I couldn't believe a rape could happen in my own home. It triggered everything in me, all my memories of abuse as a child, all the awful things I'd tried to block with alcohol and anger and sex addiction. That's when my healing really started. Once that door into the chaos of memories opened, it seemed like I was just sucked right into that tunnel where there was a thousand doors. I never opened all those doors, but I couldn't stop talking about what was behind the doors that I did open. And you know, I never will. If I stop talking, that means I'm going to stop healing and I'm going to stop helping other people from being abused.

The effects of childhood sexual abuse stay with you for a lifetime; even though the healing is deep, the memories are still there. New memories crop up, ironically when I feel stronger. Sometimes when I've remembered the sexual abuse I've gone through, even the physical abuse, I get so frightened, I get high anxiety, dizzy spells, I get sick, I get really weak. But a lot of the time I feel really strong and good talking about it.

Slowly things got better. My beautiful daughter Teri-Lynn was born, and I developed a better relationship with my older daughter, Lisa. Teri-Lynn changed my life. I say that when I had her, my chemistry changed. I didn't want alcohol any more.

Intensive therapy with a woman therapist really helped me. I've done deep healing workshops at an aboriginal women's retreat, where I was really able to scream out the pain. After I had been in therapy for a few years, I wanted to confront some of the offenders who had abused me. I told my sister about the brother-in-law who raped me when I was twenty. She believed me. He had already been charged by two other girls. But by that time, he was dead. I went to the R.C.M.P. about another male relative who had raped me. Their reaction was to call him in for a chat. Then the R.C.M.P. officer called me up, and said, "You know, he's reformed, he's a born-again Christian, and I don't think he'll do it again. Why don't you come down here and talk to him?" I wanted him charged. But I said, "All right, I'll talk to him at the police station, if an officer is present and if my therapist is present." But before the day came, he took off. They're not going to go looking for him. If they pick him up on a misdemeanour, they might try to hold him. Why didn't they charge him when he admitted to the police that he was guilty? It made me really angry.

When I started recovering, I was there for my daughter Lisa and I role-modelled that recovery to her. She finally came to me and asked me to get her counselling. She was able to say, "I hate Grandpa because he sexually abused me." I physically and verbally abused both Lisa and my son, and my father molested my daughter. She told me that he was not the only one, that there were more. She wanted to heal from the abuse.

Then that awful morning came. I will never forget it: June 11, 1989, at 7:30 a.m. A friend from the Chehalis reserve called. She said, "Sharon, there's been a bad car accident, and I think Lisa's in it." We drove right up there and the car was underwater. My girl was gone. The Creator had taken her home. I never got to say I love you, I never got to say I'm sorry. I never got to say, oh Lisa, everything is going to be all right.

I was so lonesome for her I couldn't sleep. Every day I prayed for strength from the Creator. Sometimes I think a part of me died with her. I do know that she is gone to the other side where there is only beauty and where there is no pain or suffering. We buried our beloved Lisa in the Chawathil cemetery. It was the saddest day of my life. Having lost Lisa was like losing my childhood, my chance of giving her the happy childhood I never had.

I hope that my generation will be the last to suffer like I did. In my work as a sexual abuse counsellor, I am there for the children, and there are so many more adults like me than there ever was when I was a child. We still have a lot of healing work to do, but with our traditional culture and the healthy families we've managed to create for ourselves out of the rubble of our childhood, I know we have the strength to succeed.

In the past few years, I have lost so many members of my family: my nephew, my mother, my father and stepfather. I want to be able to grieve our losses with my family of origin. I have become close to one of my sisters, and other family members, nieces and nephews. I am now able to acknowledge my mother, her sobriety later in life, and that she did her very best as a parent with the very little skills she was able to learn. I see our Sto:lo families growing stronger, more sober and healthier. I will always be the one to speak out about sexual abuse, though. I feel I did my part to initiate dealing with residential school abuse. I always make choices on the side of protecting the children. I know the families in our communities so I won't compromise when it comes to protecting children. A few years ago, I wouldn't have said our community was ready to take charge of its own child and family services. Hardly any reserves had a safe, sober home to take a child. Now we've made a lot of progress. We have role models in our communities who are disclosing about the traumas they suffered as children, and, as adults, are taking back the power and control from the adults who took it away from them. For the sake of that little crying girl on the log, the one who was dirty, ragged and never loved enough, I keep going. I have infinite comfort and time for our children today.

As First Nations communities attempt to deal with the legacy of sexual abuse, women and men are drawing strength from the widening pool of resources available in urban and reserve-based communities. Those resources range from mainstream psychotherapy to the sweatlodge, rituals and spiritual counsel. But the numbers of people needing help continue to grow. Some grandmothers and great-grandmothers are disclosing abuse for the first time, emboldened by the revelations of their daughters and the relief and peace those disclosures seem to bring.

"It will take two more generations at least before we can talk about having completely healthy families," says Lillian Howard, who serves as co-chair of the Nuu-chah-nulth Tribal Council. "But for me and my daughter, we made a decision together that the cycle of abuse stops in her generation. Because I am a survivor of sexual abuse myself, I was hyper-vigilant to protect my own daughter. Now she's a mother herself, and her two daughters, my beautiful grandchildren, will never be abused."

Aboriginal children need a chance to be carefree children again, and education is an important place to start. With the advent of First Nations–owned and operated schools, which stress cultural and spiritual education as well as the three Rs, aboriginal children of this generation are finally being educated in their home communities. The classroom atmosphere is warm and welcoming; corporal punishment and shaming are ugly memories from the past.

The Seabird Island Community School, on a Sto:lo reserve in the heart of B.C.'s Fraser Valley, has won architectural awards for its soaring exterior echoing the shape of an eagle in flight, or a salmon leaping upstream. On the side of the Seabird school are traditional salmon-drying racks designed for practical use. Inside, cedar-clad walls are hung with the work of First Nations artists.

The kindergarten, library and Halq'emeylem language classrooms are rounded, like ancient pit-houses, with modern windows and skylights. A happy clatter of children talking and laughing fills the big high-ceilinged room at the centre of the school. Nancy Pennier, an Okanagan woman who was principal at Seabird in the old "band" school, and then at the new school from the time it opened in 1990 until 1994, was a gracious host at the many ceremonial occasions held in the school's striking gymnasium. At Seabird, and at her new position as First Nations support teacher at Kent Elementary in Agassiz, Pennier was committed to tackling head-on the challenging issues of sexual abuse prevention, disclosures of sexual abuse by students, and to replacing, or at least countering, the welter of confusing, sexually permissive influences from non-aboriginal society with traditional Sto:lo values.

The availability of more First Nations teachers and administrators has led to a gradual lowering of the barriers of mistrust by many aboriginal parents, says Pennier, who is now writing her master's thesis on all-day native kindergarten. "In my early days as a teacher, you could send a notice home requesting permission to start a family life education program and the few that were returned would be marked, no, no, no, no. At Seabird, the teachers and the principal got to know the parents, because they went there for other events and they felt comfortable visiting and talking with school staff. Today, there's more widespread acceptance of personal planning, family life and sexual abuse prevention programs, and the schools can more easily begin to identify the children who might be in trouble."

Some children who are being abused don't benefit from abuse prevention programs; they have either "split off" to survive and have no conscious memories, or they're being terrorized and are afraid to tell. But the programs help almost all children to learn the boundaries of appropriate behaviour. They are encouraged to seek out a trusted adult if they are being abused.

Children can become a force for change in their own communities, Pennier says. But they should not have to carry the weight of reform. Sexual abuse prevention programs for children must be accompanied by programs for adult survivors of sexual abuse, both women and men, offenders and non-offenders alike. Maggie Hodgson of the Nechi Institute, the research and publication arm of the Poundmaker's Lodge and Treatment Centre, emphasizes that sexual abuse treatment programs must be multifaceted and based at home, run by and for aboriginal communities. Treatment requires skilled, trained professionals, Hodgson acknowledges, but "that doesn't mean a lot of Ph.D.s flown in from outside who don't know anything about aboriginal people or our experience." Hodgson says the success of the native sobriety movement that since 1969 has swept through North American reserves and urban communities "has been tremendously empowering. It's brought us out of our midnight of residential schools, alcoholism, family breakdown and sexual abuse, and into the daylight." The Carrier woman is convinced the aboriginal community has taken the crucial first steps towards vanquishing sexual abuse. "For years we tried to close up and hide the issue; now we are choosing the opposite road, to open it up and develop treatment approaches. We can become leaders in the treatment of sexual abuse," says Hodgson, "just as we did in achieving sobriety, against what people said were incredible odds."

Maggie Hodgson emphasizes that sobriety is an essential prerequisite for successful sexual abuse treatment programs. She cites a native community that has moved from 100 per cent alcoholism to 85 per cent sobriety; in just three years, the small community (which she prefers not to name) has developed a strong Ala-teen group, a youth drama group, an Alcoholics Anonymous group, and mobile treatment and sexual abuse therapy for families, as well as using the services of three therapists who come from urban areas to work with adult sexual abuse survivors. Training for front-line on-reserve workers is ongoing, and the community is now implementing a protocol to follow with police and social workers for sexual abuse disclosures.

At Gwa'Sala-'Nakwada'xw on northern Vancouver Island, children held a brainstorming session after a sexual abuse prevention program was taught at the reserve-based school. Incest and sexual assaults on children had begun in the community after a violent social upheaval caused by the forcible relocation of two groups of Kwakiutl from remote villages to a tract of land outside a small lumber town. Many dozens of children had been apprehended from the reserve, and very few of those who stayed behind escaped abuse. One father, a member of the band council, openly had sexual relations with his teen-aged daughter and produced two children with her.

Children in the town knew how vulnerable they were when drinking parties started and predatory adults descended on their houses. They came up with their own self-preservation techniques, developing a buddy system and a phone tree for kids to call when they were stuck in a house with an offender. And they marched through the reserve one Sunday with yellow arm-bands and signs proclaiming, "No More Abuse!" and "Offenders, We're Watching You! We Know Who You Are!" The children's vigilance helped to spark the community into action. Gwa'Sala-'Nakwada'xw Chief Paddy Walkus now speaks openly and publicly about stopping sexual abuse and restoring traditional morality in his community. Two elders, including the incestuous father, were prosecuted for sexual abuse and served time in jail, "to send a message that abuse will not be tolerated here, no matter who you are," Chief Walkus says. "It was the children who led the way for us."

The National Indian Child Welfare Association, a Portland, Oregon–based organization, is dedicated to combatting child abuse and neglect in Indian country. NICWA director Terry Cross, a Seneca father and grandfather with two decades' experience in social work, says it is crucial for aboriginal communities to begin talking clearly and directly about child abuse. "In the boarding schools and foster homes, we didn't learn about boundaries at all," says Cross. "Children grew up not knowing they had a right to privacy and to control their own bodies. They had people in positions of trust preying on them. Now, as adults, they may have their own boundary issues, like not realizing it is abusive to let kids watch porn videos. We talk clearly about what behaviour is okay in a healthy family and what is not. We want to give the younger generation the strength and clarity that maybe some of the older folks did not get."

For aboriginal survivors of sexual abuse, reconnecting with their culture is a critical step on the journey to recovery. A clinical study of aboriginal women survivors found "the women realized they had to deal with their profound sense of cultural shame." They needed to transform their negative experience of aboriginal culture into "something more life-affirming if they were to heal and to begin to feel whole and valuable," says Vancouver therapist Maureen McEvoy, coauthor of the study. Part of that transformation was understanding clearly that aboriginal societies were no more predisposed towards sexual abuse or incest than were families in the mainstream. As one aboriginal survivor told McEvoy: "I came to understand it wasn't because of me that all these things happened, it was because this had happened to my aunt and uncle and grandfather and great-grandfather . . . all the way back . . . it was being collected from the point of European contact and being spilled out on the youngest generation each time."

Some aboriginal adults abused while in foster care have begun to seek redress through civil lawsuits against not only the foster parents, who seldom have significant financial assets, but also the federal and provincial governments. Lawyers have argued that foster care for Indian children, like the residential school system, was the direct result of a deliberate government policy to separate First Nations children from their parents, with inadequate care and attention paid to where children wound up. In May 1994, two aboriginal sisters obtained an out-of-court settlement of between $50,000 and $100,000 after suing the R.C.M.P. and the B.C. Ministry of Social Services and Housing. Donna Lewis and Dianne Marie, both now in their mid-thirties, were taken away from their aboriginal mother, who had a history of alcoholism, when they were seven and four. Their adoptive father, former federal bureaucrat John Lewis, now a seventy-seven-year-old man living in an Ontario nursing home, pleaded guilty in a criminal case to sexually abusing the girls.

The sisters' lawyer, Megan Ellis, was able to show in court that social workers in the small B.C. town where the family lived knew John

Lewis was abusing the girls. Yet neither they nor the R.C.M.P., who took direct complaints from the sisters about Lewis's acts of rape, did anything about the allegations. Donna Lewis says both the financial damages awarded by the court and the act of seeing her abuser convicted in court were empowering, and will help the sisters in their healing.

There have also been several recent high-profile criminal convictions of abusive residential school officials. The charges brought by five Shuswap women against Catholic Bishop Hubert Patrick O'Connor, the former principal of St. Joseph's residential school and the highest-ranking cleric in Canada to be charged with sexual abuse, were a breakthrough in healing for the Cariboo communities whose children O'Connor had jealously guarded for his own use. O'Connor was a priest, a father figure and the only man in the lives of most Shuswap girls while they were at the school, usually for most of their childhood. When he began to sexually exploit the girls to whom he was guardian and spiritual leader, it was a devastating form of incest and a profound betrayal of trust.

After a difficult preliminary hearing in Williams Lake before then B.C. provincial court judge Cunliffe Barnett, the five women who had charged O'Connor held a sweatlodge ceremony on the banks of a creek at the Secwepemc village of Alkali Lake. Marilyn Belleau, who had been raped by O'Connor as a student and then subjected to a sexual relationship for years while in his employ as a secretary, was able to release some of her suffering in the ceremony. The volatile heat of the sweatlodge brought forth vomiting and tears. After a plunge in the icy-cold creek, Belleau said she "felt as though I was getting all the contamination of O'Connor out of my body at last."

On September 13, 1996, four long years later, after prosecution squabbles, a stay of proceedings and a Supreme Court of Canada decision ordering a new trial, O'Connor was sentenced to two and a half years in jail for raping Marilyn Belleau and sexually assaulting another Shuswap woman. While O'Connor's lawyers scuttled into another court to file an appeal, First Nations people who had gathered to support the women held a healing circle in a nearby hotel. A Shuswap pipe ceremony was led by Margaret Gilbert of the Sugarcane band, and the drums rang out to put an end to thirty years of trauma. Marilyn Belleau, now the chief of her Alkali Lake community, gestured to her daughter, who was sitting in the circle with three of her young friends. "This is the age I was when O'Connor began to prey on me," said Belleau. "Look at these beautiful young women here, and know that they won't have to go through what our family has gone through to get rid of O'Connor. These girls are safe."

At first, Belleau had thought, as most aboriginal women did, that Bishop O'Connor was too powerful to be held accountable. "I felt like little me taking on Goliath," said Belleau. "But we took him on together, and we won! We have gone through the whole court process and it has forced us to do our own healing, and we are stronger. We can take anything they throw our way now."

Charlene Belleau, the provincial coordinator of B.C.'s First Nations-R.C.M.P. investigation into residential schools and Marilyn's sister-in-law, was both relieved and elated. The court case had drawn the whole community together and strengthened her own resolve, she said: "Every damn priest that ever hurt any one of our children is going to be held accountable, until the day I die." Canoe Creek Chief Agnes Snow, one of the original complainants against O'Connor, said the court process had strengthened the Shuswap people. "We stuck it out to the end. Now I can rebuild my health, help rebuild my community and get on with my life. We're a strong people, we come from a great heritage."

Access to healing resources at home was key in the decision by the tiny Shuswap communities to take on the powerful Catholic Church. Sweatlodges, drumming and pipe ceremonies were held at each stage of the court trials, but there was also federally funded, structured recovery provided by the Nen'qayni Treatment Centre, set up in 1992 outside Williams Lake primarily to accommodate the five area Shuswap communities. A network of treatment centres throughout B.C. and Canada has become the front-line refuge for adult survivors of child sexual abuse, just as schools, social agencies and community health workers are helping children today.

But First Nations leaders stress that economic power and self-esteem must be restored to aboriginal communities, at the same time as healing programs are put in place. And they want these programs to address sexual abuse through an integrated, family-centred model. As Lynda Prince of the Carrier-Sekani tribal council in northern B.C. explains in the 1992 B.C. aboriginal legislative review: "One thing we object to in government funding, both federal and provincial, is that the government funds programs on an individual basis. They break everything up. Drugs and alcohol is one funding. Sexual abuse is another category. Family violence is another. We want to be funded for a holistic approach."

A slow consensus is building among First Nations that the corner-stone to the restoration of aboriginal communities is the eradication of the modern cancer of child sexual abuse. Increasingly, the political leaders coming to the fore are people such as Alkali Lake Chief Marilyn Belleau, a survivor who has not only faced her own abuser in court but is also a professionally trained counsellor committed to com-batting sexual abuse in her community. "I have been a terrorized little girl at residential school, but today I am a strong leader, and I believe my community elected me because they know they can always count on Marilyn to speak out when it comes to stopping child sexual abuse," says Belleau. "We've been through some dark days here at Alkali, but everyone saw us kick alcohol out of our lives and now they can see we'll get rid of sexual abuse, too. Our elders talk about the old days when all children were protected, and nowadays that's just what we're doing: putting the kids first."

5

"I AM RESPONSIBLE, I AM ACCOUNTABLE"

Healing Aboriginal Sex Offenders

THE circle of healing in First Nations communities has grown to include sexual abuse survivors of all ages, from children to teen-aged boys, young women to middle-aged men and elders. Yet outside the circle there is still a large body of unsafe aboriginal sex offenders, locked in a dance of suffering and pain with their victims. Front-line workers have wearied of helping survivors only to see them revictimized by the vicious cycle of abuse that seems to have a stranglehold on some communities. Across North America, there has emerged within the last decade a conviction that it is time to heal the offenders, to bring them back into the circle.

First Nations are by no means alone in facing a massive incidence of sexual violence and child sexual abuse, including the perplexing, painful problem posed by offenders who may violate literally hundreds of children before they are caught and stopped, usually only briefly, by imprisonment. But aboriginal communities have been particularly hard hit by the phenomenon. After generations of sexual abuse at residential schools and in foster care, young aboriginal men and women brought this learned behaviour back home. Elders could no longer enforce the old ways, and the clan system, with its rigid rules of behaviour and association, had begun to dissolve. Traditional spiritual laws and practices that emphasized respect for elders, women and children had been under vigorous assault by non-native legislation for decades.

"A rapist or a murderer used to bring disgrace to a village," Tsartlip councillor Manny Cooper told the Victoria *Times-Colonist* in 1992. "In traditional society they would put him in a canoe and ship him out and he wouldn't come back. Or they would tie you to a reef, and if you drowned, you were guilty. Those were our laws." Among the Sto:lo people, responsibility for preventing abuse traditionally resided with "watchmen," elders who could send their spirits through the walls of an extended family's house to make sure children were safe. By blowing into a medicine bowl, the watchmen could also create a mist that would reveal a vision of what was happening to a certain child. If any adult doubted the guardians' power by risking a violent or sexual act with a child, he or she would inevitably be found out and publicly identified.

Pam Jack, a Comanche who works with aboriginal sex offenders in the federal prison system in British Columbia, describes how pedophiles and molesters were traditionally controlled. "Sanctions were severe," Jack says. "Banishment, never allowing that person to come near a child again; for repeated offences, even death." But the removal of aboriginal children from their communities broke the strong bonds that permitted the transmission of teachings and put children outside the protective mechanisms of their own culture. "When a child is away from her parents or grandparents for ten months a year, for five or ten years, and then returns home as an adolescent and a stranger, is it likely the incest taboo is going to kick in? I don't think so," says Jack. "The breakdown of our cultural ways led to the breakdown of all the ways that kept our children safe."

By contrast, the rigid Christian nuclear family model imposed on aboriginal communities allowed a perpetrator in an incestuous family to isolate himself and his children from public scrutiny. Aboriginal men who had been deprived of natural authority through impoverishment and the theft of land were handed in exchange the weapon of absolute possession and control over their wives and children, a dynamic in complete opposition to the traditional pattern. In matrilineal cultures, women wielded power directly; even in male-led societies, women directed major decisions and held key elements of practical knowledge, succession, spirituality and child-rearing. Metis leader James Penton, a senator from Lethbridge, Alberta, told the Royal Commission on Aboriginal Peoples he believes the powerlessness of aboriginal men is the chief cause of violence in aboriginal families today.

All across Canada, aboriginal men face high unemployment, dependence on welfare and displacement from traditional methods of hunting and fishing. "Men in the prime of their working life may be the most dispossessed group of people in the community," noted Lynda Lange in a 1994 study of Fort Resolution, Northwest Territories, for the Royal Commission. While aboriginal women face many challenges, there are often opportunities for them to work on reserve as public health nurses, teachers, social workers and counsellors, jobs through which they also feel part of a vast and vital healing network of health professionals. Aboriginal men still dominate elected positions and the upper echelon of national organizations, but the job of an Indian politician is an onerous one that in the past has seldom emphasized personal growth. Devalued and dismissed, carrying around the baggage of unhealed sexual and physical abuse, aboriginal men "begin to adopt our oppressors' values, and . . . become oppressors ourselves," a Dene man named Roy Fabian told the Royal Commission on Aboriginal Peoples. "Because of the resulting self-hate and self-shame, we start hurting our own people."

There are few who would deny the disturbingly high incidence of sex offenders in First Nations communities today. The mainstream justice system has responded by jailing these offenders in ever greater numbers. Most communities initially cooperated. They were not equipped to cope with offenders; it was easier to submit them to the outside justice system and send them away. It was only after these offenders began to come home from jail, even more angry, and with their deviant sexuality even more entrenched, that aboriginal communities began to see the solution to sexual abuse had to come from within the community itself.

In 1988, University of B.C. law professor Michael Jackson warned in a report called "Locking Up Natives in Canada" that prison had become the anticipated and actual future for young aboriginal men in the same way that non-native youth looked forward to high school or college. "Placed in a historical context," wrote Jackson, "the prison has become for many young Native people the contemporary equivalent of what the Indian residential school represented for their parents." Jackson, an educator who also led landmark aboriginal rights and title litigation from in the Delgamu'ukw cases, also predicted that as the sexual and physical violence of residential school and foster care was brought home to native communities, aboriginal men would continue to go to jail in record numbers.

Jackson's predictions have more than come true. Nationally, according to a 1996 federal report, almost 17 per cent of people in prison today are aboriginal, although less than 4 per cent of the general population in the 1991 census reported aboriginal ancestry. In provincial institutions, the proportion of aboriginal inmates is even higher: a staggering 73 per cent of all incarcerations in Saskatchewan, 57 per cent in Manitoba and 17 per cent in B.C. While non-natives go to jail primarily for crimes against property, aboriginal people are incarcerated over and over for crimes against "the person," most of them repetitive, violent, frequently sexual assaults by aboriginal men on their wives, daughters, sons, friends and relatives.

Aboriginal women have reacted to the violence against them by committing crimes that injure themselves or others. For decades, more than half the inmates in Canadian prisons for women have been aboriginal. Their children, another aboriginal generation separated from parents, often perpetuate the cycle by becoming government wards or delinquents themselves.

A 1995 Correctional Services Canada survey found that close to a third of all aboriginal men in jail were there for sexual offences. (Of the prison population of aboriginal men from northern communities, one of every two had been convicted at least once of a sexual offence.) Virtually all were repeat offenders, back in prison for "Schedule One" violent crimes against people. A majority reported having been sexually abused as children. Fewer than one aboriginal offender in four had been raised by his own parents. Tragically, four out of every ten aboriginal sex offenders are under the age of thirty.

Despite their preponderance in the federal system, few aboriginal sex offenders are "DSO'ed," a label for an offender who is levied an indefinite sentence by the courts because he is seen to be a "dangerous sex offender" who would continue as an indiscriminate predator if released from jail. DSO designations typically arise from a public outcry, often one stirred up in the media. But there has been little public outcry regarding aboriginal sex offenders; the women and children they typically victimize are in less than powerful positions and lack access to the mainstream media. Instead, the majority of aboriginal sex offenders who draw a federal prison sentence tend to be "gated" from jail on mandatory release after serving two-thirds of their sentences. (Prisoners are "gated" if they fail to win any form of early parole; they're let go simply because the prison has no legal right to retain them any longer.)

As is the case with most sex offenders, many aboriginal offenders receive no treatment at all in prison. Yet when they return to their home communities, they are perceived as "cured." N'laka'pamux paralegal worker Brian Chromko, executive director of the Native Courtworker and Counselling Association of B.C., recalls a courtworkers' program that traced one pedophile, whose offences had been repeated and vicious, back to his home reserve. The man had been gated after serving a long stretch in prison; he didn't qualify for any form of parole since he'd received no treatment. "To our horror, this pedophile had been received with open arms because they figured he'd paid his debt, done his time and he was all over that business," said

Chromko. "They'd given him a job working in the elementary school."

The B.C. courtworkers group is part of the cross-Canada Native Criminal Courtworker Program, funded jointly by the Canadian and provincial governments. The program provides in most provinces advocacy and support services for aboriginal people who come before the courts. In recent years, provincial courtworkers' associations have begun to emphasize prevention. The B.C. courtworkers led the way. "As long as Aboriginal children go to bed at night crying because of violence in their homes, there can be no authentic self-government," the B.C. association stated in 1993 to explain its new priorities in a pamphlet addressed to victims of family and domestic violence. "We believe in the right of Aboriginal women and children to live their lives free from fear and violence . . . we are ready to help stop the violence and begin the healing."

Brian Chromko supports his organization's decision to address the root causes of sexual abuse. "If you removed all the sex offenders from our communities and put them in jail, the reserves would be emptied out," he says. "Our children would be abandoned all over again. We have to deal with the epidemic of sexual abuse in First Nations communities; so far we've had to focus on the victims' needs, but we won't make real progress in breaking the cycle of abuse until we turn our attention toward helping the offenders. If we want to move forward, we have to heal our sex offenders, and we have to educate communities to understand the perpetrators have to be helped, and monitored for the rest of their lives."

Like many First Nations community leaders, Chromko admits he strongly resisted confronting the issue of what to do about the legions of aboriginal sex offenders who are either incarcerated or living without supervision among women and children. It took a long time, he says, for Doreen Sterling, a Shuswap social worker who has pioneered aboriginal family therapy in B.C., to convince him his organization had to come to grips with sex offenders.

STOLEN FROM OUR EMBRACE

Sterling, who served as coordinator of the Aboriginal Sex Offender Retraining Program in 1995-96, the first comprehensive program in Canada to train counsellors to work exclusively with aboriginal people convicted of sex crimes, isn't on a crusade to "cure" offenders; like most experts well versed in the field, she believes it can't be done. But neither is she ready to abandon to jail or to complete ostracism the scores of aboriginal offenders she feels confident can be helped by their whole community to lead more effective, responsible lives. First Nations can no longer hide behind their history of suffering to rationalize neglecting children or failing to provide protection for them, Sterling says in a 1996 pamphlet about her program to train people to work with sex offenders. "Aboriginal people must be able to stand up and say: 'I am accountable, I am responsible for the safety and health of our children.'"

Offenders must be told they can't continue to use as an excuse the argument that "I abuse my kids because I was abused," says Sterling. It is true that many of those who commit sex crimes have been sexually victimized as children themselves, but far more sexual abuse survivors—three-quarters, most therapists agree—never abuse. Their own suffering makes them even more resolute that no child should ever suffer as they did. When offenders can be taught to look forward to the future instead of dwelling in the painful past, responsibility kicks in, Sterling says. "For the sake of our grandchildren, the cycle of sexual abuse has got to stop. We've got to start healing ourselves. We need to make the world a better place for our children and grandchildren yet to come. And we will—just watch."

The path to healing sexual abuse within aboriginal communities is not an easy one, and those on the front lines often meet with profound and powerful opposition. "There are leaders who say we have to focus on land and title issues. They say that to identify a whole bunch of sex offenders in our community, while we negotiate treaties, is the last thing we need at this point in time," says Pam Jack, who is employed by the Aboriginal Programs division of Correctional Services Canada.

"I say to that, denial is something we learned from non-native society and it won't help anyone heal. Also, self-government won't mean a thing if we have leaders who won't argue for funding for social programs and then dedicate those funds if we ever get them. And I say you have to consider the source: a lot of leaders are still either offending or protecting sex offenders."

The impetus to develop effective treatment methods for aboriginal sex offenders—both within prisons and outside—has come primarily from First Nations. Non-native pedophiles hounded by increasing public opposition to their presence in the community tend to switch identities and move from city to city, but a Gitksan, Sto:lo or Cree offender can't change his cultural identity, nor the fact that he is often from a small reserve full of relatives. Even in an urban setting a First Nations person tends to retain a cohesive sense of family and community. The aboriginal sex offender who leaves prison inevitably will want to return "home," forcing his people to deal with him one way or another. Some First Nations now have enough resources in place to monitor sex offenders; even those communities who have sent members convicted of sex offences to jail do not want to write these men off.

Although the prison system all across North America has attempted to devise effective treatment programs for sex offenders, most of these have met with little success, especially where fixated pedophiles are concerned. And even where there are effective programs in place, they can be problematic for aboriginal offenders. At Mountain Prison near Agassiz, B.C., a medium-security jail where up to 95 per cent of inmates are imprisoned for sex offences, therapist Faye Chato Manchuk offers an intensive three-month program that helps sex offenders explore the sexual abuse most of them suffered as children. Manchuk's program is widely seen by inmates as the ticket to parole, but it also provokes therapeutic responses that are hard to fake, since the program requires daily journalling, the reading of books, articles and first-person accounts by survivors, and, ultimately, writing a letter to one's victim or victims, whether or not the missive is ever sent.

Yet Manchuk's program, as do most intensive counselling programs for sex offenders in federal jails, stipulates that participants must have reading and writing skills at at least a Grade 10 level, a prerequisite that excludes some 70 per cent of aboriginal sex offenders. The other disincentives for aboriginal offenders are the program's linear orientation and its reliance on externalized tools like reading and writing, or on talking to non-native strangers in group therapy, to change deeply ingrained behaviour. "That's not how aboriginal people heal," says Pam Jack. What is necessary is the development of more traditional and spiritually based healing programs for incarcerated aboriginal offenders, she and many others believe.

At the community level, a great deal of work must be done to educate counsellors, family and community members. In pre-contact aboriginal society, healthy sexuality was modelled and carefully taught by example and precept. Puberty rituals in many First Nations involved segregating adolescents with members of their own sex to receive instruction about their bodies, social behaviour, conception and childbirth. Today, many aboriginal adults are still struggling to overcome the shame, ignorance and secrecy with which sexuality was imbued at residential school.

Inappropriate sexual remarks, sexual touching during wrestling, allowing children to see adults having sex or to watch porn videos: these are all behaviours proscribed in a healthy family. Yet incestuous or sexualized aboriginal families may not recognize covert, and even overt, forms of incest as profoundly damaging to a child. "Some people, torn from their families as little children, literally don't know what a family is," points out Doreen Sterling. "What, really, is a father? What does he do? How should he act? For me, these are not rhetorical questions. They must be addressed."

Within the framework of the existing Canadian legal system, aboriginal communities have begun a wide variety of initiatives to take control over their own justice issues. Michael Jackson's 1988 report, which linked aboriginal justice to the right of self-government, gave a boost to projects all over the country. With tentative federal, provincial and territorial government support, aboriginal sentencing circles, elders' councils, diversion projects and community-based probation began to spring up everywhere. Primarily, the restorative justice projects—whether an elders' court in the northern Ontario Cree community of Attawapiskat, diversion to the South Vancouver Island Justice Education Project longhouse-based program, or an aboriginal council in urban Toronto—are supposed to deal only with minor offences.

Sentencing circles typically involve a provincial court judge as well as the victim, the offender and a wide cross-section of affected community members. There have been more than a hundred such circles held in the Yukon, taking diverse forms depending on the community involved, and the practice has spread to Ontario, British Columbia, Quebec, Manitoba and Saskatchewan. Circles may recommend a prison sentence, community probation or a combination of both. In diversion programs, offenders are diverted from court and jail to serve a sentence in the community, whereby they must adhere to community conditions.

With serious offences such as sexual assault, both judges and First Nations have been loath to divert offenders from the mainstream justice system. Yet when three men were charged with sexual assault in Alkali Lake in 1989, a strong community and a judge who knew First Nations history understood that the accused did not have to be banished to jail. Judge Cunliffe Barnett, who had presided over the sentencing of two Catholic Oblates for repeatedly sexually abusing young Shuswap men at St. Joseph's residential school, knew that two of the accused had been victimized there. Judge Barnett also knew that Alkali Lake had overcome its dark days of alcoholism, and he believed the village could combat sexual abuse as well. The community-based probation order was strict, requiring absolute sobriety from all three men, supervision, no contact with victims, individual counselling and participation in a men's group, as well as a spiritual healing regime of talking circles, drumming and sweatlodge ceremonies. All three men met the terms of their sentence, and none has reoffended.

Although sentencing circles, diversion and elders' panels have made the existing justice system more responsive to aboriginal needs, they are interim measures with inherent and imposed limits. Judgement of guilt or innocence is left up to the court, and sentences must reflect existing Criminal Code provisions. Sentencing circles, which stem primarily from prairie tribal traditions, also may not be a good fit for all First Nations. Most importantly, restorative justice projects can only be effective when there has been extensive community consultation regarding both the nature of the project and those who will be sitting in judgement.

All across Canada, aboriginal women have questioned whether male elders and spiritual leaders should automatically be trusted, since they too are products of residential schools and intergenerational abuse. In Saskatchewan and Manitoba, at least two medicine men have been charged with sexual assault, and in northwestern Ontario, the Grand Council of Treaty 3 drew up a family violence strategy in 1994 that urged: "With due respect to the elders and with recognition of the great contributions they make, it must be brought out that elders themselves are victims of abuse. It is important that the elders embark on a program of personal healing. A commitment such as this by the elders would provide an example to other people." K. Peterson, special advisor on gender equality to the Northwest Territories justice minister, points out that values are changing. "Older people may evidence a tolerance of violence against women that is no longer acceptable to younger women," Peterson said in a 1992 report. Carol La Prairie, an aboriginal corrections expert, said in another 1992 report, "The use of elders in justice systems, to the exclusion of other age groups, may reflect values not representative of contemporary community values."

Mavis Henry, a Coast Salish social worker, foster parent and mother who has lived all her life on the Pauquachin reserve on southern Vancouver Island, was among a group of women who spoke out publicly in 1992, at great personal and professional risk, against the controversial South Vancouver Island Justice Education Project. The women charged that diverting aboriginal sex offenders to the longhouse instead of sentencing them to jail was perpetuating, not breaking, the silence about sexual abuse in their community. The women also accused some members of the elders' council of being offenders themselves. Women who laid charges were persecuted and run off the reserve, they said. The corruption of the elected band council system made it easy for leaders to deny jobs, housing and other financial benefits to outspoken women, particularly those who were without a large, powerful extended family to speak for them, Henry and the other women claimed. The diversion project was quietly cancelled by the B.C. government a year later.

Mavis Henry was appointed in 1994 to a powerful leadership position as the first aboriginal deputy superintendent of the B.C. Ministry of Social Services; in early 1996 she became the aboriginal advisor to the new B.C. Ministry for Children and Families. She still believes in aboriginal-led alternative justice treatment of offenders, as long as the survivors of sexual abuse are kept safe, and she feels the south Vancouver Island women's decision to speak out put their entire community through a powerful learning process. "It also empowered us to realize we don't have to be silenced by intimidation, and that if we speak out against the dreadful history of sexual abuse and assault in our communities, other women and men will come forward to support us. Nothing is going to stop the changes in our communities."

There will always be repeat offenders, resistant to treatment, from whom First Nations will require outside protection, and jail-based programs may be the best option for some individuals. Paramount in all community-based programs must be the safety of women and children, as the Royal Commission on Aboriginal Peoples urged in its sweeping recommendations regarding independent aboriginal justice. It is also urgent that the scope of the problem faced in treating and managing aboriginal sex offenders be understood, and that adequate resources be dedicated before the government of Canada hands off responsibility for all social programs to First Nations under the rubric of self-government. "Self-government on reserves or in the city has no future if our children are not kept safe and allowed to grow up free of abuse and neglect," says Marie Anderson, the N'laka'pamux director of the Hey-Way-Noqu Healing Circle for Addictions Society in Vancouver. "It sounds simple, but to stop child abuse we have to stop offenders, and we can't do that by putting them all in jail, only to have them return unhealed and reoffend."

Peter Joe was recently released from B.C.'s Stave Lake Correctional Centre after serving eighteen months of a sentence of two years less a day. A quiet-spoken young man, Joe was well known on his reserve as a teacher of life skills, a spiritual leader and a single dad. His marriage had not withstood the test of living with his wife's abusive father, whom Joe had accused of abusing both his wife as a child and their own two children. Just as the couple was on the verge of a reconciliation, Joe's wife was killed in a car accident. In the battle that followed for custody of his children, leaders of Joe's band sided with Joe against his in-laws, and he won custody of his daughter, aged five, and his son, aged six.

Just three years later, Peter Joe was in jail for sexually abusing his young daughter and physically assaulting his son. Members of his community who attended an all-day sentencing circle, along with a provincial court judge, felt strongly Joe should serve time in jail, but they wanted him sent somewhere he would receive treatment followed by a lengthy probation, conditions that couldn't be accomplished in a federal prison.

Peter Joe's name, as well as some family details and names, have been changed to protect the identity of the children who were victimized.

We were all in the same boat together at Stave Lake. I didn't feel judged so I could open up to some of those guys and learn something about my life. There was no one at home that I felt I could talk to.

I tried to stop myself from sexually abusing my daughter, and I kept hoping she would tell someone what I was doing to her, but she never did, and as time went by, what I was doing to her got worse and worse.

Whenever I tried to tell someone what I was doing to my children, I'd run into a brick wall and my mouth would seize up and I couldn't talk. I didn't know why. Now I see it was like a wall of shame.

I know that I'm the only one to blame for abusing my kids like I did. But the abuse in my family, in our whole community, started generations and generations ago. Our great-grandparents pretty much escaped the residential school, because the first white people didn't come to our area until relatively recently. On both sides, my great-grandparents and grandparents were really strong, self-sufficient people from what I know—they had big gardens, orchards, the best fishing sites in the canyon; and they dried and preserved all kinds of fish and food. But from what I've heard, it wasn't long after hordes of white people flocked in here, like in the mid-1800s, that things started to go terribly wrong. By the time my grandparents were kids, they were being shipped off to the residential school built right outside our town. Then the school scooped up most kids in our family, my grandparents on both sides, my mom, my dad, all my aunts and uncles, my brothers, and me.

It was my older brother, followed by some of his friends, who broke the silence about the sexual abuse at the residential school, about fifteen years after it had closed. The healing programs in our villages would start and then break down, because underneath the alcoholism there was just a terrible secret that almost every man was trying to hide. All hell broke loose. The R.C.M.P. stepped in and the case went to court, with my brother and a dozen other men charging a former supervisor at the school. He was convicted of a few rapes and indecent assaults of boys, but the judge estimated it was likely this supervisor had committed more than five hundred sexual assaults. It really hit home to the judge that a whole generation of men had suffered sexual abuse at that school. He said we were a people in great pain. Meanwhile, we were living that reality. The court case blew the lid off the sexual abuse issue, because a lot of people came forward to disclose they'd been abused. Therapists were brought in at first, but then they started to get closer to home, to start looking at the fact that boys who had been

STOLEN FROM OUR EMBRACE

abused at the school had grown up to be abusers themselves. When the disclosures got close to the powerful families on reserve, the whole process was shut down. A lot of pain got spilled and there was nobody there to mop it up. It began to poison us more.

Men my age can't stand the pain when they start to remember. They can't stand the pressure of burying the shame and pain, and having that weird sexual experience burned onto their memory at an early age, so they start to act out what happened to them. Some of us started to do to our children, and ladies, too, what was done to them. It's like you want to get back some of the power that was taken away. The shame is too much. You feel like nothing will ever take the hurt away and you might as well get rid of yourself because you're just garbage on earth. Although I don't remember being sexually abused at residential school, I'm pretty sure I was abused at home. I don't even have all my memories yet.

Other guys took out the pain on themselves. A lot of us died at a very young age. At my high school grad party alone two people died. I can show you the pictures of the guys I went to residential school with, and there's not many of them left. One guy I knew, Peter, the only way he could deal with it was at the end of a gun. Another guy went off the road in a pickup truck with his two buddies. They found his body in a tree. Chuck was hit by a car in 1980, and John shot himself. Three died as a result of a head injury. Another guy walked in front of a train. One was killed three years ago on the highway after he got drunk and walked in front of a truck. A lot of guys jumped off the high bridge over the canyon, that was a real popular suicide place. It seemed like I was going to a funeral every other week. In my grad year alone—most of us started out together at the residential school—half are dead and one guy has no legs.

The community has never gone through a deep healing process to make it safe for men who were abused, and men who became offenders, to come forward and disclose and get healed. Behind all the alcoholism and drug abuse, the family violence, men are hurting pretty bad. You know, all those scenes [in residential school] come back to me, the beatings and being so scared, in my nightmares, even when I'm awake. I was kind of despised at school and picked on. I felt powerless in school and in my family, where I was mocked and ridiculed because my skin was so much darker than my siblings. I had these deep feelings of blackness about myself, and when they came up, I didn't have the courage to go out and try to relate to ladies or find a baby-sitter so I could go out. I had no self-esteem. I turned to my daughter to meet my emotional and sexual needs. With my son, I think I was beating on him because of all the boys who beat on me. The violence at school that I just absorbed deep into my body, even the blows that landed on other kids, came out in the lickings I gave my son. I'd try to stop, but then I'd get mad over something small, and before I knew it, I'd have hauled off and smacked him in the face, or punched him. I was out of control.

The abuse with Janie started with just fondling and then penetration of her with my fingers. I would always reach an orgasm, right from the beginning. It started out once every two weeks, then up to once a week, and then in the later stages it would happen three to four times a week. In the later stages I did attempt intercourse with her. It was a compulsion with me. Looking back I see myself as an extremely lonely man treating her like a little wife, looking after my needs first. She never asked me to stop until the last few times.

I know it hurt her. She would burst into tears for no reason during the day. She would have bad nightmares. I kept on telling myself, I can't do this any more, but I couldn't stop. My son started taking his anger toward me to school. He'd misbehave. He stole some money from one of the teacher's purses. The kids actually were apprehended for two weeks once, about six or seven months before the final apprehension. That time I did disclose about hitting Justin, but I didn't say anything about my daughter. I had to agree to go to therapy and I took a couple of parenting classes. I guess I learned the violence at home, too. My father was really abusive toward my mother. He would beat her up really bad.

Finally my children were apprehended right at the school by the band social worker, who had been called in by my kids' teachers. The kids were acting out in school what was happening at home. When my brother Jake and his wife Rita received the kids, they put them in family therapy right away.

The more I look at it the more I blame my loneliness. I was a very lonely man. I was looking to Janie for all my needs. I wasn't even thinking of her, I was only thinking of myself. The longer I stayed single, the closer Janie and I were becoming, in an unhealthy kind of way. I didn't really tell her to keep quiet or use any threats or anything. Part of me was really hoping that she would tell. I couldn't take the responsibility myself, and that was wrong.

I didn't talk about the abuse until after the kids had made a full disclosure, and some people in the community really held that against me, too—that I didn't spare my children anything, I made them talk first. I was part of a Sundance society in the interior, and that's where I went first to disclose, to about eighteen people in a talking circle. Then I went back home and relayed the message that I had made my disclosure. I saw it as a step toward healing. I went back to my job teaching life skills to adults, but all through that day I felt like shit, I just wanted to give in my resignation, quit pretending I had anything to teach other people. After I handed in my resignation I talked with Jake and the social worker and told them I wanted the kids to stay with Jake and Rita. I said I wanted to get the necessary therapy to deal with my problems. They were helpful.

Then I went to the chief and council and disclosed to them. I requested them to help me through it. The chief, lawyer, social worker and the Crown counsel talked about it and agreed to make my case the first circle sentencing our community had done.

There were about twenty people in the room on the day of my circle sentencing. It was held in a community hall on the grounds of the old residential school. In the room was the judge and Crown counsel, my lawyer, two ministry social workers, the band social worker, the chief and a couple of councillors, a lawyer and Jake and Rita to represent my children, their family therapist, my aunt and my mother, two facilitators and two R.C.M.P. officers from the local detachment.

It was a long day, about twelve to fourteen hours. It started out with a pipe ceremony. After that everybody introduced themselves and said why they were there. People talked about their own lives as much as about me. My mom told everybody that for quite some time our home was a home without love, with no communication. She focussed on the last few years when I'd been helping her and getting her enrolled in the adult life skills course, how her life was turning the corner. She'd started to really come out of herself and develop self-confidence after all those years of drinking and the abusiveness of her relationship with my dad. She said she had some knowledge something was happening with me and my kids but she wasn't sure. In some ways she was blaming herself for not talking to me or somebody else. Both my mother and Jake suspected me, I think: in fact, Jake had seen me touch Janie sexually. But it wasn't our family's way to talk.

I had already done a family disclosure before the sentencing with my mom and aunt and my sister and brothers. They reacted with shock, but they still love me. It was really hard on my mom. During my teaching she saw a side of me that was really good. It helped her, and then I turned out be in need of serious help myself. I felt like I'd really let her down.

When it came time to talk about the sentencing, I was silent. I left it up to the group. The judge said an appropriate sentence would be prison for more than three years, but in a federal institution he was concerned I wouldn't receive any treatment. Everyone else thought two years less a day was appropriate so I could get help. There was one person who felt I should be banished from the community for up to four years. A lot of people, including the chief, were angry about that. The chief said his goal is family growth and healing, and he meant our whole family, me and my kids, my brothers and sisters. Our family needs to heal and learn how to bond.

I got involved with the Native Brotherhood in prison, and we had sweats on a regular basis while I was there. We got some hassles from one or two of the guards, but most of them were cool. In the sweat-lodge, I felt like I could really open up and let out some of the pain. Elders came in to help us. I could be more open than I would be at home. I felt some comfort with the guys. They knew where I was coming from. We had been wanting to bring in a traditional healer.

I still place a lot of faith in the traditional ways, because the elders have explained to me how the strict rules maintained community values and order. The residential school and the priests undermined all of that, and at the same time introduced sexual abuse to our communities. The elders told me that the strict rules dictated even who you could associate with or marry. The elders told me there was strict disciplinary measures taken if sexual abuse did occur. A group of the strongest men in the community would act as police. They would take whoever it was who committed the abuse and take them high into the mountains. For the first offence, they would build a big bonfire and put the offender on his knees on the very edge. They would tell him why he was there and what he'd done wrong and what would happen if he was ever brought back for the same thing. The second offence, they would build a big bonfire and tie fresh rawhide around his forehead. As the rawhide dried in the fire it would shrink and cut a deep ridge into his forehead. It was very painful and it scarred, marking him for life. On the third offence, a person was taken into the mountains far away and left alone without food or clothes. He was told never to come home.

If I'd had a choice between the traditional punishment and being sent to Stave Lake, I guess I'd have chosen jail, but the old cultural rules were what kept our people strong for thousands of years. At Stave Lake I had the chance to go back into my whole life and look at all the issues that caused me to offend with my children. It was safer there than in the community to talk about myself. I do have some goals for myself and for the future. I know I need a lot of therapy and healing.

It's my goal to get some training and work as a resource person with the Native Brotherhood with sex offenders doing time.

It will be a long road before I can have contact with my kids again. The court order prevents me from contacting them in any way unless they want it, so it's their call, not mine. It does hurt to know I might not see them for a long time. Right now I don't deserve to see them; I'm not safe for them yet and the community doesn't feel I'm safe. In the future I do want them to know their father, even if they never live with me again. At some point my children did love and respect me. I have a lot of love and compassion for them, how they're hurting now.

My community still has a long way to go. We need a family treatment centre, total family treatment, not just alcohol and drugs. This chief and council seem more motivated to have that happen, although a lot of our leaders haven't done their own healing. Whether there's money for family treatment at the provincial and federal levels is another question. Until our community can go through deep healing together, a lot of offenders and sexual abuse survivors won't feel safe to come forward, and the cycle will just keep repeating itself over and over. The suicides and the suffering of little children like mine won't stop.

I was released from jail after eighteen months and allowed to come home to serve my probation, which has pretty strict no-contact rules with my kids, and I can't be alone with other children. Some people in the community were pretty hostile, but most see me as someone who made a big mistake and is trying to deal with it. Most of my family has shown me they still love me. I still haven't seen my children, but I understand it has to be their decision whether I'll ever be a dad or see them again. I take a lot of comfort from sweats and the traditional healing. It's my way of starting over.

After two decades of testing both prison-based programs and alternatives to imprisonment, First Nations all across Canada have concluded

STOLEN FROM OUR EMBRACE

that culturally appropriate treatment on both fronts holds out hope for the future. Although incarceration in "iron houses" was historically anathema to First Nations people, some of the most progressive developments in aboriginal justice have occurred in Canadian prisons. Aboriginal prisoners began to argue in the late 1970s that they had the right to practise their own spirituality. By the mid-1980s they were able to argue they were entitled to those practices under Section 35 of the 1982 Canadian constitution and under the freedom of religion provisions of the new Charter of Rights and Freedoms. Finally, in 1992, federal legislation was amended to require Correctional Services Canada to "provide programs designed particularly to address the needs of Aboriginal offenders" and to create aboriginal advisory committees at the national, regional and local levels. Implementation of the new law has been inconsistent, but it has brought some encouraging changes.

An Aboriginal Programs section within Correctional Services Canada develops and administers spiritual and cultural healing programs in prisons. Some federal jails, recognizing the healing power of the sweatlodge, have set up structures on prison grounds. Under the guidance of elders and other helpers, aboriginal prisoners are led gently on a journey back to a traditional foundation of moral values. Thick steam clouds rise in the sweatlodge as water is splashed onto red-hot rocks, forcing the body to abandon poses and rationalizations adopted for the outside world. What is true and right rises to the surface of a person's consciousness. Offenders emerge from the sweats feeling cleansed and purified, says Frank Settee, a Manitoba Cree elder contracted by Correctional Services Canada to work with aboriginal offenders in B.C. Settee and at least two other elders now visit medium-security institutions at Mountain, Mission, Kent and Agassiz, and also Elbow Lake, a minimum-security aboriginal-specific prison camp.

A central component of the aboriginal offenders' treatment program in B.C.'s federal jails is a five-month course of native studies developed by Manitoba consultant Dr. Neil Macdonald. "This is a very, very critical part of the program, because many offenders don't know our own history, how our communities became dysfunctional," says Pam Jack. Next, offenders take instruction in how to lead a "balanced lifestyle," to achieve physical, mental, emotional and sexual health. "Gradually, offenders become more amenable to treatment," Jack says. "We see them sharing their native studies and balanced lifestyle binders with their family and visitors." Similar programs operate in other provinces.

For aboriginal prisoners who grew up in dysfunctional, acultural settings, prison programs are their first real acquaintance with the ways of their own people, and they can provide a pathway to follow out of jail for the rest of their lives. One of the few researchers to study the issue, James Waldram of the University of Saskatchewan, concluded that spirituality programs "have a significant effect on the mental health and well-being of offenders." Reduced recidivism among aboriginal sex offenders who have participated in these programs is marked, Waldram found. Although these traditional programs are of great benefit to all aboriginal prisoners, many feel that aboriginal sex offenders particularly need deep spiritual and emotional healing, since so many are acting out an unresolved sexual abuse history of their own. If they can confront their own memories and expunge their feelings of shame and contamination, they are on their way to a state of emotional health in which they will not need to continue to victimize others.

Elder Frank Settee also helps aboriginal sex offenders who are released from jail to return to their home reserve, which is often reluctant to receive them. In December of 1996, he accompanied two released sex offenders to remote Gitksan and Nisga'a villages in northern B.C. "I hold a workshop for everyone in the community who wants to attend, not just the professionals like the probation officer, police and social worker, but everyone, including the victim's family if they're from the same reserve," says Settee. "I tell them about the spiritual healing I have done with this man, and that he will always be Gitksan, or Nisga'a, or Cree. He has nowhere else to go and they don't have the option to kick him out, because he's home. At the same time, I tell them what he needs in order not to reoffend." Once understanding replaces fear, and communities know what they must do to monitor the offender and establish safety, Settee says the aboriginal sex offender often can live on reserve without ever reoffending. In the last decade, he's conducted several successful homecomings.

Two First Nations in Canada are leading the way in North America in community-wide programs to halt sexual abuse by identifying and treating offenders as well as survivors. At Hollow Water, Manitoba, the reserve-based program is in its ninth year, with only two cases of recidivism. (In non-native offender populations, half to three-quarters of all pedophiles and sex offenders can be expected to reoffend, even after treatment.) At Canim Lake, B.C., an ambitious treatment program for sex offenders on reserve, offering amnesty for those willing to take a polygraph and undergo aversion therapy, is in its second year of operation.

Disclosures of sexual abuse started a decade ago in Hollow Water, an Ojibwa village of 650 people three hours north of Winnipeg. A father had raped his two-year-old daughter. Uncles and aunts had sexually abused their nephews. A mother had held down her daughters so the father could rape them. A father had repeatedly punched his daughter in the stomach to try to force a miscarriage after he impregnated her. More than three-quarters of community members had been sexually abused as children, and 35 per cent of them were known to be victimizers.

The profound dysfunction at Hollow Water began in the 1970s after highways and electricity punched through the reserve, leading to the extinguishment of hunting and trapping as a way of life and limiting employment to seasonal forestry work. Cultural practices ebbed and eventually died. The economic losses were compounded by the loss of children; whole generations were taken by truck or train from Hollow Water to the residential schools, where many were repeatedly sexually and physically abused. By the end of the 1980s, every household was crippled by alcoholism, and sexual abuse had infected the whole community.

Starting in 1984, Ojibwa social workers began to combat alcoholism at Hollow Water using the personal growth programs pioneered in the sobriety movement at B.C.'s Alkali Lake, which blend non-native techniques with aboriginal values. Alcoholism fell dramatically, from 80 per cent of band members to less than 20 per cent, where it remains today. But with sobriety came a flood of painful memories.

By 1987, a resource group had been formed, and the Community Holistic Healing Circle was established to serve a population base of about 1,500 people living in Hollow Water and the surrounding Metis communities of Manigotagan, Aghaming and Seymourville. The community acronym adopted for the project, matching the first letter in the name of each village, was M.A.S.H., which suited its challenging mandate. "We live in a war zone," team members said in a 1993 statement. "It's not the guns and bombs kind of war. Ours is a more insidious conflict that has consumed the best energies of our best people for several generations. The enemies in this war are alcohol and drug abuse, sexual abuse, interpersonal and family violence, welfare dependency, dysfunctional family and community relations and extremely low self-esteem."

As in the television series, humour, tireless commitment and optimism would be needed to keep the team alive. "M.A.S.H. is also a good name for us because we are in the business of healing our communities and . . . as a team continually struggling to cope with casualties of the war while planning and executing strategies for winning it."

Hollow Water gained the cooperation of the area R.C.M.P. as well as the Manitoba attorney-general's ministry. "Our system is replete with recidivism," says Michael Watson, director of regional prosecutions for the Manitoba Justice Department. "It was clear the service we had been providing was not working at Hollow Water. It was the community perspective that the people coming out of the jails were more of a danger to their community than when they had gone in, that they just came out angry and were more likely to commit offences. If an entire commmunity thinks the system is not working, we have to listen."

The Hollow Water team of Ojibwa social workers and specially trained community members swings into action with military precision and organization once a disclosure of sexual abuse is made. The victim's needs come first; he or she is provided with counselling and support systems. The offender is confronted by team members as discreetly as possible and given the option of defending himself in a court of law. If he wishes to go the community route, he must first be charged by the R.C.M.P., but he will stay out of jail, on probation, as long as he participates in the community-based program. Initially, the Hollow Water program resorted to incarceration of offenders in "more serious" cases. Lately, it has begun to question whether any incarceration at all is helpful for an offender. The Hollow Water program's 1993 "Position Paper on Incarceration" says: "Removal of the victimizer from those who are best able to hold him/her accountable and offer him/her support adds complexity to already existing dynamics of guilt and shame. The healing process of all parties is therefore at best delayed [by incarceration] and most often actually deterred." Counselling, including sex education and anger management, can start immediately for the offender and his extended family when he is on community-based probation. Nor is the offender segregated from the rest of the community; he can assist at feasts and other events as long as he is never alone with children and does not approach his victim or victims in any way.

The key to the Hollow Water program is the often gruelling healing circle, where eventually the offender must face his family, other offenders and counsellors—and the survivor, if she or he so chooses. Berma Bushie, an Ojibwa child and family worker who coordinates the healing program, admits sitting an offender down in a gut-wrenching circle confrontation is not easy for anyone. But healing comes from digging out the pain. Sending people to jail is not the Ojibwa way and accomplishes nothing, Bushie believes. She told the *Globe and Mail*'s Peter Moon, "In our culture, it's not our way to punish. But that does not mean that we do not hold people accountable. There have to be ways of measuring that these people will not be a threat to anybody else."

Underscoring the use of the circle is a return to reliance on Ojibwa spirituality. The traditional clan structure has been resurrected, and Ojibwa medicine man Betson Prince was brought in from Winnipeg to be Hollow Water's director of culture for ten months in 1991. Prince reintroduced the sweatlodge as the most powerful part of the healing. Marcel Hardesty, an elected member of the Hollow Water band council and a victim of abuse himself, emphasized to Moon that "the spiritual program is the key. It helps people to understand why they have hurt and been hurt and makes them feel better. The ceremonies, the sweatlodge, even the prayers in the circle. And the burning of the sweetgrass, the sage, cedar, the tobacco. It's all part of the spiritual healing process."

The Holistic Healing Circle program has restored pride and self-reliance. Local probation authorities and police note the village has begun to rely on its own resources instead of depending on continuous outside intervention by police and social services agencies. Everyone—village residents and outsiders alike—agree the program has breathed new life into Hollow Water. Overall, crime and violence are down. By June 1995, the Hollow Water program had helped 409 clients, including 94 victims and 52 offenders, of whom only two have reoffended.

There are some caveats about the Hollow Water process. The greatest strength of community-based treatment, the circular structure closed to outsiders, can also be its greatest weakness, cautions Maggie Hodgson of the Nechi Institute. Hodgson was dismayed to find that a young rape victim and her mother had left Hollow Water after experiencing harassment from the family of the man charged. "Healing within a small community can be very powerful, but it's also subject to the on-reserve power structure, where certain families have more influence and can make the lives of victims who disclose abuse very miserable," Hodgson says. "Our offenders are not being healed in jail, but I'm concerned that keeping rapists and child molesters in the community can make women and children feel very vulnerable, as though their needs are not being addressed. It's a very difficult balance."

Another bold experiment in community-wide treatment of sex offenders is taking place at Canim Lake, a Shuswap settlement in British Columbia's rugged Cariboo district. The people of Canim Lake are one of seventeen modern-day Shuswap bands, speakers of a distinctive aboriginal language who call themselves the Secwepemc.

The residents of Canim Lake launched Canada's first reserve-based university program, which saw thirty-one members of their community graduate in 1992 with Bachelor's degrees granted by Gonzaga University in Washington State. Canim Lake also commissioned the first study of the effects of residential school on survivors and convened Canada's first national residential school conference. When the community hosted a meeting of the Royal Commission on Aboriginal Peoples at its school gymnasium in March of 1993, the band's family violence coordinator, Charlene Belleau, announced a bold plan for dealing with the community's epidemic of sexual abuse, in particular its offenders.

Canim Lake knew from the study it had commissioned, produced by University of Guelph sociologist Dr. Roland Chrisjohn, that two-thirds of its members had suffered sexual abuse at St. Joseph's residential school. The fallout included sexual dysfunction between marital partners, problems with intimacy, intense family violence, "and 40 to 50 other measurable negative impacts," Chrisjohn reported. As well, he wrote, "intergenerational effects . . . such as childhood sexual abuse are a problem of the first magnitude."

Speaking on behalf of the Canim Lake community, Charlene Belleau told the meeting that amnesty would be offered to all offenders who voluntarily disclosed and agreed to submit to community-based sentencing and treatment. Belleau outlined the phases of the program. "Being with children is a privilege, not a right," she emphatically told the Royal Commission. "A person with a history of offending will not be allowed to be with children until he has proven over a long period of time he poses no risk to our children's safety."

Canim Lake initially hired Phoenix, Arizona-based clinical psychologist Robert Emerick to spend one week out of six on the reserve, but is now administering the program with its own trained personnel. At first, Emerick ran up against a wall of denial and resistance. "There was a time when even I, and I've worked with sex offenders most of my adult life, was afraid to come up here," he admits. "My life was threatened. I got phone calls telling me to leave it alone."

But by the middle of 1995, the Canim Lake program had received funding and political support from the B.C. Attorney General's ministry, the provincial Women's Equality ministry and the federal Department of Indian Affairs. Dozens of Canim Lake members completed a sexual trauma inventory to gauge the extent of abuse on reserve and the need for counselling. Seventeen abuse survivors went through a year-long intensive course of therapy based on traditional talking circle groups and peer counselling. "From the results we got in a year of peer counselling and group therapy, it is evident that the traditional cultural healing and peer support is far superior to the expensive, one-on-one professional therapy a few band members got before," notes Emerick. "People were not healing with fly-in, fly-out non-native therapists." Finally, even before the amnesty phase was ready to proceed, eight men voluntarily came forward and confessed that they were sex offenders.

Belleau, who strongly believes in the healing power of the sweatlodge, has offered ceremonies on reserve to police officers, judges and provincial bureaucrats. Emerick believes just as strongly in conventional methods of treating sex offenders, including the polygraph, or lie detector, to reveal an offender's pattern of lying and evasion; foul-odour aversion therapy; and phallometric testing, in which a clamp is attached to the penis of an offender to measure his response to sexual material. He favoured using both methods in the Canim Lake program.

Once the first eight men had come forward, all band members—survivors, offenders and family members—were advised of their rights under the Canadian Charter of Rights and Freedoms and told they were free at any time to seek redress from the legal system or to elect to stand trial in a court of law. Offenders who chose on-reserve treatment were warned they would face not only a gruelling course of therapy and confrontation but also an electronic check of their veracity.

Before taking the polygraph, which was operated by an R.C.M.P. officer, the eight Canim Lake offenders admitted to assaulting 144 different victims. After polygraph results disclosed some prevarication, the men confessed they had abused 277 victims and been far more violent than they'd first admitted. Most were still offending up until the time they self-identified.

Sex offenders at Canim Lake who do not voluntarily come forward can be charged and sentenced in the outside justice system. Those who do participate in the community-based system must meet strict terms of on-reserve probation, including being housed at Letwilc Lodge, a large log building slightly isolated from the main part of the reserve. If offenders successfully complete treatment, there is provision for gradual, highly monitored reunification with families. The Canim Lake program is currently under close scrutiny from justice officials and First Nations across Canada, who are interested in using it as a blueprint.

The community-based treatment program at Canim Lake does have its flaws. At least one influential leader has turned his back on the process, defying both other band members and the R.C.M.P. "Many men in this community, as in others both native and non-native, have a very long history of offending and a strong resistance to stopping their behaviour," Emerick explains. "They are financially secure, have positions of power and respect both in the aboriginal community and outside, and they will go to any lengths to avoid being identified."

Even without the participation of a few powerful offenders, the sexual abuse prevention program at Canim Lake is succeeding, insists Charlene Belleau, who presented the first outcomes of the program at a national conference on aboriginal offenders in the fall of 1996 in Winnipeg. "Survivors of sexual abuse are feeling at Canim Lake for the first time that they are heard, and respected, and that they will get help." Almost all the accused offenders have cooperated with the treatment program, and of those who are in the program, no one has reoffended. Antoine Archie, Canim Lake chief and a social worker himself, knows the offender treatment program has its detractors on reserve, but he is also convinced no one wants to go back to the old alternatives of secret child sexual abuse or jail. "This was not our way, in the old days, to harm our own children, and it hasn't been that long since the non-natives brought us alcohol and sexual abuse, compared to how long we have been here. Together we can find the path back to the old cultural strengths we relied on. And if we have a few slips along the way, that's nothing compared to where we've been."

6

(OMMON, EXPENSIVE AND PREVENTABLE

Fetal Alcohol Syndrome

ALONE among almost all peoples on earth, First Nations living in the northern half of North America neither made nor drank alcoholic beverages before contact with Europeans. Even among pre-contact agricultural tribes in the southern half of North America and in South America, where more than forty kinds of alcoholic beverages were fermented from as many plants, intoxication was rare. "[Aboriginal people] used alcohol as they did other drugs, in a primarily religious context," notes Jack Weatherford in his book *Indian Givers*. Introduced by early European fur traders to grease the wheels of trade and erode the resistance of native women, alcohol was as deadly a "gift" to northern First Nations as the smallpox blanket.

The history of the fur trade is rife with reports of the avid interest aboriginal people displayed in "firewater"; it is just as clear that those reports were exaggerated, minimizing drinking by non-native fur traders and often omitting reference to the deliberate use of alcohol to manipulate and cheat native men and women. Over the next century, alcohol became deeply entrenched in aboriginal communities all over North America. It combined with despair, dislocation and unemployment to create a deadly cocktail that robbed aboriginal families of pride, self-respect and their future. It is doubtful whether contemporary Canadian society could have accomplished to the same degree the destabilization of aboriginal communities without the lubricant of alcohol. Certainly alcohol paved the way for the legalized abduction of aboriginal children that has continued apace to the present day.

Aboriginal communities today are plagued by an influx of modern intoxicants and drugs, including marijuana, cocaine and heroin, and the deadly spectre of solvent abuse stalks many reserves, inflicting permanent injury to the brain and other organs in children as young as six. Yet the Royal Commission on Aboriginal Peoples, after touring Canada and conducting research for five years, concluded: "Alcohol is the addictive substance presenting the greatest number of problems to Aboriginal people and communities in Canada." The National Native Association of Treatment Directors estimates about 80 per cent of aboriginal people in Canada are affected by alcoholism, either through being addicted themselves or through dealing with the addiction of a close family member.

Brian Maracle, Mohawk journalist and author of the book *Crazywater*, puts it succinctly: "If people don't understand native alcoholism, they don't understand native people." Alcohol psychosis occurs among aboriginal people at five times the national average; one in five hospital admissions for alcohol-related illness in Canada is an aboriginal person, according to the Canadian Centre on Substance Abuse. Almost three-quarters of the people living on B.C. reserves have identified alcohol abuse as their single most significant problem. In a 1991 federal survey, 60 per cent of aboriginal teens aged twelve to fifteen admitted to drinking beer regularly, compared to 80 per cent in the sixteen- to twenty-year-old age group, of whom more than half admitted to intoxication and even blacking out in the two months prior to the survey. The impact of excessive alcohol consumption on the already challenged state of aboriginal health is severe: higher incidences of heart disease, cirrhosis and liver disease, gastritis, gastrointestinal cancers and hepatitis. As Brian Maracle points out, the destruction created by alcohol is vast: "We are paying the legal, medical, financial and social consequences in the form of beatings, accidents, injuries, suicides, murders, arrests, jail terms, fires, drownings, sexual abuse, child abuse, child neglect, poor health, child apprehensions, unemployment and welfare dependency." For many aboriginal communities, alcoholism is the first hurdle to overcome before other reforms can be accomplished.

Perhaps the most acute pain felt by aboriginal communities is the damage alcohol abuse has done to their children. Thousands of First Nations children removed from the homes of alcoholic parents may never be reintegrated. But even more devastating and permanent is the damage done directly to children before they are born. Aboriginal children are disproportionately damaged by the most long-lasting suffering inflicted by alcohol: the wide range of birth defects known as Fetal Alcohol Syndrome (FAS), and the related syndrome Fetal Alcohol Effects (FAE). Both are caused by drinking alcohol during pregnancy. Fetal alcohol syndrome is a precise medical diagnosis of a child with prenatal alcohol exposure who meets these minimum criteria: prenatal and postnatal growth restriction; central nervous system dysfunction, such as neurological abnormalities; developmental delays; behavioural dysfunction; learning disabilities and other intellectual impairment; and skull and brain malformations. The three key clues to the full diagnosis are growth delays, central nervous system involvement and facial anomalies.

The facial anomalies in children with full-blown FAS make them appear as similar to one another as siblings: small eyes and head, flattened mid-section of the face, short, turned-up nose and thin upper lip. As preschoolers, FAS children may exhibit hyperactivity, attention deficit, language and motor skill problems, acting-out behaviour and inappropriate socialization. By the time they progress to their school years, the afflicted children are described as having attention and short-term memory deficits as well as problems with language, learning and behaviour. FAS adolescents are vulnerable to exploitation of all kinds; they may display inappropriate sexual behaviour or endanger themselves with indiscriminate friendliness. They are vulnerable to drug and alcohol addiction, and they may be easily drawn into criminal activities through their innocence or lack of judgement. Not every child with FAS will exhibit behaviour problems, especially those fortunate enough to be raised in a loving, supportive, culturally strong home. FAS children can be loving, gentle, talented and wise, even if they lack common sense or concrete life skills.

For every child with full FAS, there are ten times as many children who suffer from the often invisible disability of FAE, also described as "possible FAE" since it can be difficult to diagnose. FAE children have reduced or delayed growth, birth defects and behavioural disorders that may not be noticed or attributed to prenatal alcohol until months or even years after the child's birth. Yet some FAE children may actually function more poorly in some areas than children with the full syndrome. Since their appearance is usually conventional, they run an even greater risk than do FAS children of being characterized as disobedient, defiant and disorganized rather than brain-injured. Many social workers and physicians, including Vancouver pediatrician Dr. Christine Loock, prefer to speak of a continuum of Alcohol-Related Birth Defects rather than the misleading categories of greater and lesser syndromes.

In aboriginal communities that are developing a heightened awareness of FAS/FAE, many adults are slowly starting to realize that they, too, have been damaged by prenatal alcohol. "It may be quite subtle, such as an inability to reason abstractly or organize oneself, difficulty learning and remembering, or trouble in imposing discipline and structure as a parent," says Susan Little, a nurse in charge of a community prevention program among the Ktunaxa-Kinbasket people in the Kootenay region of B.C. "I had a young mother who attended one of our prevention meetings come in to tell me later that she had just realized that she, too, is alcohol-affected. It can be quite a shocking revelation." The oldest person to seek an FAS/FAE diagnosis in the Ktunaxa program was well into his sixties, Little says, "and there are many more adults and elders affected who aren't diagnosed."

Bathing a fragile fetus in alcohol is like spilling a drink on a computer: the circuitry is scrambled in ways that are hard to predict and impossible to repair. A fetus does not have the liver cells or blood circulatory system to process alcohol even in minute amounts. Mothers who had less than a drink a day during pregnancy were found in a University of Pittsburgh study to have cost their children five IQ points. Researchers agree that just one binge of five or more drinks during pregnancy can inflict on the unborn child a range of learning difficulties for life. Yet not every drinking woman will produce an FAS child; studies of alcoholic mothers who gave birth to fraternal twins found that only about half of the children had FAS. Knowing the risk, few unaddicted women would choose to play Russian roulette with their baby's life. But as Washington physician Dr. Sterling Clarren, who in 1978 identified FAS as "the most frequently known teratogenic cause of mental deficiency in the Western world," points out: "If I said to you, you have a 50-50 chance of having an FAS baby, would you consider that good odds? No. But an alcoholic might."

Clarren has interviewed and treated hundreds of alcoholic mothers over two decades, and he emphasizes, "None of them intended to harm their babies." Yet denial and rationalizing are part of the alcoholic's behaviour pattern. Each successive child born to a drinking mother will be more severely damaged; as her alcoholism continues, her body will have fewer resources to bestow upon the fetus. Factors such as smoking, drug use and poor nutrition also play a role in determining how severely a drinking mother's children will be affected. Says Dr. Clarren: "The only clear message we know is true is: Don't drink."

More than two decades have gone by since a University of Washington team—pediatricians Dr. David Smith and Dr. Kenneth Jones, and psychologist Ann Streissguth—coined the term "Fetal Alcohol Syndrome" in a study of eleven alcohol-damaged children published in the British journal *Lancet*. There are still no accurate statistics on the extent of FAS/FAE in Canada. Few Canadian doctors have been trained to include in their regular practice a thorough, accurate FAS diagnosis. Nor is there any systematic federal or provincial tracking of FAS or the more subtle FAE, except for the figures provided by the minority of diagnoses performed in a hospital.

Consequently, a somewhat arbitrary and certainly conservative incidence estimate that "one to three children in every 1,000 is born with FAS in industrialized countries, and [a number] several times higher than that for possible FAE" is accepted in this country, and was officially cited in the 1996 federal policy statement on FAS/FAE.

FAS/FAE is by no means only an aboriginal problem. Its incidence crosses all class and race boundaries, from the stereotype of the skid road alcoholic to the martini-tippling white middle-class matron. But the few formal studies conducted to date indicate that the aboriginal incidence of FAS/FAE is much higher than the mainstream, and that there are some aboriginal communities in B.C. and the North that have FAS/FAE incidence rates as high as one in six to ten births. In the Downtown Eastside of Vancouver, a predominantly aboriginal neighbourhood, almost one in two babies is born affected by alcohol or drugs, the highest rate in North America.

Perhaps the most accurate snapshot of the aboriginal incidence of FAS/FAE can be gleaned from medical institutions. The Kinsmen's Children's Centre in Saskatchewan, which has the most comprehensive data base in Canada, has identified in the past decade more than 450 children with FAS/FAE, of whom 75 per cent are aboriginal. Vancouver's Sunny Hill Health Centre for Children, the main diagnostic centre for B.C., documented more than 440 FAS/FAE cases from 1992 to 1996, more than 50 per cent of them aboriginal children.

First Nations have become understandably wary about being the subjects of fetal alcohol studies, especially since their communities usually reap few tangible benefits from having the lives of women and children put under a microscope. The publicity that accompanies such studies can be hurtful and counterproductive for all concerned, but especially for the First Nation. In 1985, Dr. Geoffrey Robinson, Dr. John Conry and Dr. Julianne Conry of the University of British Columbia embarked on a three-phase study of FAS/FAE incidence, which was to be followed by proposals for prevention assistance, with the residents of Canim Lake, B.C. The research was aborted by the band after early results led to sensational media headlines. Other com-

STOLEN FROM OUR EMBRACE

munities have had similar experiences. First Nations have concluded that they must take ownership and control of FAS/FAE research to ensure that studies meet their needs first. At the same time, many aboriginal health professionals feel there is an urgent need for good epidemiological research, both to combat community denial and to provide the evidence governments demand before they release funds. The goal is to find successful community/academic partnerships.

Of the children diagnosed at Vancouver's Sunny Hill Centre, more than three-quarters were not living with their biological parents. Eight of ten children with the full syndrome grow up away from their birth mothers, for a host of reasons. They may be apprehended at birth to allow hospitals to proceed with medical intervention or taken from their parents as preschoolers. A twenty-year study in Seattle found that three-quarters of the mothers of FAS babies had died of alcoholism and its complications before their children reached their teens.

The proper care of alcohol-affected children is tremendously expensive. Each tiny shivering baby born in a delivery room reeking of booze will cost at least $1.5 million over his or her lifetime. Dr. Geoffrey Robinson, a leading researcher in the field and founder of the B.C. FAS Resource Society, tells medical students and native community nurses that "preventing one child from being born with FAS more than earns you your life salary." Underfunded First Nations health care systems, both on reserve and in the inner city, have difficulty getting and allocating funding to take care of their own fetal-alcohol-damaged children and adults. Yet when a native child is taken into care, it appears that funding suddenly kicks in to take him or her on the round of medical appointments that the child will need for the rest of his or her life. Diagnosis and visits to a psychologist can be more readily organized and reimbursed when a child is in government care. Birth parents struggling to take care of their own alcohol-affected children may feel discouraged and ultimately be defeated by the lack of diagnosis, counselling, tutoring and respite care, and by the need for ceaseless advocacy to achieve services for their child and to keep the family intact. On an isolated reserve, access to good health care and diagnosis is a challenge, unless the First Nation has specifically developed programs for alcohol-affected children. Frustrated aboriginal parents may surrender a child to government care so that he or she can get the medical and social help needed. Rather than stimulating a flow of funding to help First Nations take care of their own, FAS/FAE is too frequently used as another justification for separating aboriginal children from their parents and extended families.

The high aboriginal birth rate in the last twenty-five years has produced a demographic bulge of FAS/FAE adolescents and young adults. Lodged in non-native homes or drifting in and out of government foster care, these young adults pose an urgent crisis. One of four juveniles in Canadian jails suffers from fetal alcohol syndrome, according to a 1996 study by Dr. Julianne Conry and Dr. Christine Loock. Aboriginal adolescents frequently comprise more than 50 per cent of all residents in Willingdon Juvenile Detention Home in Burnaby, B.C., and they are found in equally high numbers in juvenile facilities on the prairie provinces and in northern Canada.

Fortunately, there are now some judges who have become aware they are jailing alcohol-afflicted children simply because there is nowhere else for them to go. At a 1996 conference in Whistler, B.C., health professionals from western Canada and the U.S. listened as former B.C. provincial court judge Cunliffe Barnett expressed concern that courtrooms are increasingly clogged by alcohol-disabled adolescents who have been failed by the social services network and the justice system at every crucial juncture of their lives.

Barnett told conference delegates about a court case involving Ronald, a fifteen-year-old Shuswap boy with FAS. Barnett was asked by probation officers and Crown counsel to sentence Ronald to a lengthy term in closed custody. A tough-talking boy who covered up his insecurity and nonexistent self-esteem with foul language and threats, Ronald was seen by most authorities as the deliberate author of his own misfortune, yet he was clearly brain-injured. He was frequently ill and lacked any stability or consistent parenting in his life. Repeatedly victimized, gang-raped by several men at age eleven,

Ronald had begun to hand back some of the abuse he'd received, graduating from petty crime to stolen cars and guns.

Although a pediatrician had written, "Failure-to-thrive, query FAS?" on Ronald's chart at three weeks of age, it took a court order by Judge Barnett to get Ronald, a government ward, his first thorough medical exam. Dr. Kwadwo Asante at Sunny Hill Centre diagnosed him as having a very low IQ and full fetal alcohol syndrome. Judge Barnett sent officials scrambling with a court-imposed deadline of three weeks to find Ronald a safe place to live, an order which in itself drew brutal attention to the fact that there is nowhere in all of Canada or the U.S. to send young adults with FAS/FAE. Native courtworker Amy Sandy finally got Ronald a six-month berth at the Poundmaker's native treatment centre in northern Alberta, but the conundrum posed by Judge Barnett remained: how can troubled FAS adolescents like Ronald ever lead peaceful, productive adult lives?

First Nations across North America are starting to address that issue. As the Aboriginal Nurses of Canada emphasized in their 1997 report, "It takes a community to raise a child with fetal alcohol syndrome." Aboriginal health-care providers emphasize that FAS/FAE is not one woman's issue but a communal responsibility, and some of the most successful FAS prevention and outreach programs in North America are now underway in aboriginal communities. Although some FAS/FAE aboriginal children will continue to require substitute care, many First Nations today are determined to place children with relatives or extended family. The goal is to keep the birth mother in contact with her children while she is assisted to recover from her alcohol addiction. Although FAS/FAE children can prove an enormous challenge for an alcoholic mother, she is often the afflicted child's best hope of forming any lasting human bond. If birth parents can be provided with a solid support structure of addiction counselling, parenting courses, respite care and educational assistance for their children, an aboriginal family can be saved instead of split up into damaged, hurting pieces that will inevitably be more of a burden on the public purse.

FAS/FAE activists point to a crippling lack of coordination between provincial and federal governments on FAS/FAE prevention. There is no national strategy, and the Canadian government maintains it can address all the needs of FAS/FAE-afflicted children "under existing programs," according to a 1996 statement by then Liberal health minister David Dingwall. "Foetal Alcohol Syndrome: A Preventable Tragedy," a 1992 report produced by the federal Standing Committee on Health Issues, called for "aggressive public information campaigns" in aboriginal communities as well as "more effective and appropriate community-based ways of dealing with learning disabilities, of which FAS is the major portion of demand." The Conservative government of the day ignored the report's recommendations, arguing that no one group in Canada is at greater risk for FAS/FAE than any other, and that programs targeted specifically to aboriginal people would only stigmatize them further.

The position of Jean Chrétien's Liberal government has scarcely evolved from that of the previous government. Although Dingwall insisted in his 1996 statement that the federal government had done much to prevent FAS/FAE, concretely their involvement consisted of funding five conferences, producing a pamphlet and a video, and directing only one initiative specifically at First Nations—a health providers' manual. In fact, the Liberal government has been singularly derelict in devising strategy or in funding anything but piecemeal parts of existing programs for the thousands of aboriginal children afflicted with FAS/FAE, for whom it retains fiduciary and financial responsibilities.

The Standing Committee on Health Issues also recommended mandatory warning labels on liquor bottles and in bars, along with a legislated ban on glamorous "lifestyle advertising" of liquor. But powerful booze barons appear to have been successful in backhanding all attempts by politicians, health professionals, aboriginals and other activists to label alcoholic products as hazardous to the health of unborn babies. Alcohol is labelled as a danger to pregnant women and their fetuses in almost every industrialized country in the world, including the Scandinavian countries, the United States, Mexico and

Colombia—but not in Canada. Instead, in his 1996 statement, Dingwall promoted the liquor industry's own 1-800 number, which provides "lifestyle" advice to women. The Canadian Distillers' Association, which dispatches a young female executive to FAS symposiums to argue against labelling, maintains warning labels on liquor aren't necessary because everyone already knows about the dangers of drinking while pregnant, a position contradicted by most surveys and every tenet of health promotion ideology. (The American National Health Interview Survey, for example, reported recently that fewer than 57 per cent of people under forty-five have even heard of FAS.) Some Canadian provinces have introduced limited labelling, but in the absence of federal political will on the issue, some women's groups and health activists have taken the initiative by plastering their own warning stickers in women's washrooms in restaurants and bars.

As the Royal Commission on Aboriginal Peoples concluded, First Nations need to "determine their own health and social services needs," and to be delegated "full control over aboriginal health research and special education campaigns," such as those to combat FAS/FAE. With the programs they have in place today, First Nations are proving they can do a better job than Ottawa in looking after their own people. But they need the resources to continue. Federal leadership and funding is required to develop a national aboriginal strategy on FAS/FAE, which should include provision for epidemiology and monitoring on and off reserve through a scientific but culturally responsive structure; access to confidential diagnosis for alcohol-affected children and adults; culturally appropriate community- and school-based education for alcohol-affected children and their caregivers; a prevention campaign that speaks sensitively and effectively to First Nations women and men; more training for aboriginal professionals in FAS/FAE issues; and day-care, respite care and support for birth parents and substitute caregivers of alcohol-affected children. A national aboriginal clearinghouse for FAS/FAE information, such as the National Organization on Fetal Alcohol Syndrome's data base in the U.S., is also long overdue. Above all, aboriginal activists say First

Nations families need support to look after their FAS/FAE infants, children and young adults in a culturally intact setting. "We urgently need to find the resources to create a safe setting at home or near home for our young alcohol-affected adolescents and adults, to help them overcome the deficits they can't do anything about; and to help them have fulfilling and productive lives," says Sophie Pierre, administrator of the Ktunaxa-Kinbasket Tribal Council. "We believe we know best how to raise our FAS/FAE children as an integral part of our own community. It's a priority for us as First Nations."

Kandice Boudreau, heir to a high-ranking title of the Gitksan nation, was born in a Vancouver hospital to a severely alcoholic mother. Diagnosed at birth with full-blown fetal alcohol syndrome, Kandice has been lovingly raised and legally adopted by her maternal aunt Margaret Boudreau. Now a teen-ager, Kandice Boudreau is a child who speaks from the heart. She has a large, ready smile shining out from a small face framed by thick black hair often brightly tinted in accordance with the latest teen style. She has spoken all over North America, from Inuit communities in the North to Navajo and Pueblo communities in the American Southwest, about what it is like to be a child living with FAS.

This is Kandice's story, followed by the voice of her mother Margaret.

I'm never going to drink because I've already lost too many brain cells. I don't mind talking about how alcohol hurt me if it will help another kid. My birth mom's drinking hurt my brain really badly. She was drunk when I was born. I was born drunk. I have to go to the doctor and the dentist so, so much. I'm sick a lot and I have to work really, really hard at homework to keep up. I've met lots of FAS kids like me, and I don't think kids should have to go through what we do. Once my mother Margaret asked me, "Kandice, if you had three wishes, what would you want?" And I thought and thought, and I said I'd like a horse, or another dog, or lots of money, but more than anything I want a new brain, like the brain of a baby whose mother didn't drink.

MARGARET (*left*) & KANDICE BOUDREAU

At school I'm in the Strategies program, with kids who have mental or physical disabilities. We go to regular classes, too, but one of our teachers always goes with us, because some of the kids have real behaviour problems. They freak out or get really angry and frustrated because they can't learn and they start hitting out or smashing up things. It's a bit scary. I get really angry and frustrated too, but I don't act out like that.

My biggest problem is that I'm still lonely. In elementary school I was lonely and now, in high school, I'm lonely. I don't have anyone to hang out with after school. It's very frustrating at school, too. I keep saying, "Why can't I do things other kids can do? Why can't I learn like them, go to movies like them or think like them, or remember anything?" I start crying. I wish oh, so bad, that my brain could work, that it could be fixed. None of the regular kids want to be friends with me, because I can't really follow what they're saying. They talk so fast, and if I ask them to repeat it, they say, like, See you around, Kandice. They don't mean to be mean, but it really hurts me.

I also lose time from school because I'm sick a lot. That's not my fault. Once in elementary school I had the flu for a whole week and when I came back the teacher said to me, right in front of everybody, "Kandice, if you're sick any more this year, I'm going to have to fail you." I felt so bad I couldn't speak. If she had said that to me in private, maybe I could handle it, but in front of everybody! I told my mom and she talked to the teacher, but the teacher never apologized to me. She doesn't know about FAS, that we have a lot more sickness and operations and stuff than other kids.

When people give me three or four instructions I can't keep them all in my head. I still don't know money very much, the coins really confuse me. My teachers try to teach me about real money because for a long time all the money was really the same for me. Then my mom started allowing me to go into stores and give the right money and remember to wait for change. All the store people know me and they'd call out, "Kandice! You forgot your change," but like my mom says, there won't always be nice people, so I have to figure out what money I'm supposed to get back.

Common sense is a complicated thing for me. I have to remember to turn off the bath before it overflows. I guess I have to be told a lot not to touch strange animals because they might bite me. Like I have trouble to learn life skills. We did a whole unit on safety in elementary school and now in high school, we still talk about it. Before, I always used to get lost, but I take the bus to school by myself now and I can go to McDonald's after school, buy food with the right money, and then come home by myself.

Math is hard for me, but I have a tutor and I can do math with a calculator. One time in elementary school, a substitute took my calculator away. I told her I was allowed because I can't do math without a calculator, but she didn't care. I came home all upset and crying. I wanted to crawl away and hide. Then the teacher promised she'd always leave a note for the substitute saying, "Kandice is allowed to have her calculator." With my tutor, we use menus and pretend we're going to a restaurant, then I decide what I'm going to have, how much it will cost and what money I get back.

My birth mother, Sandra, never really stopped drinking. She'd come to visit me with Larry, my real dad, and grab my cheeks and pinch them, saying stuff like, "Oh, Kandice, you're so cute, cute little Kandice." It seems like they thought I was about two years old still. They weren't supposed to visit me when they were drinking. I tried to talk to Sandra when I was little about why she drank alcohol when I was inside her but she didn't want to talk about it. Finally, when I was about thirteen, she called me one day when she was sober and she said, "Kandice, I'm sorry." I said, "That's all right, Sandra." I said I forgive her and I really do. But I said, "Sandra, now that you know what happened to me, don't ever do it to another little kid." She promised she wouldn't, but she still kept on drinking.

All last spring Sandra was really sick with flu. The ambulance came and they told her to go to the hospital, but she refused. On Good Friday, we got a call from Larry, my birth dad, and he said Sandra had died in her sleep. It took me a few minutes, and then I really started crying and crying. My mom and I believe in angels, and for the first few days I missed Sandra so bad, I could see her and talk to her. She wasn't so sad any more, and she wasn't drunk, either! It makes me really sad that in her life, Sandra never could stop drinking. We got to be really close the last couple of years, but it makes me sad, too, that she could never be my real mom.

I think a lot about when I grow up. I really love animals, and when we go up to the farm in the summer, I love to be with the horses, dogs and chickens, and even to listen to the coyotes and wolves howling at night. Sometimes you can even hear bears in the bush. I'd like to be a mom myself if Mom could stay with me. I really love babies and I'd like to babysit. Even though I'm FAS, I will never have a baby with an injured brain because it doesn't get passed on to your baby unless you drink. My mom and Dr. Loock have told me that I will have a really hard time not drinking too much alcohol, so the best thing for me is to just never get started. I know how hard it is to be FAS, so I don't ever want to hurt a baby like my mother hurt me.

I wrote something myself for this book. Here it is:

My Life with FAS and How I Live with It

Well, when I was in my birth mother's tummy, she did some heavy drinking and my aunt that turned into my mom tryed to stop Sandra drinking because she was going to have baby. That was going to have something wrong with it and a damage brain but Sandra didn't know that. And then the baby was born and Sandra wanted Margaret her sister to name the baby so Margaret loved the name Kandice. And when Kandice grow little more she did not know why she was so slow in class. And then her mom told her at Mcdonald's when she was seven years old and then Kandice knew what was wrong with her.

Kandice grew to be a lot older. One day Kandice decided to make something happen to this world today, she decided to tell people about something she had that she knew wasn't going to leave her body. She Kandice started to do talks with her wonderful mom Margaret. They did conferences and told people a lot of stuff about her and went on t.v. lots of times. And be came fammos like stars on t.v. and people thought that was good and Kandice's family was proud of her and loved her so much. Kandice was very happy and proud of herself too. Kandice could some time not be all happy but that's not how she makes her life, she try to make it more exiting to live in. Kandice's mom told her it's not good to live in deprresion and kids with FAS like Kandice doesn't want to live that way.

Margaret Boudreau:

Margaret Boudreau was born into the Frog clan of the Kispiox community, in the heart of Gitksan territory, a vast area in northwest B.C. Her earliest memories are of growing up in the wilderness with her paternal great-grandmother, a medicine woman who lived off the land, and her maternal grandmother. Margaret believes her life came full circle with Kandice's birth, allowing her to reforge the strong spiritual bond she had with her beloved grandmothers. Margaret and her husband, Gary, live in a large Vancouver home, where they provide foster care to aboriginal children affected by prenatal exposure to alcohol or drugs. In addition to Kandice, they have two adult children, four grandchildren and several foster children.

Kandice and I come from a long line of female healers. One day she'll be able to live without Gary and me, she says, but I don't know if I could survive without her. Kandice is a spiritual throwback to my great-grandmother. Kandice and I have special ways of communicating and we both rely on our spiritual beliefs for strength. When I took her home to Kispiox when she was just seven, the elders all saw her gifts right away. "She's a medicine woman, that one," they said.

As soon as Kandice was born, they put her in an incubator where Gary and I could see her. I talked to her and called her by name. As a baby, Kandice was a tiny, shivering, shaking thing, never at peace in her own body, even when she was asleep. The alcohol had her in its grip. For the first few months, Kandice was like an alcoholic or drug addict going through withdrawal, except she was a newborn baby. She didn't come home from the hospital until she was two and a half months old.

When Kandice went home from the hospital with Sandra, we were devastated. Kandice needed surgery and a lot of care. We often took over Kandice's care completely. It was very hard for me to see Kandice so damaged and Sandra still drinking, unable to care for her, because I loved them both. Sandra was my baby sister and I basically brought her up.

We fostered Kandice for ten months and she settled down and began to thrive. Sandra went to detoxification and alcohol treatment and counselling for almost a year. When she got out, she managed to visit Kandice without alcohol on her breath whenever the social worker was there. Two days before Kandice was scheduled to go back to her, Sandra started drinking heavily again. I warned the social worker but they gave Kandice back to Sandra and Larry. I felt grieved as though I had lost a child.

We went back to having Kandice on weekends, but it was very confusing and upsetting for her. It all came to a head when Kandice was twenty-five months old. I had driven over to check on her and I could hear her crying. Finally my sister answered the door, visibly very drunk. Kandice was sobbing in her crib, covered in poo, her face, her hair, everywhere. There were people passed out everywhere on the floor. I cleaned Kandice up as best as I could, then wrapped her in my coat and took her home.

Finally we were designated Kandice's foster parents by the court. We felt convinced Kandice's life would be at risk if she returned to her birth parents while they were still drinking, and finally the courts and the ministry agreed. We legally adopted her. Sandra remained a part of Kandice's life, when she was able to be.

My sister Sandra died this year. I believe she finally just gave up on life. She was tired of all the pain and suffering. She made a choice to keep on drinking. She knew it was hurting her, but she'd tell me, "Margaret, nobody can save me, don't even try." Sandra did love Kandice, but she never could have parented her. For me, it was very sad—she was the little sister I had tried to bring up, who gave me the gift of Kandice, and now she's gone.

I was the second of four children born to Cora Morrison and Phillip Crosby. Cora was a strong, dignified lady who helped all the women in our village, but I believe even when she was pregnant with me, there was secret heavy drinking by the women who would gather together in the afternoon. I believe I've been affected too by fetal alcohol, not the full syndrome like Kandice, but I'm sure I have fetal alcohol effects in many respects.

I was adopted into the Gitksan House of Delgamu'ukw, and there are lands and forests back home that are part of Kandice's birthright, too. Even if we never return to live there, Kandice is very aware of her heritage. As the eldest daughter, I was very privileged to be brought up by my great-grandmother, Ulles, until I was seven, in a tiny cabin way up in the mountains. I remember each day with her perfectly clearly, as if it were yesterday, hunting and trapping fox and marten to trade for staples like flour and sugar. Ulles was the oldest person ever to have lived in the Kispiox/Hazelton area, about 139 in English numbers when she died.

After my Ulles died, I went a little strange for two years. She was my anchor in life, and my spirit left with her when she died. The rest of the world was superficial, day-to-day things that didn't touch me or mean anything to me. I believe that's what it's like for some of us who are affected by our mothers' use of alcohol; we need deep, deep bonding, and we form one bond for life. Now Kandice has that same deep spiritual presence.

Sandra never had that traditional upbringing with the elders that my brother and I did. She had no one, and as the youngest child, she was more affected by our mother's drinking. I was able to deal with my own alcoholism. I had my kids and I loved them dearly. Gary and I began to foster children, most of them aboriginal children who were born alcohol- or drug-affected, which was very challenging and rewarding.

Even though Kandice has disabilities, she is very smart. She's very perceptive and accurate about people. I believe her insights and her spirituality are a gift that will stand by her in her life. It's as though the Creator took away with one hand and gave with the other to make up for the way Kandice was born.

I'm not a teacher, I'm not academically inclined at all, but I know how to help Kandice learn. By constant advocacy and a lot of battles with the school board and schools, we've got tutors for Kandice and our FAS/FAE foster kids. I help Kandice with her lessons at home, breaking them up into small parts so she can understand them. Kandice likes to withdraw to her room and colour, listen to music or write letters. She has over two hundred penpals all over the world, and she keeps all their letters in a binder. She'll rejoin the family when she's relaxed again. We respect that privacy of hers because she's learned on her own how to manage the FAS overstimulation.

I've always allowed Kandice to make the choice about whether to speak in public, and now we've spoken to First Nations people all over North America. Kandice is a teacher and a healer. People come up to her to hug her after we speak; they can sense her healing gifts.

Kandice loves little children; she dotes on her nieces, and there's a very loving, nurturing side of her that would make a wonderful mother. But Gary and I won't be around forever to help her, and that does worry us. We are confident that this fetal alcohol that has plagued three generations in our family will end, right here and now, with Kandice. Kandice's children will never have FAS. She is our new beginning, and if she is where a Gitksan hereditary title now rests, people must understand and accept Kandice. Her wisdom is a gift from our ancestors, and I thank the Creator every day that Kandice came into our lives.

The goal of combatting fetal alcohol syndrome has brought together First Nations people from all tribes and regions of North America. The first, seemingly insurmountable shared goal has been to loosen the grip in which alcohol has held aboriginal people for centuries. Significantly, it was a child who launched one of the most powerful social movements of the twentieth century: First Nations' sobriety.

In 1972, in her Alkali Lake kitchen, Phyllis Chelsea poured her liquor down the sink, devastated that her seven-year-old daughter Ivy had refused to come home because she was terrified by her parents' drinking. Chelsea, who now works with Shuswap children in reserve and mainstream schools, kept her vow of sobriety to Ivy, braving scorn and resistance in a village where 95 per cent of adults drank to excess. Alkali Lake had moved in a now well-documented process to almost total sobriety by the early 1980s, using a blend of traditional aboriginal values and techniques from the modern human potential movement to create a powerful, effective formula that soon was being shared with aboriginal nations from Australia to Inuvik, from New Mexico to Nova Scotia.

Today, the rates of aboriginal sobriety are steadily rising all over North America, from remote reserves where alcohol is banned to urban aboriginal communities where young people, provided with role models for sobriety as well as ample evidence of the pitfalls of addiction, never start drinking to excess. Aboriginal treatment centres report results that are more lasting and profound than mainstream addiction treatment. Maggie Hodgson of the Nechi Institute on Alcohol and Drug Addiction wrote in a 1992 study that "seventy-six per cent of the [former drinkers] we have surveyed [now have] two to ten years of sobriety." The sobriety movement has received financial support from all levels of government, including $60 million annually from the National Native Alcohol and Drug Program. Still, aboriginal sobriety is a success story largely because it is a grassroots movement initiated and directed by First Nations. It is now the case that far fewer aboriginal people in Canada drink daily or weekly than do non-natives. Total abstinence is twice as common among aboriginal people than in the general population.

The Ktunaxa-Kinbasket people, five communities of 1,200 people who live in the Kootenay region of B.C.'s southern interior, resolved in the early 1990s to embrace and integrate their generations of alcohol-affected people, from infants to elders, instead of surrendering them to hospitals, foster care, jails and institutions. "We knew we had an epidemic of FAS/FAE, but we decided to meet the challenge through a community-wide approach," explains Sophie Pierre, who is chief of the St. Mary's band as well as administrator of the Ktunaxa-Kinbasket Tribal Council. With funding assured for five years, the

Ktunaxa hired nurses, educators, elders and life-skills tutors, and in 1992 launched their comprehensive Community Healing and Intervention Program, known as CHIP.

Pierre, a capable administrator who has been provincial co-chair of the B.C. First Nations Summit, points out that in the aboriginal tradition, children are the community's future, so preventing FAS is everybody's business. "Our First Nations approach is different from the mainstream because we don't single out the individual woman," says Pierre. "This involves the whole community; it's not just a case of trying to stop Mom drinking." The Ktunaxa maintain their own alcohol treatment and wellness centre, and Pierre believes sobriety for everyone greatly furthers FAS prevention. She also believes that the key to halting FAS/FAE is to draw on traditional cultural values, a view reinforced by the experience of two decades in achieving aboriginal sobriety. "We're healing our whole community—alcohol has done enough damage," Pierre says.

As part of the CHIP program, Florence Phillips convenes the Kitquwxaxam, which means "a gathering" in the Ktunaxa language, every second Tuesday. Women, children, and frequently men and elders come together to talk about pregnancy and alcohol, to share parenting concerns, to practise budgeting and other practical issues, and sometimes just to pickle beets or share a big meal of stew and bannock. "We allow ourselves to be guided by what the people want to do; we bring in speakers from the community, elders often, and we work on life skills, but we don't preach or dictate," says Phillips, a non-native married to a Ktunaxa hereditary chief. "We recognize that there are a great number of people of all ages, three generations, affected by fetal alcohol, but we also believe they have many gifts and skills to contribute. It's a question of patience, and learning to help people learn."

For the Ktunaxa, a gentle, culturally based approach to educating community members about FAS is the only one that has a chance of success. "Fetal alcohol is still a very sensitive, painful subject for most First Nations," Sophie Pierre says. A medical team headed by U.B.C.'s

Dr. John Conry assessed 167 Kootenay-area schoolchildren in the early 1990s, finding that the incidence of severe learning disabilities and mental retardation was more than seven times higher for aboriginal children, with the largest single cause most likely FAS/FAE. The U.B.C. study did not proceed and is now the subject of litigation; Ktunaxa-Kinbasket leaders felt the study put scientific goals ahead of the needs of their community and would cause more harm than good. Instead, the Ktunaxa-Kinbasket community elected to move towards intervention and prevention rather than gathering statistics. "We are still trying to get people to say the words 'fetal alcohol syndrome,'" says Susan Little, the non-native registered nurse hired as CHIP coordinator at the program's start-up. "After five years, we're just getting comfortable with those words, but at the same time we've accomplished an excellent level of preventing more FAS/FAE babies; we're supporting our school-age children, helping alcohol-affected parents cope and working with alcohol-affected elders." Today the community's program is widely recognized as the most comprehensive and successful FAS/FAE outreach and prevention program in North America, says Little.

Although CHIP workers identify FAS/FAE as the root cause of many learning and behaviour problems, very few children and only a handful of adults have ever been formally diagnosed. There is no funding to transport children to Sunny Hill Children's Health Centre in Vancouver for diagnosis, and there are as yet few area physicians trained to make the diagnosis. But the Ktunaxa do not wait for formal medical diagnoses before intervening. Says Little: "We had one little boy formally diagnosed last week. The doctor said he had classic FAS, behavioural problems, learning difficulties, an attachment disorder and Tourette's syndrome. From working one-to-one with this little boy, we already knew that, and were treating him accordingly." Little notes CHIP has advantages many doctors do not: "We know the parental drinking history. We don't have to wait for a formal diagnosis before we start to work with kids whose history and appearance and behaviour are all very familiar to us."

Since the B.C. education ministry has no specific funding category for FAS/FAE, a costly diagnosis does not trigger any extra resources for the affected child in the school system, either. So CHIP workers go into schools to educate teachers and to work on a one-to-one basis with alcohol-affected children. Their mandate is to assist any aboriginal child, whether Ktunaxa or not, in the tribe's traditional territory. Most are status Ktunaxa children living on reserve, for whose health care the federal government is financially responsible, yet CHIP's funding of $260,000 annually has come entirely from the B.C. health ministry. The federal policy is not to stigmatize aboriginal people by singling them out for FAS/FAE funding—no matter how critically needed. Ottawa's contention is that the needs of FAS-afflicted children can be met "under existing programs." The Catch-22 behind this bureaucratic bafflegab is that there is no provision in federal funding categories for First Nations to do community-wide FAS/FAE prevention and outreach, no matter how demonstrably successful this approach has been.

Florence Phillips spends several days a week in the reserve-based elementary schools and also visits mainstream elementary and high schools attended by children of Ktunaxa or other aboriginal ancestry. "Children who have fetal alcohol, attention deficit, hyperactivity or all three have a lot of trouble learning in a regular classroom full of bright pictures and noise," says Phillips. "It's just too much stimulation for them. I take them aside to a quiet area to calm down, or even go outside and kick a ball around to release energy, until they're ready to settle down and try to learn. Having me there to support them is better for their self-esteem than spending half the day outside in the corridor on a chair, which many of them were doing before we started CHIP."

Educators across North America are constantly developing new curricula and techniques adapted to the specific learning difficulties of fetal alcohol children. Patricia Tanner-Halverson, in her fifth year as a district psychologist for the Indian Oasis School District on the Tohono O'Odham Indian Reservation in Arizona, has published scholarly research on FAS, but just as importantly, she passes on practical advice through handouts eagerly traded around at FAS/FAE conferences. Tanner-Halverson works with and teaches alcohol-affected students every day on the southern Arizona reservation, which has 1,800 families with 5,000 children under sixteen years of age. Although the IQs of FAS/FAE children are not always low, Tanner-Halverson notes that almost all struggle with issues such as poor judgement in social situations, trouble staying on task, impulsiveness, memory problems, difficulty with abstract thinking, impaired learning, lack of problem-solving strategies, and the inability to learn from mistakes or understand the consequences of their behaviour.

The key to educating such children is to catch their elusive attention and hold it. Learning about their traditional culture can help alcohol-affected aboriginal children ground some of the emotional chaos inside. Other strategies, which help alcohol-affected children of any cultural background, include organizing the classroom environment to be calm, clear, consistent and as free of distractions as possible; teaching time management and organizational skills; controlling hyperactivity; and judiciously using discipline and rewards. Tanner-Halverson strongly believes there is an educational process for alcohol-affected children; it just has to be developed, refined and put into practice. She notes that thirty years ago, it was thought severely retarded people could not be helped. "When these people were treated as if there was no hope, there was no hope," she says. "The truth is, we just did not know to educate them. The same can be said for alcohol-affected children."

The challenge facing educators is how to find sufficient resources for all special-needs children, not only those with FAS/FAE. As in many other provinces in Canada, the B.C. education ministry insists FAS/FAE children can be taken care of through programs designed for children with vastly different physical or mental disabilities, or simply plunked down in a typical classroom. The result can be chaos. In schools with large numbers of alcohol-affected children, a high special-needs population and complex social problems including poverty, the education system appears to throw up its hands and abandon every child equally. It is only the most determined advocates who can fight the school and ministry bureaucracies to obtain learning assistance, diagnosis and counselling support for alcohol-affected children.

At a March 1997 meeting at Sir William Macdonald Elementary School on Vancouver's east side, parents and teachers pleaded with school-board officials for more resources to help the enormous number of undiagnosed, untreated special-needs children. Parents estimate that more than half of the three hundred students at the school, which has an aboriginal enrollment of about 45 per cent, are not getting either the diagnosis or the learning assistance they require. Although Macdonald school participated in a pilot program to develop a curriculum for FAS/FAE children, alcohol-affected kids in the school typically received little extra counselling, tutoring or special teaching suited to their condition. Teachers, too, felt the strain; forced to cope with large classes of children with varying special needs, they could not provide the extra help so many children required.

Parents spent forty-three days camped in tents on the grounds of the Vancouver School Board, but it was left to an aboriginal parent, a thirty-year-old Wet'suwet'en mother named Lana Wright, to embark on an ambitious 1,500-kilometre walk from Prince Rupert to Vancouver to raise consciousness and money for the beleaguered school. "If we can get everyone together on this, who knows?" Wright said to reporters before she left. "Perhaps we'll move a mountain." On June 13, 1997, the day before her son Michael's sixth birthday, Wright triumphantly returned to Macdonald school, having worn out nine pairs of running shoes, raised a great deal of awareness and gathered stories all along her route about the tragic educational experiences of aboriginal adults. Wright, who has an education degree and plans to continue her education at the University of B.C., urged aboriginal children to stay in school despite the pain their parents endured and the challenges they face.

In her own way, Wright did move a mountain: she raised several thousand dollars for the school, and the Vancouver School Board agreed to add a teacher, to situate a district special-needs class at

Macdonald and to keep a special-program worker whose job was originally to have been eliminated by budget cutbacks. The B.C. Ministry for Children and Families agreed to fund a social worker to begin at the start of the 1997-98 school year. Lana Wright's "Messenger of Hope Walk" was an aggressive modern tactic designed to win support for FAS/FAE children and those with special needs, but the inspiration for her walk was traditional and cultural, she explained. Her grandfather Joe Tom was a Wet'suwet'en messenger who could run 160 kilometres in twenty-four hours to deliver important messages to northern aboriginal settlements. "To me, the walk was difficult, especially being away from my son, but it's important to stand up for our children so they get the support they need," Wright said. "Hopefully, other parents won't have to go to the lengths I did to get help for their children."

In Vancouver's predominantly aboriginal Downtown Eastside, one of every two babies is born damaged by drugs or alcohol. A ten-block radius boasts 1,800 drinking seats and is responsible for two-thirds of the entire city's public alcohol consumption. In this neighbourhood—Canada's poorest postal code area—women typically seek medical care only twice during gestation: to confirm their pregnancy and to have their baby delivered, says Betty MacPhee, director of Crabtree Corner, a drop-in day-care located in the heart of the district. The day-care's mostly aboriginal clientele share lunches, clothes, toys and healing circles. Initially, alcohol-affected aboriginal children were almost always apprehended from their mothers at birth, MacPhee says. "Mothers were seldom provided with grief counselling or alcohol treatment, so a high percentage got pregnant again within the year to replace their lost child. Their alcohol and drug use was accelerated to numb the pain of their loss, so each subsequent baby was being born more and more damaged." MacPhee was determined to reverse that pattern, and in 1990, the day-care began an ambitious FAS/FAE prevention and outreach program that has become an integral part of the transformation of the downtown mean streets into a neighbourhood of families.

From 1990 to 1993, Crabtree Corner did pioneering prevention work with federal funding of less than $75,000 a year. Although the day-care's work won national and international acclaim, its FAS prevention project was cut off by Ottawa and it had to seek a bridging grant from the provincial government. "What does that tell you about government or society's priorities?" demands MacPhee. "Surrounding this day-care we have the highest incidence of FAS/FAE babies in North America, but we have difficulty getting adequate, guaranteed core funding, particularly from the federal government. We should be trying to give this generation of First Nations children the best head start that we can in life." Despite the obstacles, Crabtree Corner has managed to keep a full-time FAS/FAE outreach and prevention worker and a funded aboriginal trainee position while running a busy day-care, referring women and children to a new nearby health clinic or obtaining medical assessments on site, and holding weekly healing circles, potluck meals and support groups.

Along with other advocates, MacPhee has also lobbied long and hard for detox centres to give priority to pregnant women. All detox centres in B.C. now do so, although there are seldom spaces immediately available, and delays of even a few crucial weeks can forever alter a child's future. Barbara Panter, a social worker who now heads Crabtree's FAS/FAE prevention and outreach program, points out there's still a major Catch-22 hindering women of child-bearing age from kicking drugs and alcohol: "The bottleneck happens with the long wait list to see B.C. health ministry alcohol and drug counsellors, because it's still a mandatory prerequisite for detox and residential treatment."

Aboriginal women will often avoid detox rather than surrender their children into even the "temporary" care of the B.C. Ministry for Children and Families. It can be almost impossible for a single mother to complete addiction treatment on a welfare income, meet all the social workers' conditions for getting her children back and somehow get the approval and money to rent an apartment suitable for herself and her children. Yet many women have managed to persevere and succeed, assisted by Crabtree and programs like Sheway, a midwifery program and drop-in centre—jointly funded by the provincial health ministry and the city health department—for women at risk of giving birth to a baby with FAS or FAE.

Each year, MacPhee notes, more and more healthy babies are born to moms who have stayed closely tied to the lifeline provided by Crabtree. Instead of attending support groups for parents with apprehended children, these moms talk parenting techniques over lunch while their babies and toddlers play in the next room. "At our last conference, a First Nations woman who has given birth to two FAS/FAE children she lost to social services got up with tears streaming down her face and talked about conquering her addictions for the sake of her future children," says MacPhee. "She now has a little daughter who is quite fine."

In the United States, aboriginal people have led the way in FAS/FAE prevention and outreach, spearheading in 1990 the formation of the National Organization on Fetal Alcohol Syndrome (NOFAS), a dynamic nonprofit organization based in Washington, D.C. NOFAS has developed the first medical school curriculum on FAS, piloted at the University of New Mexico and now being taught at Georgetown and Northwestern Universities; set up bilingual public awareness campaigns in six states; published books for adults and children; established an information clearinghouse with a toll-free line; and kicked off a vast range of grassroots community initiatives, including a special teen program. The organization unashamedly seeks maximum publicity for its prevention message, using radio and TV spots featuring such high-profile entertainment figures as musicians Bonnie Raitt and Queen Latifah and actor Jimmy Smits. Each year, NOFAS hosts a national conference and a network of community conferences for professionals and caregivers.

At the 1992 NOFAS conference in Albequerque, New Mexico, one of the keynote speakers was a Navajo woman named Shea Goodluck, herself the mother of a young man diagnosed with fetal alcohol effects. Shea Goodluck lives in a Navajo government adobe subdivision in

Fort Defiance, New Mexico, with her second husband and their children, teen-agers Rex and Crystal, and little Ray, who is still in elementary school. Rex, who has been given the Navajo name Dancing Hair, has fetal alcohol effects. For Goodluck, after years of hard drinking and living on the street, it has been a bittersweet homecoming to the Navajo life. She was invited back by a Navajo Nation government agency to work with women of child-bearing age who are facing the same issues Goodluck has dealt with in her own life.

Born in Lukuckachai, a wide valley "between the four sacred mountains of the Navajo Nation," Goodluck was left by her alcoholic mother in the care of her grandmother and step-grandfather, who sexually abused her throughout her early childhood. At the age of nine, she fled across miles of open plain and desert to find her mother, who believed her daughter's disclosure because the same man had victimized her as a child. But her mother abandoned Goodluck again, this time to a Bureau of Indian Affairs boarding school that had already claimed the childhood of three generations of the family. Here Shea grew up and then, following her mother's pattern, became a young alcoholic mother.

Goodluck's two oldest sons were born unaffected by alcohol. But she was living on the streets of Denver, eating from a dumpster and waiting for the liquor store to open at six in the morning, during the first four months of her pregnancy with Dancing Hair. "I was drinking so heavily my menstrual periods were disrupted. I didn't even know I was pregnant until it was too late for my baby," she says.

Goodluck managed to sober up briefly after Rex was born, terrified she would lose him and her two older sons. After several relapses, she finally checked into the Tule River alcoholism treatment centre in 1987, where she faced her pain with the help of Theda New Breast, an aboriginal healer and activist. It wasn't until two years later that the emotional impact of what Goodluck's drinking had done to her son actually hit her. She'd rationalized his rages and learning difficulties as dyslexia. Then she read *The Broken Cord*, a seminal book by the late academic and author Michael Dorris, a part-Modoc Indian who adopted his FAS-afflicted aboriginal son Adam in the days when there were scant resources or insights for parents of FAS/FAE children. "It took many weeks and many tears to read that book," Goodluck remembers. "I realized why Dancing Hair had trouble learning, why he had rages of frustration, why he couldn't read and write as well as other kids his age. I relapsed. For the first time in many years I went right back to the bottle. There was no room in that book for compassion for the biological mothers, the women like me who had been driven from Indian reserves by incest and violence and sexual abuse, and grown up with alcohol as a fact of life. We drank with no knowledge of what we were doing to our children. But to conquer my own alcoholism, I knew I could not deny the reality of my son's disabilities."

As Goodluck regained control of her drinking, she became convinced that "we have to work as a team against alcoholism. We've got to quit pointing the finger at the mothers. Yes, we have to get them to take responsiblity and we have to educate, but we are not going to get anywhere by shaming and blaming. As Indians raised in the boarding schools, we know all about that. It don't work."

Now a counsellor, Goodluck organizes weekly mothers' meetings where she has captured the trust of young women—several of whom have babies with full fetal alcohol syndrome—by telling her own story and relying on traditional Navajo values to advise and counsel. "Our people, the Dineh, have a life theme, to restore the harmonious balance within oneself, to walk in beauty," Goodluck says. "My strength came when I returned to the old Navajo ways and realized that I was out of balance and harmony, that to walk in beauty I had to put alcohol behind me forever. When I returned to my traditions I recovered the 'sacred birth' concept which celebrated each new child as a sacred gift."

Living with an FAE-afflicted child is not easy. Rex suffers from attention and learning deficits. After a trip out of town, Goodluck will sometimes return home to find holes punched in the bathroom wall or a door off its hinges from one of Rex's rages, usually caused by his frustrations in learning or adjusting to school and social situations. Goodluck knows she will always have a second full-time job as advocate for her son, even when he is an adult. "I abandoned Rex emotionally when I drank while I was pregnant with him," she says. "Now he needs me, so the cycle of abandonment that's gone on for generations in my family ends here: I'll never abandon him again."

First Nations FAS/FAE programs are making great strides forward, not only in helping their alcohol-affected members but in preventing any more damaged children from being born. Antonia Rathbun, an Oregon art therapist and birth parent of a child with FAE, suggests maybe it's modern society that is dysfunctional, not these exceptional children. They challenge our values, says Rathbun, because "they cannot, despite the urging of industrialized society, move, think and live harder, faster and increasingly abstracted from things connected to the natural world. People with FAS/FAE simply cannot maintain this whirlwind of life, and realistically, they prevent us from keeping pace with it as well." Indeed, First Nations educators have noticed that what FAS/FAE children need to thrive is very close to a traditional aboriginal life: calm, healing, a sense of belonging, demonstration of practical skills, connectedness to nature and community, and a solid cultural identity.

FAS/FAE children are growing up at home to become fine young men and women. "One young woman has amazing organizational skills; she could easily run a small office. Another is a concert pianist and one young man is a very talented artist," says coordinator Susan Little of the Ktunaxa's Community Healing and Intervention Program. CHIP hopes to build a rural ranch within Ktunaxa territory where FAS/FAE adolescents and adults can live in a safe place, on their own land, with the healing influence of the natural world all around them. "More of our babies are being born healthy now," says Little. "We build on community strengths, so it's not a doctor or nurse preaching, it's the pregnant mom's peers, parents and grandparents who support her in not drinking. More of our babies are born alcohol-free than you would find in a comparably sized non-native community."

7

"WE CAN HEAL"

Aboriginal Children Today

"I believe now is our time. Now is our time. We are starting to be looked at now and I believe we can really make a difference now because we are finally standing up."

— Randy Nepoose, Hobbema, Alberta

FIRST Nations people in Canada agree that the next two decades will belong to aboriginal youth. Today a strong young generation is struggling to emerge from the dark colonial days into the bright hope of autonomy and self-determination. All across the country, aboriginal young people are making themselves heard: in schools and universities, in native politics, at protests over education cutbacks, at community marches to combat child abuse, and in healing circles and sobriety treatment centres.

Young First Nations athletes are cheerfully clashing at basketball games, hockey playoffs, lacrosse tournaments and canoe races; there are rowers, runners and hockey players of national reknown. Angela Chalmers of Manitoba's Birdtail Sioux First Nation, the first woman in the history of the Commonwealth Games to win both the 1,500-metre and the 3,000-metre races, in 1990, credits her aboriginal roots for teaching her patience and perseverance. "Look at my grand-mothers, how tough they had to be, and my mother, the discrimina-tion I saw her deal with," says Chalmers today. "I've faced racism too, and I tell the aboriginal kids I speak to as part of the native role model program [sponsored by the federal Indian Affairs department] that you can put that anger to good use: in physical exertion, in confidence and passion. Find out what you care about and prove you can excel as well or better than anyone; for the community, your family, but above all for yourself. Don't forget, I say when I talk to young aboriginal kids, because we've been through a lot, we're strong people and we have a deep, deep well of strength to draw on."

At the Splat'sin day-care in Spallumcheen; at Xitolacw school in Mount Currie; inside a kukeli hut or traditional pit-house in Alkali Lake's elementary school; in the Nisga'a school board districts from kindergarten to Grade 12, First Nations children are learning their lan-guage and culture along with their math and science. At Keremeos Senior Secondary School, in B.C.'s southern interior, almost all the teens from the Lower and Upper Similkameen bands who enroll also graduate, and some rank among the school's top achievers. An ever-increasing number of aboriginal youth are going on to university and college and actively seeking careers. They are speaking out in aborigi-nal and mainstream media. They are connecting with indigenous peo-ple all over the world via the Internet through hundreds of websites, such as the popular Canadian-based Aboriginal Youth Network. And they are flocking by the thousands to the youth conferences held over the past few years everywhere from Inuvik to Regina, Ottawa, Montreal, Halifax, Edmonton and Vancouver. A young aboriginal man named Randy Nepoose spoke for all when he declared at a northern youth conference in 1992: "Now is our time."

There have never been, in recorded history, more aboriginal young people than there are now in Canada. Today, more than 36 per cent of the aboriginal population is under the age of fourteen, compared to 21 per cent of the non-native population. Another 20 per cent of aborig-inal youth is aged fifteen to twenty-four. The population of young

STOLEN FROM OUR EMBRACE

aboriginal people will continue to grow until there are almost 200,000 First Nations youth in the fifteen- to twenty-four-year-old age bracket by the year 2011.

The traditional values that sustained First Nations for thousands of years before contact are emerging as the foundation that will carry aboriginal nations to recovery and renewal. After five centuries of a cultural and economic war waged primarily against their children, First Nations still believe it is the young who will prove to be the mainstay of the renaissance now underway. The aboriginal birth rate, in itself a sign of hope, is almost twice that of the rest of Canada. More and more aboriginal children are being raised by sober parents connected to their culture. Children who require substitute care while their families are in recovery are increasingly cared for by aboriginal child welfare agencies in all parts of the country. Although aboriginal children still face immense challenges, there are generations of young people ready to become politically astute future leaders and contributing members of autonomous nations.

The Royal Commission on Aboriginal Peoples emphasized Canada's responsibility to aboriginal youth in their 1996 report. "Their numbers in the population of today and their role in shaping and leading their communities and nations tomorrow make it essential for governments—aboriginal and non-aboriginal alike—to listen to their concerns and act on their priorities," the commissioners wrote. "They are the current generation paying the price of cultural genocide, racism and poverty, suffering the effects of hundreds of years of colonialist public policies. It's as though an earthquake has ruptured their world from one end to another, opening a deep rift that separates them from their past, their history and their culture. They have seen parents and peers fall into this chasm, into patterns of despair, listlessness and self-destruction. They fear for themselves and their future as they stand at the edge. Yet aboriginal youth can see across this great divide. Their concern about the current crisis is leavened with a vision of a better tomorrow."

Canada stands on the brink of a momentous decision that no

national government has yet had the political will to make. First Nations need not only Canada's official acknowledgement of their inherent right to self-government but also adequate resources to allow them to govern in the future and to compensate them for decades of damage inflicted in large part by Canada's misguided and morally tarnished Indian policies. Restitution does not mean more piecemeal government programs, dollars doled out to perpetuate a climate of dependency. As Ovide Mercredi, the former chief of the Assembly of First Nations, declared in 1994, this is a nation of young people that is "moving beyond the psychology of grievance." This is a nation of young people with high expectations, seeking not handouts but empowerment.

Still, the landscape is littered with mines that aboriginal young people must somehow dodge in order to succeed: systemic racism and higher rates of illness, disease, suicide, substance abuse, school dropout levels and unemployment. From the very moment of birth—even in the womb—aboriginal children face infinitely more challenges than non-native babies. Higher rates of smoking, alcohol and polydrug use among aboriginal mothers compromise the health and survivability of the fetus, as well as the child's long-term future. Almost twice as many aboriginal babies die in infancy than do other Canadian infants, despite a steady improvement in aboriginal infant mortality over the last forty years. In the 1960s in Canada, 60 aboriginal babies died for every 1,000 live births. That improved to 23.7 deaths for every 1,000 aboriginal births by 1980. Today, the deaths of aboriginal babies average about 12 to 14 per 1,000 births, but that is still far higher than the national mortality rate of about 6 per 1,000. Premature births and low birth weight, both of which are far more common in aboriginal babies, can impair an infant's ability to thrive and may even lead to lifelong health problems. Aboriginal babies are three times more likely to die in the first six months of life from Sudden Infant Death Syndrome.

Poverty is a scourge that stalks aboriginal children as they grow up. It is a well-documented fact that poor children suffer more health problems of every kind, and aboriginal children in Canada are among the poorest of the poor. They suffer and even die from Third World conditions that are relatively rare among mainstream Canadian children. Substandard housing conditions, unsafe drinking water and inadequate sewage treatment can cause serious and sometimes fatal diarrhea, gastroenteritis and malnutrition. Native children are three times more likely to suffer bronchitis, pneumonia and croup than are non-native children. They endure far more chronic ear and respiratory tract infections, and more flu, which can in turn cause serious illnesses like rheumatic fever, according to a 1996 review of aboriginal health care by Dr. Harriet MacMillan of McMaster University. Deaths from injuries are four times greater for Indian infants than for those in the general population, five times greater for aboriginal preschoolers and three times greater for aboriginal teen-agers up to nineteen years of age. The average life expectancy for aboriginal children as they reach adulthood is eight years less than the national average.

By almost every measure, aboriginal children's health and well-being lags far behind that of the mainstream. "Dental decay is almost universally prevalent among aboriginal children and it may not be improving," says James Leake, who conducted the Oral Health Survey of Canada's Aboriginal Children in 1992. Poor hygiene due to lack of education, inadequate dental care, lack of fluoridated water supplies on reserve and the high-sugar junk food diet often associated with poverty are the causes of these high rates of dental decay; all are entirely correctable conditions in an industrialized country like Canada.

Perhaps the most disturbing challenge to the health of aboriginal young people is the phenomenon of inhalant abuse. The chemicals sniffed are common and accessible: typewriter correction fluid, nail polish remover, felt pens and, most widely available of all, gasoline. In exchange for a giddy high that makes a child dizzy and numb, a growing body suffers harm ranging from slowed reflexes, double vision and hallucinations to long-term damage to the brain, kidneys and liver.

In the B.C. First Nations Solvent Abuse Study, an as-yet-unpublished survey conducted in 1995 by the Community Health Representatives Association of B.C. (CHR), community health nurses reported that the average age of solvent sniffers was thirteen and that a fifth of all solvent users were children under eleven. Information collected in 166 of B.C.'s 204 aboriginal communities showed that, of the 235 solvent users identified, 61 per cent were under nineteen years old and a majority (70.5 per cent) were male. Despite these disturbing figures, the CHR study concluded it had uncovered just the tip of the iceberg; it estimates there could be as many as 2,000 chronic solvent abusers in B.C., a staggering number of them young children. "Denial is high in many communities," the study points out. "People do not like to talk about solvent use and in particular do not like to identify users." Solvent use is more chronic and serious in isolated northern regions of the province, the study says, although reserves across the province concurred on what the social problems were that led to sniffing: "Young people not having enough to do, drug dealers in the community, intense rivalry in the community, lack of spiritual/cultural traditions and geographical isolation," as well as serious health issues such as alcohol and drug abuse, diabetes, domestic violence, suicide and fetal alcohol syndrome. The B.C. study provides alarming proof that hundreds of aboriginal children are quietly doing permanent damage to their brains and their bodies just to achieve a brief escape from their harsh reality.

The epidemic spectre of suicide also faces aboriginal children as they reach adolescence. Their sisters, brothers, relatives and friends are hanging themselves, blowing their heads off with guns, jumping from bridges and stepping in front of speeding trains. To a young aboriginal person in Canada, it's like growing up in a war zone with an enemy that attacks from within. Suicide is six times more common for aboriginal youth than for their non-aboriginal peers. It is "a blunt and shocking message," the Royal Commission on Aboriginal Peoples warned in *Choosing Life*, its special report on suicide, that "a significant number of aboriginal people in this country believe they have more reasons to die than to live." Suicides tend to occur in clusters, each death leading to a rebound despair expressed in copycat acts. A spate of suicides can strike an aboriginal community anywhere in the country, leaving the best and the brightest dead. Pitangikum, a northern Ontario reserve, experienced eight suicides and more than a hundred attempts in 1994 alone. At Whitedog, near Kenora, Ontario, four young people died by their own hand in April of 1995 and another in July.

There is no more telling indictment of the future Canada has handed First Nations children than their rejection of life itself. First Nations caregivers say their children are killing themselves in record numbers as an expression of self-hatred induced by the intergenerational assault, in many guises, on the very core of aboriginal identity. Research confirms that the early separation of a child from family, followed by emotional deprivation, puts him or her at high risk for self-harm. Children who remain with parents and grandparents do not necessarily emerge unscathed; their caregivers may react to trauma they themselves have experienced by lashing out with abuse, violence and addictive behaviour. Adolescents who have been physically and sexually abused were found in a recent study to be ten times more likely to kill themselves. Alcohol and drug use are also more closely associated with aboriginal suicide than with suicides in the general population. In a recent B.C. study, 74 per cent of aboriginal people who killed themselves did so while intoxicated, compared with only 36 per cent of a comparable sample of non-native suicides.

Like alcoholism, suicide is a symptom of underlying malaise; denial must be confronted and causes understood before the deaths will stop. The tiny Pacheenacht community on the west coast of Vancouver Island suffered a rash of suicides between 1993 and 1995. The day after Christmas in 1993, a young mother wrote a good-bye letter to her baby daughter, then hung herself from a beam. Another group of Pacheenacht youths were discovered to have struck a suicide pact; all in all, there were five suicides within three years. A scheduled inquest was cancelled because the band feared the rebound effects of more adverse media publicity. Band councillors blamed alcoholism and a complete lack of recreation or career opportunities for young people; the federal government responded by identifying Pacheenacht as one of five "communities in crisis." B.C. Chief Coroner Vincent Cain issued his own inquiry report, citing lack of role models, poor education and employment prospects, low self-esteem, unresolved grief, welfare dependency, alcohol and drug use, poor parenting skills and loss of cultural identity.

It soon became clear that the solution to the suicide epidemic lay with the Pacheenacht people, however, not with outside "experts." The small community began a concerted drive to provide options for its young people: language and cultural training for the very young; recreation, volunteer and employment opportunities for older children and young adults. A year later, Pacheenacht youth were hard at work building part of the new Juan de Fuca Marine Trail. The local health centre, rejuvenated by some federal funding, was offering social development and health programs, while the provincial government funded a "Kids at Risk" program that used recreation to teach self-esteem and conflict resolution skills to children of elementary-school age. The Pacheenacht and other First Nations have found that gently introducing their young people to the longhouse, powwow dancing or the big drum—cultural activities that require sobriety and commitment—can bring children back from the brink of despair. There is an urgent need all across the country for suicide-prevention programs like these, with support from all levels of government and even from the private sector, to help First Nations prevent the loss of their most precious resource.

AIDS among young aboriginal people is also of grave concern. Although there were only 176 confirmed cases of AIDS among aboriginal Canadians by January of 1997, First Nations leaders speculate those numbers simply illustrate Ottawa's difficulty in collecting statistics in the aboriginal community. Aboriginal health activists point to conditions that could allow AIDS to spread rapidly, such as the disproportionate number of aboriginal people in and out of jail, where anal sex and intravenous drug use are common. Aboriginal people also tend to die of AIDS up to twice as fast as non-natives, as the Vancouver Native Health Society documented in a 1995 study conducted at St. Paul's Hospital in Vancouver. Aboriginal people were admitted to hospital far less frequently and tended to have briefer stays, although this was often due to non-compliance with medical advice. The median age of death for aboriginal people with AIDS in the study population of ninety-six people was twenty-nine, compared to forty-one for non-native AIDS patients.

The Royal Commission on Aboriginal Peoples was restrained when it suggested in its final report that a very real potential for violence also exists if the urgent needs of First Nations youth, already exacerbated by the wrongs visited upon their parents and grandparents, are shunted aside by government. In almost every large city or town in Canada, young urban natives face a crisis of rootlessness. Most of Winnipeg's 65,000 aboriginal people have emigrated from Manitoba's 62 reserves and 120 Metis communities. They may be fleeing poverty or seeking a job, education or more social contact. Whole families leave the reserve to escape the cronyism and elitism of many elected chiefs and band councils. Teen-agers and young adults on their own are also leaving rural reserves in ever-increasing numbers, attracted by the allure of the big city.

Unfortunately, what many people find in an urban setting is more grinding poverty and an environment even more scary and isolating than the one back home. "People come thinking they will have a better life in the city, but they end up trapped," Dave Chartrand of the Manitoba Metis Federation told *Maclean's* magazine. "The kids see what's happened to their parents, and don't see any hope for themselves." Employment prospects for aboriginal people in the city, particularly youth, are scarcely better than on reserve. "In this economy, it's more and more difficult for young people," says Wayne Helgason, a Cree from Manitoba's Sandy Bay Reserve who is executive director of the Winnipeg Social Planning Council. "They don't see finding a decent job even if they get an education, and so other forms of activity become their only choice."

In Winnipeg, aboriginal youth gangs with names like the Manitoba Warriors and Indian Posse have attracted an estimated eight hundred young, disadvantaged and angry natives. Not merely a nuisance, the gangs are involved in criminal activities such as prostitution, assault, armed robbery, drive-by shootings and even murder. Since the Winnipeg police formed its fifteen-member gang unit in the summer of 1995, they have made 440 gang-related arrests. Native youth gang violence has also spread to other prairie cities, including Regina, which saw 71 gang-related arrests in 1996, and Saskatoon. In Vancouver, although there is little organized native gang activity, aboriginal youth dominate the street kids' scene, especially in the poorer Downtown Eastside and east-end neighbourhoods, where young aboriginal girls have been recruited into prostitution by Latino gangs.

In March 1996, Manitoba's aboriginal affairs minister David Newman declared himself determined to reduce gang activity by increasing opportunities for young urban natives through a coordinated approach involving all levels of government, community groups and the private sector. Despite Newman's apparent good intentions, the Conservative provincial government of which he is a member cut funding to the Winnipeg Indian and Metis Friendship Centre by 85 per cent that same fiscal year. It was left to five Manitoba aboriginal organizations and former Manitoba Cree MP Elijah Harper to set in motion a series of youth conferences designed to entice young people away from gangs. In the trenches of Winnipeg's inner city, aboriginal street workers and an order of Catholic sisters try to deter aboriginal youth from crime and violence.

But aboriginal youth activism, a vital alternative to apathy and violence, has begun to assert itself all over Canada. Both urban and on-reserve aboriginal communities have been forced to address the urgent crisis facing their youth, pressured by young activists with no particular allegiance to any aboriginal political organization. "I call them runners, these organizers for the Native Youth Movement, because they'll work with whatever organization can give them access to their members and resources to advance their issues, which are all very real—like education, housing, employment, social and medical care," says Viola Thomas, president of the United Native Nations, an organization representing off-reserve aboriginal people in B.C. "A lot of the young people are second- or third-generation urban and a lot have blended aboriginal heritage, so they don't identify with one particular First Nation or reserve. They're disenfranchised from treaty settlements and status benefits if they don't have a relationship with their home band; and if they're in the city, they are being told they don't have any more rights and benefits than non-natives. They live with the legacy of generations of grief and pain, parents damaged by residential schools and foster care, but they don't qualify for education or housing assistance, or even counselling. No wonder they're angry."

Tim Fontaine, a young Manitoba Cree organizer and nephew of Assembly of First Nations National Chief Phil Fontaine, explains: "The Native Youth Movement offers the same things to aboriginal kids that the gangs do—belonging, a sense of family and empowerment. But we try to make sure we don't fit the profile of the young aboriginal man who's more likely to go to jail than university in this country. We're not into crime. We're channelling anger into seeking change, and that's really positive. The only thing we can't compete with the gangs on is the money, and that's hard, because almost all of us have grown up in poverty."

The youth wing of the United Native Nations has begun to play a vital role in the B.C. provincial organization and even at meetings of the UNN's national organization, the Congress of Aboriginal Peoples. "Every time we have an important meeting with politicians or aboriginal leaders, we take a member of our youth group, because this is their future—they're going to have to fight long and hard for what they need," says Viola Thomas.

In the early summer of 1997, a busload of aboriginal youth urged B.C. cabinet ministers and members of the Legislative Assembly in Victoria to rebuff attempts by the federal government, as it moves to off-load its responsibility for health, welfare and education services, to transfer financial responsibility for off-reserve aboriginal people, both status and non-status, onto the provinces. The premiers of Manitoba, Saskatchewan and Alberta had also strongly protested this federal initiative, which could cost the provinces billions of dollars annually, at a first ministers' conference in October of 1996. "When Ottawa decided to say off-reserve, non-status treaty Indians are no longer being funded by the federal government, they broke a fiduciary relationship," said Saskatchewan Premier Roy Romanow at the time. "That hurt the provinces and it hurt the other First Nations." But by April 1997, when the premiers met again—this time with off-reserve aboriginal representatives present—cuts to the Canada Health and Social Transfer Agreement were virtually a fait accompli, affecting not only off-reserve aboriginal people but many other Canadians as well. By mid-1997, urban aboriginal people and their children were beginning to feel the pinch of the new financial restrictions. Worried that the federal government was returning billings for the care of off-reserve aboriginal people and advising practitioners to seek reimbursement directly from patients, doctors' offices stopped accepting status Indian cards. Off-reserve aboriginal people were left with a choice of getting medical coverage under provincial welfare schemes, paying their own premiums or seeking coverage from their bands, most of which were quietly serving notice to people living away from home that the band could not afford to cover their medical bills.

The attempt to disqualify aboriginal people from federal benefits based on their place of residence was compared by one First Nations leader to "negotiating by entering the room with a loaded gun." Others likened the move to the pass system that endured until the 1950s; no Indian could leave a reserve without permission from the Indian agent. Viola Thomas of the United Native Nations calls the federal government's actions a human rights violation. "Nowhere does it say in the Canadian constitution or in the Indian Act that aboriginal rights depend on where you live. As ever, it will be aboriginal children who are primarily hurt, because they will have no entitlement to federal health and welfare benefits or education dollars unless they have a good connection to an elected band council," says Thomas, a Secwepemc from Kamloops who has lived in Vancouver for most of her adult life. "In B.C., more than one-half of aboriginal people live off-reserve, and 65 per cent of urban aboriginal families are single parent, female-headed, living in poverty. Women flee reserves with their children to escape violence, and now the federal government is telling them they have to go back to that same band—to the same powerful male leaders they're afraid of—to get the financial help to which they're legally entitled." Aboriginal "graduates" of foster and adoptive care face the additional Catch-22 of being legally severed from their band of origin but unable to access federal funding except through that same band.

The Royal Commission on Aboriginal Peoples called for a twenty-year commitment to the renewal of the relationship between Canada and First Nations, particularly the 405,200 children and youth under twenty-five who make up 56 per cent of the country's aboriginal population. In 440 specific recommendations, whose implementation would cost an estimated $1.5 to $2 billion a year in addition to the $6.2 billion spent annually on aboriginal people, the commission urged Canada to close the gap between mainstream and aboriginal standards in health, housing and education. Former federal Indian Affairs minister Ron Irwin promised to study the report, yet publicly disparaged the commission's cost estimates. Irwin and former Assembly of First Nations' chief Ovide Mercredi, locked into a long-standing feud, disagreed over the importance of the $58 million report. When Irwin retired from elected office in 1997, he remarked that he didn't see the need for a major restructuring of government relations with aboriginal people.

With the advent of two new leaders who are bound to dominate national aboriginal politics in Canada—both of whom have pledged to bring a fresh commitment to negotiation rather than confrontation—hope has recently revived that the commission's thorough research and analysis will not go to waste. Jane Stewart, appointed Indian Affairs minister when Jean Chrétien's Liberal government was reelected in June 1997, has already called the commission's report a "wonderful framework" and pledged her willingness to discuss its recommendations with aboriginal groups. As MP for the southern Ontario riding of Brant, which is beside the high-profile Six Nations reserve, Stewart is well versed in the importance of establishing cooperative relationships with First Nations. "I do really believe this is about a partnership," Stewart told reporters after she was named to the post. "We need a continuation or a new beginning in terms of our relationship with aboriginal peoples that builds a bright future for us all. I think it begins with consensus and with mutual respect and recognizing the need for us all to treat each other with dignity."

Stewart will soon confront a cordial but formidable counterpart in aboriginal politics. Phil Fontaine, the new national chief of the Assembly of First Nations, was elected in a hard-fought battle in the early morning hours of July 31, 1997. Fontaine, the former grand chief of the Assembly of Manitoba Chiefs, made it clear at the outset that the relationship between the AFN and the federal government "must be government to government" and stressed the importance on the federal government's side of being "open, accessible and flexible." One of Fontaine's first acts was to speak directly to Prime Minister Jean Chrétien; following their conversation, Fontaine told reporters: "There is a desire on the part of the government to work with us." He also stated his intention to seek unity among the six hundred chiefs of the Assembly of First Nations.

Both Fontaine and his closest competitor for national chief, the Musqueam Nation's former chief and treaty negotiator Wendy Grant-John, are committed to making the future better for aboriginal youth. "I appreciate the deep frustrations our young people feel and we want to give them an opportunity to set their own path," Fontaine said. "We have to find ways and means of bringing them into the circle."

Although she lost her bid for the position of national chief, Grant-John will continue to play a key role in provincial and national aboriginal politics. One of her most heartfelt personal and political priorities is to achieve implementation of the Royal Commission's key recommendations while hope and promise are still alive for the 56 per cent of the aboriginal population under the age of twenty-five. "We need to empower our youth by providing strong education and employment options, to overcome with concrete action and goals the

STOLEN FROM OUR EMBRACE

growing feeling of hopelessness, the unacceptable levels of suicide, poverty and other signs of despair," Grant-John says. "Never before in our history can it be more strongly said that our youth is our future. We have got to empower them to succeed."

Nowhere is the future of young aboriginal people more clearly hanging in the balance than in the field of education. In 1972, the National Indian Brotherhood urged in its landmark paper "Indian Control of Indian Education" that schools should not only educate aboriginal children to modern standards but also play a central role in the revitalization of native languages and cultures. To accomplish that, the NIB stated, schools would have to come under First Nations influence and control. The NIB position paper signalled the dawning of a new day in aboriginal education, but since then it has been a long and difficult struggle to establish aboriginal-directed education. Aboriginal education bodies have been kept on a short leash with a rudimentary structure of federal funding that supports the basic curriculum but provides few resources for cultural instruction or special needs. The federal government now typically provides education dollars directly to each First Nation, which can choose to set up its own school or reimburse the local school board for children sent to its facilities. By 1993-94, 51 per cent of all federally funded schools on reserve were band-owned and operated. But more than half of all aboriginal children living on-reserve still have to travel off-reserve to attend schools. Of the 60 per cent of all First Nations people in Canada now living off-reserve, 95 per cent send their children to conventional schools. In the census year of 1991, 68.7 per cent of all aboriginal students were still in provincial public school systems.

The overall education of aboriginal children lags far behind that of other Canadian children. Fewer aboriginal youth complete their studies at any level of the education system. Among aboriginal youth aged fifteen to twenty-four, 68.5 per cent have not completed Grade 12. Three times as many aboriginal Canadians as non-natives have less than a Grade 8 education; fewer than 1 per cent of aboriginal Canadians possess a university degree.

Nevertheless, in the years since First Nations made a deliberate decision to be major players in the field of education, there has been significant progress in curriculum development and language and cultural teachings; the development of versatile programs to suit aboriginal learning and lifestyles; and a general improvement in educational levels attained. In 1981, 63 per cent of aboriginal people older than fifteen had completed primary school, while 29 per cent had a high-school education. A decade later, 76 per cent of aboriginal people over fifteen had completed primary school and 43 per cent had completed high school.

Role models are invaluable to young aboriginal students battling shaky self-esteem and uncertainty about their goals. In May of 1997, a young woman from Kamloops named Nadine Caron became the first female First Nations medical doctor to graduate in British Columbia. While she was attending medical school at the University of B.C., Nadine's off hours were spent not packing up skis and heading for the slopes but loading her car with microscopes, stethoscopes, preserved fetal pigs and tissue samples to accompany her talks to schoolchildren on reserves around the province. "I'd let the younger kids try on the stethoscope and see how it worked, or look at some pond water through the microscope, while the high-school kids could try their hand at dissecting the fetal pigs," says Caron, who first attended Simon Fraser University on basketball and soccer scholarships.

Caron, whose heritage is Ojibway and Italian, was determined from a young age to excel at everything she did. "I encourage the kids I talk to to set their sights high—there's such an urgent need for aboriginal people in science and medicine careers," she says. Now, following in Caron's footsteps, there are two more aboriginal women in U.B.C.'s medical school.

Three young aboriginal women who began at an early age to address conflicts and pursue their career goals are Rose-Marie Francis, Bessie Austin and Gaylene Henry. All attended Vancouver high schools, although each of them is a member of a First Nation far from the west-coast city, and all took part in a special graduation

Left to right: ROSE-MARIE FRANCIS, BESSIE AUSTIN & GAYLENE HENRY

ceremony held in June 1997 for First Nations graduates of the
Vancouver school system. Rose-Marie Francis, a nineteen-year-old
Kwakiutl born in Bella Coola but registered to her mother's band, gave
the valedictory at the ceremony. Bessie Austin, a seventeen-year-old
Gitksan member of the Frog clan, spoke to Grade 11 students to
encourage them to make it all the way to graduation. Gaylene Henry,
an eighteen-year-old born to a Sioux father she knew briefly as a child

and a Cree mother from the Ochapowace band southeast of Regina, celebrated her graduation from Vancouver Technical, the city's largest high school, with a well-formed plan for her future.

In the fall of 1997, Francis will follow the lead of her father, Ted, by becoming a student at the Institute for Indigenous Education, which now offers two-year diplomas but soon will offer full university-level degrees. Started in 1995 by the Union of B.C. Indian Chiefs, the institute provides twenty-five First Nations students at a time with the opportunity to learn about their own history and culture, as well as to pick up conventional subjects. "I want to be a science teacher," says Francis. "I got straight As in biology and I'd love to work with kids. Ultimately, though, I plan to get my doctorate in science." She is passionately interested in aboriginal politics and in the negotiation of modern-day treaties in British Columbia, particularly since her father is involved in the treaty process as an urban representative of the Sliammon band. "As urban people, we have to stay on top of what's going on in the treaty process, because there is no formal way for us to participate, and yet it's our future that is being negotiated too," Francis points out.

Francis's father has always been the primary caregiver for her and her brother. Because her mother is an unrecovered alcoholic, Francis seldom sees her. "I don't agree with her lifestyle," she says. Both her parents and her grandparents were the products of residential school, and in her early years, Francis lived with the unhappy patterns created by that family history. She recalls the New Year's Eve when, as a child of four or five, she walked up to her father and demanded: "Why do you drink and smoke like that all the time?" Recalls Francis: "He poured his liquor down the sink and threw his smokes in the fire—my mom was screaming at him not to—and from that day on, he never smoked or drank again. He told me years later that he suddenly saw he was choosing booze over his children, and that he couldn't do that ever again." As a single father, Ted Francis often worked several jobs at a time to support his children, while making sure they did well in school.

Francis also has a new concern: day-care. Her first child was to be born just a month before she enters the Institute for Indigenous Education. Her father has invited the child's father, a N'laka'pamux man with whom Francis has been involved for four years, to move in with the family while Francis finishes her schooling. Grandpa has offered to help look after the baby. But Francis anticipates she will be going to school for a long time. "The first thing I plan to do at the institute is lobby for more student day-care," she says. The prospect of having her own child, at an age young for mainstream society but not unusually so for First Nations, has strengthened Francis's resolve to succeed. "Children are the future, that's what I was raised to understand. I appreciate what I was given in life, despite what both my parents have gone through, and I feel I'm in a much better position to provide for this child and make sure she or he grows up knowing our history."

Gaylene Henry will be twenty-one at the turn of the millennium, just entering full adulthood, but she has a lot of living planned between now and then. In the summer of 1997 she returned to the Prairies, where she will attend the University of Regina in the fall. "I missed my grandmother, and I missed the prairie, just what it smells like and feels like back home—it took me a long time to get used to the coast," she says. She often visits her Saskatchewan reserve to see her beloved grandmother, who helped to raise Henry. Her grandmother and her grandmother's siblings sometimes talk about their days in residential school, which shocks Henry: "They talk about how they'd get hit with a ruler for talking their language. If somebody tried that with me, I'd hit them right back." Powwow dancing, a prairie tradition, has sprung up on the west coast, so even while Henry lived in Vancouver she was able to keep up her fancy dancing and jingle-dress competition dance.

After moving to Vancouver when she was ten years old, Henry attended several schools, including the alternative Tumanos program for aboriginal students at Van Tech. "I got all screwed up in Tumanos because you were allowed to work at your own pace and really fall behind," she says. "My marks were better in the regular school program so I switched back." Henry will take an undergraduate degree in anthropology in Regina. "I want to study all the indigenous people in the world, in Central and South America, New Zealand and Australia, the Maoris and the Aborigines. I want to study their customs and beliefs and history." Then she plans to return to the University of B.C. to study law. "I'm totally determined to get my Ph.D.; if I could, I'd go to school all my life," she says. "If the federal government wants to help First Nations young people, it should support our education, then we'll be able to help ourselves for the rest of our lives."

Henry believes the federal government should support First Nations youth through full funding for post-secondary education, skills and trades training, and provide career counselling, instead of doling out "handouts" to kids who fail. "To me, First Nations kids are given so many opportunities to screw up that they fulfill that expectation—there's a program for everything when you screw up in life. I'm trying to be straight and get educated and I get doors slammed in my face. We need to be empowered and self-determining, and the best way to do that is through education." Friends and family members have attended school dropout programs for native kids "where they get money to go to school, and if they skip, they still get the fifty bucks," Henry says disgustedly. "What does that teach anyone about responsibility? We want to be in control of our own destiny, not getting money to fail."

Henry has stuck to her plans even when her family life at times became chaotic, even dangerous. Her mother, Nowela Henry, has been very supportive, but Gaylene has seen other close family members succumb to high unemployment and easy drugs. "With some of my cousins and uncles doing hard drugs, it got so that everything of value to us is gone; anything that wasn't nailed down in our house was stolen and sold," says Henry. In her last winter of high school, Henry sank into a deep depression, and began to drink. She attended school enough to avoid expulsion, but in every spare moment she reached for alcohol. "I finally stopped because my mother was going to commit me to detox and treatment," she says. Henry snapped out of her depression and drinking in time to finish high school with good enough grades to get into university, but the experience frightened her enough to decide to return home, where she feels most comfortable among Cree-speaking peoples.

Bessie Austin, who attended a Vancouver alternative secondary-school program called Total Education, claims she can sum up her cultural knowledge in one sentence: "I'm Gitksan and I'm a member of the Frog clan." All through her school years, in three regions of B.C., Austin was taught very little about aboriginal culture. Although her grandmother and her great-grandmother are fluent Gitksan speakers, neither of them was with Austin consistently enough to pass the language on to her, a fact she laments. Yet when the three high-school girls begin to talk about traditional aboriginal values, Austin expresses a well-articulated point of view. "Every time a teacher calls us 'Indians,' I'll put up my hand and say, 'Excuse me, we're aboriginal or First Nations, or if you must, native Indians, but we are not Indians. The only reason we're called Indians is that Columbus got lost and thought he was in India.' "

Austin's only memory of her father, an American of German and Apache heritage, was of the police coming to deport him when she was three, "but he was really abusive to my mother and used to hit her around, so she was glad to get rid of him." Bessie's mother, an alcoholic, left Hazelton, B.C., for Vancouver Island with one of Austin's many "stepfathers," leaving her daughter and son with their grandmother, Ina. Ina cared for many children with the help of her own mother, Austin's great-grandmother Eliza, whom Austin called Mamma. Though Austin recalls her Mamma with fondness, her life with her grandmothers came to an abrupt end when she was just eight years old. Austin and her brother John were apprehended by social workers after it was discovered that an uncle living with them was sexually molesting some of the children in Ina's care, including Austin.

"After that, I bounced from foster home to foster home, but I refused to let go of John; I hollered that he had to go with me no matter what, so we stuck together," says Austin. "All of the foster homes were non-native, except for once, when we were put with an auntie, but it didn't matter because we kept running away. I wanted to go home although I wasn't sure where home was. I'd go back to Mamma's." During brief periods of sobriety, Austin's mother would reclaim her children from "the welfare." Finally, she moved Bessie and her brother to Vancouver. Austin attended several Vancouver schools, trying to stay awake and learn despite her mother's chaotic, alcoholic lifestyle. "When I was fifteen, I realized my mother would never look after me properly, that I would never eat healthy with her or be able to finish high school," says Austin. "I went to ASU [the Adolescent Street Unit of what is now the B.C. Ministry for Children and Families] and signed myself into care." This time, Austin was determined to make the system work for her. "I convinced them to let me try 'independent living.' A support worker came around once a week or so and helped me buy groceries and talked to me about school and everything. She was really more like a friend." After a year, Austin convinced the social worker to allow her to live with her boyfriend, a young non-native tradesman.

Austin plans to be a social worker, or perhaps a letter-carrier; she likes the idea of fresh air, independence and exercise. There is no trace of self-pity as she talks about her life, nor does she blame her mother. "I am who I am because I want to be here and I want to succeed," she says. "My mother's made her choice to keep drinking. I always nagged her about quitting and then, about four years ago, I just stopped. It's her life." Austin understands her mother's alcoholism even as she rejects it as a choice for herself. "My mother and her family all went to residential school, where they were abused physically, sexually and emotionally," she says. Yet through all the Gitksan family's travail, Austin has emerged with a strong sense that she is loved. "I'm a strong First Nations person I think because I absolutely have always known that I was loved. As for my grandmothers, especially Eliza, I know she adored me and put me first in everything, because that's the aboriginal way. I have a great mother who taught me to be truthful and honest. Even though she's an alcoholic, I know my mom loves me with all her soul and heart." Austin believes the key for her generation is to overcome the lingering damage done by residential schools and foster homes: "For me, my goal is to figure out ways to stop it, to stop the abuse and alcohol, to prevent the stuff that happened to me from ever happening to my children."

Gaylene Henry agrees: "When you're raised in residential school or foster homes, you don't get parenting skills. Even our parents who went to public schools had to deal with a lot of racism. There's a lot for our generation to overcome, but we also have a lot more opportunities. I really want my life to be solid and settled so I can give my children the love and the cultural knowledge that I got, but also what I didn't have—safety and security." Both Henry and Austin are emphatic that they won't be ready to think about motherhood for several more years; they have their own urgent needs and goals. Says Austin: "I'm still working on bringing up myself; I just don't have the patience to work with little kids yet." Rose-Marie Francis is joyfully looking forward to the birth of her baby. Her partner has taken training as a counsellor at the Hey-Way-Noqu Healing Circle for Addictions Society in Vancouver, and Francis envisages the couple offering their combined skills to both of their First Nations in turn, without severing ties from the city where they grew up. "I guess we're a First Nations family of the future, because although both of us want to live in our home territory and stay involved there, we both know we have to live in the city to reach our education goals. We really want our child to have the best of both worlds."

To Lorna Williams, the St'at'yemc educator who is the Vancouver School Board's First Nations education specialist, these three young women represent the strong potential of aboriginal youth. Williams documented the problems aboriginal schoolchildren face in a 1993 study. Asked what kept them from staying in school in Vancouver, native students replied: "Ashamed and embarrassed to be Indian," "racism," "alcohol and drug abuse," and "no support from home." Williams, a proponent of establishing an aboriginal high school within the Vancouver school system, says such schools can be refuges from racism and the sometimes unhelpful attitudes of mainstream educators. Even more important is the positive role that a separate school could play in revitalizing the aboriginal languages and cultures that were "virtually destroyed" by the educational system.

In the decade that she has worked with the Vancouver School Board, Williams has encouraged First Nations educators, helped to develop a home-school support system and hired close to twenty school-based First Nations support workers. Five special programs are situated in regular schools to meet the needs of about 150 aboriginal children. Williams knows all about attitudes that prejudge aboriginal or immigrant children as "slow" learners. Sent to a residential school when she was only six, she recalls being placed in a class of forty-five students where the teacher assessed Williams and all except two of the other aboriginal children as mentally retarded. As an adult, Williams has become a linguist, educator and an administrator of renown.

Among Lorna Williams's most far-reaching accomplishments has been her pioneering work with Feuerstein Intensive Enrichment, a mediated learning method. FIE uses the simple "instruments" of shapes, dots and lines to help children reason both concretely and abstractly without having to puzzle through value-laden lessons. As the instruments become more difficult, the child's brain subtly increases its reasoning power, imperceptibly overcoming emotional and cultural blocks. The method is ideal for children who have suffered a cognitive loss due to trauma or have learning disabilities, language and cultural differences, or behaviour issues. FIE was created by Dr. Reuven Feuerstein, who developed the technique for children of the Jewish diaspora who had survived traumatic and tumultuous life events before they came to Israel. Williams saw instantly the usefulness of such a method to aboriginal children, who were dealing with staggering events of grief and loss in their own lives. She travelled to Israel to meet with Feuerstein, and over the years, the two educators developed a warm professional relationship, the Jewish elder sometimes coming to Canada to work with aboriginal children. "It was through

Feuerstein and his work that I began to see that I have, as a teacher, a very, very significant and powerful role in the lives of children," says Williams. "The stronger that I can make these children—to understand how to problem-solve, to make decisions and to understand their actions and behaviour—I can only make them stronger for all the things they have to contend with outside school." Williams has taught FIE to hundreds of teachers all over North America and Europe.

A First Nations graduation ceremony was Williams's brainchild. Although in 1985 only two aboriginal children graduated from high school in Vancouver, a decade later there were fifty-six. Now each June brings together a whole auditorium of bright, excited First Nations graduates to the ceremony, full of plans for the future.

In late May of 1997 about eight hundred parents, teachers and elders gathered at the Walnut Grove Secondary School in Langley, B.C., in another ceremony to honour aboriginal students, including close to a hundred Grade 12 graduates. Among the students who received awards of excellence was fifteen-year-old Karrmen Crey, Ernie Crey's second oldest daughter and a Grade 11 student who has topped the honour roll in every year of high school. Karrmen has experienced all the benefits as well as the downside of her aboriginal heritage. "It is nice to know that I'm a part of a culture so diverse, so elaborate and meticulously beautiful," says Karrmen, who appreciates "perks" such as "government education sponsorship, the cultural experience and everything therein such as art, language and history." Karrmen has also witnessed the racism and resentment directed at aboriginal people over fishing rights, "land claims" and "what people perceive as a free ride for us just because we're aboriginal." She is happy that she was raised "with full knowledge of my cultural background," but she is primarily focussed on her future, which to her lies in continuing her education. "I like learning and reading and accumulating my resources educationally. I want to keep learning so that my abilities are far-reaching," Karrmen says. "I want to know that I will be able to provide for myself in the future no matter what the circumstances. I was born with an instinct to write, but you can't survive in the woods with a pen and parchment, so I'll need something more substantial than my status card—an education and the ability to provide for myself."

Later in the same ceremony, the Pam Koczapska Award was presented to Lakahahmen community member Kenneth Lancaster, a twenty-six-year-old Sto:lo man who graduated with a biochemistry degree from McGill University in 1995 and plans to enroll in medicine at the University of B.C. Koczapska was a non-native teacher respected for her long and honourable relationship with the Sto:lo people, and the elders presenting the award also acknowledged the presence in the audience of Ernie Crey, for whom Pam remained a lifelong mentor after she briefly welcomed him to her home as a foster child.

After centuries of the compulsory surrender of their children to strangers, First Nations all across Canada have made their highest priority acquiring the legal, social and financial resources to care for their own. The Micmac in Nova Scotia and the Cree of northern Ontario have established sophisticated child and family support systems that depend on professionally trained aboriginal social workers and have strengthened cultural traditions by seeking extended family support. In Manitoba, control of aboriginal children was delegated to several aboriginal agencies in the 1970s, and today more than 90 per cent of aboriginal children needing protection in the province are placed in First Nations homes, most within their own extended family or culture.

Some of the Manitoba agencies have had to battle political interference from elected chiefs and councillors who may have a vested interest in obscuring child protection needs among their immediate family and friends. The Dakota-Ojibway Child and Family Services (DOCFS) agency in southern Manitoba was shaken to its core in 1992 by the death of Lester Desjarlais, a thirteen-year-old boy who had been tied to a tree and sodomized by a relative of the chief of his community. The perpetrator received more protection than Desjarlais, who committed suicide after he was repeatedly revictimized. A scathing indictment of the DOCFS was delivered by Judge Brian Giesbrecht, who headed a 1993 inquiry into Desjarlais's death. But Giesbrecht was also highly critical of the federal and Manitoba provincial governments, which he said had off-loaded an enormous responsibility for aboriginal social services onto Manitoba First Nations but provided meagre financial resources and virtually no professional support.

In B.C., tripartite negotiations are underway among the federal and provincial governments and at least eleven separate First Nations seeking to administer their own child and family programs. The size of aboriginal groups represented ranges from an individual band to an entire nation of twenty-five communities. The groups are at varying stages of negotiation, ranging all the way from a simple protocol that requires provincial social workers and the R.C.M.P. to notify a band social worker before entering the reserve for a child apprehension to the complete delegation of the statutory authority to apprehend children and certify foster homes.

Among the first tribal groups in B.C. to set up its own social services agency was the Nuu-chah-nulth Tribal Council, representing fourteen communities on the west coast of Vancouver Island, which in 1985 created the Usma Nuu-chah-nulth Child and Family Services Program. "Traditionally it was everyone's responsibility to protect our children because they were Usma, the most precious one, the cherished ones," notes Usma director Debra Foxcroft, who grew up on the Tseshaht reserve just outside Port Alberni, where the Usma offices are located today. Usma was a mandated agency almost from the outset; its social workers were soon able to apprehend children from homes without having to call in a provincial social worker. This authority, combined with the agency's proactive sexual abuse prevention program and aggressive child protection goals, initially provoked resentment as well as appreciation among its member communities. "It's been very hard for me as a Nuu-chah-nulth woman to work in my own community—there were times when I was threatened to my face at events that were supposed to be traditional feasts or peaceful potlatches," admits Foxcroft. After Usma had been in existence for several years, however, "the community settled down and realized we weren't there to be brown government social workers and take their children away. We put more emphasis on family support and tried to set up committees in each of the member bands to work with us."

Usma has been able to significantly improve the overall well-being of Nuu-chah-nulth children, offering parenting workshops, counselling resources and sexual abuse prevention programs. It has certified dozens of safe aboriginal foster homes for children requiring care, and returned many Nuu-chah-nulth children from all over Canada and the United States to their home territory. The agency has been able to place the majority of children in care—about sixty in 1996—in the homes of extended family members or in another community within the tribal council's mandate.

Even so, Usma has had to defend its child protection actions in at least two ongoing court challenges launched by disgruntled parents and caregivers. Although a brief produced by Usma in 1992 for the provincial legislative review panel declared that "the court system is too adversarial, intimidating and imposing," ironically the agency has had to spend time and money in court defending its own policies. "That's all part of the growing pains," Foxcroft says philosophically.

Among other First Nations proceeding in various phases to child protection authority are the Gitksan and Wet'suwet'en, the Nicola Valley, the N'laka'pamux, the Burns Lake, the Sechelt, the Cowichan, the Squamish Nation and the Sto:lo Nation. Unique among all the agreements is that of the small Spallumcheen band, which first asserted its right to control its children's destiny in a 1979 band council resolution made under the provisions of the Indian Act; the federal government has declined to challenge the resolution. Although Spallumcheen social workers, with the assistance of the chief and council, now make most key decisions about the community's children, the band has left the mandated child protection function to provincial social workers.

The Sto:lo people, as one of the tribal groups most impacted by close proximity to non-native settlement, have sought wide-ranging jurisdiction over their children, with a strong conviction that child protection must be culturally based. In the spring of 1994, the Sto:lo issued invitations, first to the community and then to the B.C. social services minister and an array of provincial and federal bureaucrats, to attend information sessions about the Sto:lo child and family services program, known as Xolhmi:lh.

"Xolhmi:lh???" the invitations read. "Say what? How is that pronounced? 'Zolmeet?' 'Ex-ol-mee-l?' 'Hoth-meeth?' 'Ha-clear your throat-meeth?'" In Halq'emeylem, the Coast Salish language of the Sto:lo, Xolhmi:lh—the last pronunciation is the closest—means the special relationship of caring, respect and love that exists between a caregiver and a child. The daytime open house was the public representation of a private ceremony that had taken place in a Sto:lo longhouse a year earlier, when the talks first began. There, according to Sto:lo custom, the name Xolhmi:lh was bestowed by Sto:lo leaders upon the honoured members of the community who would uphold the mission of the sacred undertaking: to bring Sto:lo children home and raise them in a safe, loving environment. The name was given not only to Sto:lo hereditary chiefs but also to the federal and provincial employees who had helped to negotiate the initial agreement, and to Xolhmi:lh's first executive director, Dan Ludeman, a non-native social worker.

After three years of operation, the Xolhmi:lh Child and Family Services Agency is emerging as a strong and healthy model of First Nations administration, praised by everyone from former B.C. social services minister Joy MacPhail to federal Health and Welfare administrators, including Pacific Region director Paul Kyba. Of 3,800 Sto:lo children, of whom about 1,500 live on reserve, there are about 140 children in the care of the agency at any given time, a ratio of about one in ten. "If that seems high, it's because Sto:lo people are still in recovery and a lot are still living in poverty," says Ludeman. "Also, our social workers know the community much better and are trusted more. The vast majority of children in care are there because of neglect. Neglect is a function of poverty and the fact that parenting skills skipped a generation or two with residential schools and foster care." Now, about 70 per cent of the Sto:lo children who require substitute care can be placed in approximately eighty Sto:lo foster homes; the rest are placed in non-native homes scattered throughout the Fraser Valley. The agency receives funding from the federal government at the same per-diem rate paid to provincially run foster homes, group homes or institutions.

The most recent First Nation in Canada to move towards full responsibility for child and family services is the Nisga'a Tribal Council, the first aboriginal body in British Columbia to have negotiated an agreement-in-principle for a modern treaty with the provincial and federal governments. The Nisga'a are also the first nation to sign a delegation agreement with the B.C. government under the new Child, Family and Community Service Act enacted in 1996. The signing of the initial child protection agreement on May 13, 1997, was announced in a joint press release by B.C. children and families minister Penny Priddy and Nisga'a Tribal Council president Joseph Gosnell. "This is one of the last stepping stones on the path to Nisga'a autonomy under self-government," said Gosnell. "Our mission is to ensure the physical, mental, emotional and cultural well-being of all Nisga'a children and to maintain families according to Nisga'a tradition."

Nisga'a authority will be phased in in three stages. First, while the Nisga'a develop skills and resources, they will be responsible only for preventive and support services, including foster homes. In the second phase, they will take on child protection services, including the right to apprehend children. In the third and final phase, the Nisga'a will appoint a director who will have powers and responsibilities equal to the B.C. ministry's own director of child, family and community services. Once this stage has been achieved, the Nisga'a will be well along the road to the restoration of full self-government in a contemporary context. Ultimately, the Nisga'a—and other First Nations—will be able to write and administer their own child welfare legislation.

In July 1997, the Sto:lo Nation's Xolhmi:lh Child and Family Services achieved a breakthrough in tripartite negotiations with federal and provincial governments by inking an agreement that would allow aboriginal families of any nation living inside Sto:lo traditional territory to choose to be served by Xolhmi:lh rather than by the B.C. Ministry for Children and Families. "In the vast majority of cases, aboriginal families prefer an aboriginal agency, even if it is a different First Nation, because there is a commonality of values and an understanding of the obstacles which parents have to overcome to raise healthy families," says Xolhmi:lh director Dan Ludeman. "This recognizes the right of aboriginal families to live where they choose, and should they get into difficulties while living away from home and be in need of family support, addiction counselling or temporary care for their children, they have the option of working within an aboriginal value system." Ludeman notes aboriginal people still harbour immense mistrust of the mainstream social services system; even in the face of modest reforms, memories have not faded of "the welfare" and its predatory history.

In the years to come, First Nations in B.C. and across Canada intend to negotiate full jurisdiction over their own children and those of other aboriginal families living in traditional territory, in a bid to ensure not only cultural integrity but a more efficient and humane means of serving diverse aboriginal families. In order to properly discharge their responsibilities, First Nations are adamant that they must receive the same funding levels that have been channelled to provincial governments for decades as federal reimbursement for the care of aboriginal children. Indeed, the resources need to be far greater to repair the devastating effects of Canada'a failed Indian policy on aboriginal families and to bring the health and future prospects of aboriginal children up to the level enjoyed by other Canadian children. It is here that the funds from redress or restitution are most urgently needed.

A blanket of First Nations jurisdiction covering aboriginal children all over the country would have been unthinkable in Canada at almost any point in the last several hundred years, since Europeans first began to "cultivate the young plants" of the New World. Yet it is only half a millenium since aboriginal children were the vital, cherished soul of strong societies that had endured far longer than the European nations who regarded indigenous peoples as inferior savages. Child-centred traditions never truly vanished within the collective memory of First Nations societies, and many tribes have already begun to recover—and flourish—as they restore their wise child-rearing ways. Aboriginal communities today know they face formidable challenges, but they also know that healthy, intact families are the cornerstone of self-determination. At the heart of the ongoing restoration of aboriginal communities is their hope for the future: their children.

SOURCES

As well as the publications listed below, we consulted newspapers and magazines including the *Globe and Mail*, the Vancouver *Province*, the Vancouver *Sun*, the *Toronto Star*, the *Winnipeg Free Press*, the Regina *Leader-Post*, *Maclean's*, *Saturday Night*, the Seattle *Post-Intelligencer* and the *Oregonian*; and broadcast media including CBC Radio's *Sunday Morning* and *Ideas*, and news programs on CBC Radio and Television, BCTV, CKNW, CKVU and CHEK-TV.

All interviews not credited to acknowledged or published sources are from personal interviews conducted by the authors.

Chapter 1

You Are Asked to Witness: The Sto:lo in Canada's Pacific Coast History, edited by Keith Thor Carlson (Chilliwack: Sto:lo Heritage Trust, 1997); *To:lmels Ye Siyelyolexma: Wisdom of the Elders* and *Halq'emeylem Language: Halq'emeylem Classified Word List*, by Brent Galloway, the Coqualeetza Elders' Group, the Stalo Heritage Project Elders' Group (Sardis, B.C.: Coqualeetza Education Training Centre, 1980); *The Upper Sto:lo Indians of British Columbia: An Ethno-Archaeological Review*, by Gordon Mohs (Prepared for the Alliance of Tribal Councils, 1990); *Coast Salish Spirit Dancing: The Survival of an Ancestral Religion*, by Pamela T. Amoss (Seattle, Wa.: University of Washington Press, 1978); *The Fraser Valley: A History*, by John A. Cherrington (Madeira Park, B.C.: Harbour Publishing, 1992); *Indian Healing: Shamanic Ceremonialism in the Pacific Northwest Today*, by Wolfgang G. Jilek, M.D. (Surrey, B.C.: Hancock House Publishers Ltd., 1982); *Coast Salish Essays*, by Wayne Suttles (Vancouver: Talonbooks, 1987); *The Salish People, the Local Contributions of Charles Hill-Tout, Vol. III, The Mainland Halkomelem* (Vancouver: Talonbooks, 1978); "The Children of Tomorrow's Great Potlatch," by Ernie Crey, in *The Celebration of Our Survival: The First Nations of British Columbia*, edited by Doreen Jensen and Cheryl Brooks (Vancouver: University of British Columbia Press, 1991); *Indian Slavery in the Pacific Northwest*, by Robert Ruby and John A. Brown (Spokane, Wa.: The Arthur H. Clark Co., 1993); *The Handbook of North American Indians*, general editor William C. Sturdevant (Washington, D.C.: Smithsonian Institution, 1990); *Documenting Canada: A History of Modern Canada in Documents*, general editors Dace DeBrou and Bill Waiser (Saskatoon: Fifth House Publishers, 1992); *Sqwelqwel te Sto:lo: Sto:lo Nation Newsletter*, edited by Ann Mohs (Sardis, B.C.: Communications, Sto:lo Nation, six times a year).

Chapter 2

Out of the Depths: The Experiences of Mi'kmaw Children at the Indian Residential School in Shubenacadie, Nova Scotia, by Isabelle Knockwood (Lockport, N.S.: Roseway Publishing, 1992); *Breaking the Silence: An Interpretive Study of Residential School Impact and Healing as Illustrated by the Stories of First Nations Individuals*, Assembly of First Nations (Ottawa: 1994); *Victims of Benevolence: The Dark Legacy of the Williams Lake Residential School*, by Elizabeth Furniss (Vancouver: Arsenal Pulp Press, 1992); *Residential Schools: The Stolen Years*, edited by Linda Jaine (Saskatoon: University Extension Press, 1993); *No End of Grief: Indian Residential Schools in Canada*, by Agnes Grant (Winnipeg: Pemmican Publications Inc., 1996); *Indian Residential Schools: The Nuu-chah-nulth Experience* (Port Alberni, B.C.: Nuu-chah-nulth Tribal Council, 1996); *Shingwauk's Vision: A History of Native Residential Schools*, by J. R. Miller (Toronto: University of Toronto Press, 1996); *The Oblate Assault on Canada's Northwest*, by Robert Choquette (Ottawa: University of Ottawa Press, 1995); *Chain Her by One Foot: The Subjugation of Native Women in Seventeenth-Century New France*, by Karen Anderson (New York: Routledge, Inc., 1991); *The West Beyond the West: A History of British Columbia*, by Jean Barman (Toronto: University of Toronto Press, 1991); *Indian Education in Canada*: Vol. 1, *The Legacy*, and Vol. 2, *The Challenge*, edited by Jean Barman, Yvonne Hebert and Don McCaskill (Vancouver: University of British Columbia Press, 1986 and 1987); *A Narrow Vision: Duncan Campbell Scott and the Administration of Indian Affairs in Canada*, by E. Brian Titley (Vancouver: University of British Columbia Press, 1986); *A Long and Terrible Shadow: White Values, Native Rights in the Americas 1492-1992*, by Thomas R. Berger (Vancouver: Douglas & McIntyre, 1991); *Contact & Conflict: Indian-European Relations in British Columbia, 1774-1890*, by Robin Fisher (Vancouver: University of British Columbia Press, 1977); *Reading, Writing and the Hickory Stick: The Appalling Story of Physical and Psychological Abuse in American Schools*, by Irwin A. Hyman (Lexington, Mass.: Lexington Books, 1990); *Education for Extinction: American Indians and the Boarding School Experience 1875-1928*, by David Wallace Adams (Lawrence, Kans.: University Press of Kansas, 1995); "Champlain Judged by His Indian Policy: A Different View of Early Canadian History," by Bruce G. Trigger, in *The Native Imprint: The Contribution of First Peoples to Canada's Character*, edited by Olive P. Dickason (Athabasca: Athabasca University Educational Enterprises, 1995); *Looking Forward, Looking Back*, Vol. 1, *Report of the Royal Commission on Aboriginal Peoples* (Ottawa: Canada Communication Group—Publishing, 1996); Kuper Island Industrial School: Conduct Books, Daily Diaries, Attendance Records (Victoria, B.C. Provincial Archives, Dept. of Indian Affairs and Northern Development: 1891-1907).

Chapter 3

Native Children and the Child Welfare System, by Patrick Johnston (Toronto: Canadian Council on Social Development in association with James Lorimer & Co., 1993); "Family and Child Welfare in First Nation Communities," by Andrew Armitage, in *Rethinking Child Welfare in Canada,* edited by Brian Wharf (Toronto: McClelland & Stewart, 1993); *Seen but Not Heard: Native People in the Inner City,* by Carol La Prairie (Ottawa: Aboriginal Justice Directorate and Ministry of Public Works and Government Services Canada, 1995); *Flowers on My Grave: How an Ojibwa Boy's Death Helped Break the Silence on Child Abuse,* by Ruth Teichroeb (Toronto: HarperCollins Publishers, 1997); *The Dispossessed: Life and Death in Native Canada,* by Geoffrey York (Toronto: Lester & Orpen Dennys, 1989); *Liberating Our Children Liberating Our Nation: Report of the Aboriginal Committee Community Panel, Family and Children's Services Legislation Review in British Columbia,* by Lavina White and Eva Jacobs (Victoria, B.C.: Queen's Printer for British Columbia, 1992); *Comparing the Policy of Aboriginal Assimilation: Australia, Canada and New Zealand,* by Andrew Armitage (Vancouver: University of British Columbia Press, 1995); *A Little Rebellion,* by Bridget Moran (Vancouver: Arsenal Pulp Press, 1992); *Far from The Reservation: The Transracial Adoption of American Indian Children,* by David Fanshel (Metuchen, N.J.: The Scarecrow Press Inc., 1972); *Canada's Off-Reserve Aboriginal Population: A Statistical Overview,* by the Social Trends Analysis Directorate (Ottawa: Department of the Secretary of State of Canada, 1991).

Chapter 4

Our Little Secret: Confronting Child Sexual Abuse in Canada, by Judy Steed (Toronto: Random House of Canada, 1994); *The Spirit Weeps: Characteristics and Dynamics of Incest and Child Sexual Abuse* (Edmonton: Nechi Institute, 1988); *Let the Healing Begin: Breaking the Cycle of Child Sexual Abuse in Our Communities* (Merritt, B.C.: Nicola Valley Institute of Technology, 1990); "Wounds to the Soul: The Experiences of Aboriginal Women Survivors of Sexual Abuse," by Maureen McEvoy and Judith Daniluk, in *Canadian Psychology* 36:3; *Faith Misplaced: Lasting Effects of Abuse in a First Nations Community* (Williams Lake, B.C.: Cariboo Tribal Council, 1991); *Healing Is Possible: A Joint Statement on the Healing of Sexual Abuse in Native Communities,* by Nechi Institute, the Four Worlds Development Project, the Native Training Institute and New Direction Training—Alkali Lake (Edmonton: Nechi Institute, 1988); *Child Sexual Abuse in Native American Communities* (Washington, D.C.: National American Indian Court Judges Association,

1985); *The Eagle Has Landed*, prepared by Trish Merrithew-Mercredi, Nuniyeh Consulting Services Ltd. (Edmonton: Nechi Institute, 1992); *Gathering Strength,* Vol. 3, *Report of the Royal Commission on Aboriginal Peoples* (Ottawa: Canada Communication Group—Publishing, 1996).

Chapter 5

Examining Aboriginal Corrections in Canada, by Carol La Prairie (Ottawa: Supply and Services Canada, 1996); *Bridging the Cultural Divide: A Report on Aboriginal People and Criminal Justice in Canada*, by the Royal Commission on Aboriginal Peoples (Ottawa: Canada Communication Group—Publishing, 1996); *Dancing with a Ghost: Exploring Indian Reality*, by Rupert Ross (Markham, Ont.: Octopus Publishing Group, 1992); *Returning to the Teachings: Exploring Aboriginal Justice*, by Rupert Ross (Toronto: Penguin Books Canada Ltd., 1996); *Locking Up Natives in Canada*, by Michael Jackson (Vancouver: Canadian Bar Association, 1988); *The Year in Review: 1995*, by the Native Courtworker and Counselling Association of B.C. (Vancouver: 1995); *Sex Offender Retrainer Program a Solid Success: Enters Second Year*, by the Native Courtworker and Counselling Association of B.C. (Vancouver: 1996); "Nightmare of the Shadow People," by Holly Nathan, a series of articles in the Victoria *Times-Colonist*, July 1992; *Globe and Mail* newspaper article on Hollow Water by Peter Moon, April 8, 1995; *Globe and Mail* newspaper article on Canim Lake, B.C., in January 1994.

Chapter 6

Crazywater: Native Voices on Addiction and Recovery, by Brian Maracle (Toronto: Penguin Books Canada, 1993); *Indian Givers: How the Indians of the Americas Transformed the World*, by Jack Weatherford (New York: Ballantine Books, 1988); *Fantastic Antone Succeeds: Experiences in Educating Children with Fetal Alcohol Syndrome*, edited by Judith Kleinfeld and Siobhan Westcott (Fairbanks, Alaska: University of Alaska Press, 1993); *Alcohol and Child/Family Health: A Conference with Particular Reference to the Prevention of Alcohol-Related Birth Defects*, edited by Geoffrey C. Robinson and Robert W. Armstrong (Vancouver: B.C. FAS Resource Group, c/o Sunny Hill Hospital for Children, 1988); *The Broken Cord*, by Michael Dorris (New York: HarperCollins Publishers, 1989); "Fetal Alcohol Syndrome: A Research Report for the Royal Commission on Aboriginal Peoples," by Marilyn Van Bibber (Vancouver: Unpublished background report, 1995); *Gathering Strength,* Vol. 3, *Report of the Royal Commission on Aboriginal Peoples* (Ottawa: Canada Communication Group—Publishing, 1996).

Chapter 7

Aboriginal Health in Canada: Historical, Cultural and Epidemiological Perspectives, by James B. Waldram, D. Ann Herring and T. Kue Young (Toronto: University of Toronto Press, 1995); *A Statistical Report on the Health of First Nations in British Columbia,* for Health Canada (Ottawa: Minister of Supply and Services Canada, 1995); *Aboriginal Issues Today: A Legal and Business Guide,* by Stephen Smart and Michael Coyle (Vancouver: Self-Counsel Press, 1997); *Treaty Talks in British Columbia: Negotiating a Mutually Beneficial Future,* by Christopher McKee (Vancouver: University of British Columbia Press, 1996); *Choosing Life: Special Report on Suicide among Aboriginal People,* prepared for the Royal Commission on Aboriginal Peoples (Ottawa: Canada Communication Group—Publishing, 1994); *Restructuring the Relationship,* Vol. 2, Part 1; *Perspectives of Realities,* Vol. 4; *Renewal: A Twenty-Year Commitment,* Vol. 5; *Report of the Royal Commission on Aboriginal Peoples* (Ottawa: Canada Communication Group—Publishing, 1996).

ACKNOWLEDGEMENTS

Writing this book was like embarking on a long journey. There are many people we'd like to thank who helped us along the way.

We are honoured to have been entrusted with telling the stories of Willie Blackwater; the late Julia Frank, Joyce McBryde, Glady Tenning and Faith Richardson; Sharon Blakeborough; Peter Joe; Margaret and Kandice Boudreau; and the young women who shared their goals and aspirations in Chapter 7, Bessie Austin, Rose-Marie Francis and Gaylene Henry.

We believe David Neel's sensitive portraits will help bring people's life stories alive for readers. We are grateful to George Littlechild for allowing us to use on the cover of our book his beautiful, haunting painting of his relatives in front of the Ermineskin residential school, and for sharing his remarkable life story.

We'd like to acknowledge people of the Sto:lo Nation for sharing information and providing support of many kinds: Skowkale Chief and Chiefs' Speaker Steven Point, Sto:lo Nation Education Manager Gwendolyn Point, archaeologist Gordon Mohs, historian Keith Carlson, Aboriginal Rights and Title Coordinator Clarence Pennier and Xolhmi:lh Child and Family Services Executive Director Dan Ludeman.

At the United Native Nations in Vancouver, we'd like to thank Lizabeth Hall for her valuable work on behalf of aboriginal foster and adoptive children, birth mothers and adoptive families, and the UNN's current president, Viola Thomas, for her insights and advice. Lizabeth Hall guided our search for the aboriginal birthrights of my niece Anna May Smith. The Vancouver School Board granted us generous access to Vancouver schools to interview First Nations children and teachers; the school board's First Nations education specialist, Lorna Williams, provided us with contacts, advice and context.

The North American (later National) Indian Child Welfare Association's annual conferences were a vital way for us to network with aboriginal people from all over North America. Terry Cross of NICWA and the organization's staff and board members were always helpful. Marie Anderson and her staff at the Hey'Way'Noqu Healing Circle for Addictions Society in Vancouver provided us with interviews, insights and their own personal experiences, as did Brian Chromko and his staff at the Native Courtworkers and Counselling Association of B.C. Phil Fontaine, Manitoba Cree MLA Eric Robinson, and Frank Settee and Pam Jack at Correctional Services of Canada allowed Suzanne to attend an aboriginal healing circle inside a prison and gave us their considerable wisdom on the subject.

The work of many other journalists informed us along the way; Terry Glavin was an inspiration and an example, and we shared ideas and information with Ruth Teichroeb of the *Winnipeg Free Press* and Holly Nathan, formerly with the Victoria *Times-Colonist*. I'd like to thank my employers at the Vancouver *Province* for accommodating me in a series of absences, and the Communication, Energy and Paperworkers' union contract for making such leaves possible.

We attended a host of aboriginal conferences and visited many First Nations communities. Margaret Gilbert and her sister and brother-in-law Victorine and Willie Alphonse, Sr., welcomed me into their homes and sweat-lodges at Alkali Lake and Sugarcane; their mother, Amelia Dick, gave me a bed many times in her log home at Alkali Lake. Freddy Johnson, Marilyn Belleau and Josie Johnson helped me put everything into perspective; my "buddy" Noel Johnson faithfully kept in touch with me. Shea Goodluck insisted I stay with her family and shepherded me around the Navajo reservation. We appreciate the long-standing support of our Nuu-chah-nulth colleague "Wamesh," George Hamilton, and his family. We were welcomed by people at Canim Lake, in the Similkameen, at Spallumcheen, in Gwa'Sala-'Nakwada'xw, in Nuu-chah-nulth territory, and by members of the Ktunaxa-Kinbasket Tribal Council, the Lummi Nation and many other First Nations. Their generosity in sharing their lives will stay with us forever. If not all of their names and stories appear in this book, it is due only to limitations of space; each person played a role in shaping our ideas, and we remember and honour their contribution.

We'd like to acknowledge Scott McIntyre for seeing in Ernie's life story the roots of a book, and for bearing with us throughout the lengthy process of bringing a more complex and detailed book to reality. Barbara Pulling's thorough and professional editing stood us in excellent stead. We would also like to acknowledge financial assistance from the Canada Council Explorations program.

Ernie would especially like to acknowledge Roberta and Jim Wilson of the Lummi Nation, who provided friendship and a steadfast commitment to his work in child welfare while he was president of the United Native Nations Society of B.C.; he also appreciates the members of the United Native Nations Society of B.C. who supported his efforts to change the way governments respond to aboriginal children and families. He would also like to acknowledge Chief Lester Ned of the Sumas First Nation for listening to him hold forth about child welfare in the midst of conducting "fisheries business."

From the very beginning of this book, some people were steadfastly in my corner, and it is because of them that this book finally came to be. Naida Hyde believed in me. Shirley Turcotte not only showed an unflagging faith and commitment to this book but also gave me a sanctuary in which to write, while her son Jeff cheerfully put up with me. My women's group, Heather, Signy, Mary and Vicki, were the wise "midwives" who helped bring this book into the world. My extended family in Cargary—my mother, brothers and sisters, and the much-loved next generation of nieces and nephews—are always in my heart and my thoughts. And the most important people in my life, my wonderful children, Naomi and Zev, who made many sacrifices to allow me to complete this project; and my husband, Art Moses, my comfort and mainstay in life but also my tireless editor who brought to bear his patience and professional skills in helping to read and edit the manuscript—this book is for you, because you understood why I had to remember and write about aboriginal children.

Suzanne Fournier

INDEX

STOLEN FROM OUR EMBRACE

File Hills industrial school, 58
First Nations Summit of B.C., 73, 79
Fontaine, Phil, 72, 218
Fontaine, Tim, 215
Fort Providence mission, 119
Fort Resolution, 119, 145;
Foster care, 32–9, 81, 84; abuse in, 32–3, 37–8, 42–3, 100–01, 111, 113; impact on children, 84–5, 90–1, 106–7, 110–14; sexual abuse in, 121–2, 139
Fournier, Suzanne, 9–18
Francis, Rose-Marie, 220, 221–3, 227
Frank, Julia, 93–5

Giesbrecht, Brian, 231
Gilbert, Margaret, 10, 141
Gitskan people, 73
Gitwinsihlkw, 78
Gonzaga University, 168
Goodluck, Shea, 201–4
Gordon reserve residential school, 77
Gosnell, Joseph, 234
Grand Council of Treaty 3, 153
Grant-John, Wendy, 61, 218–19
Grinstead, Const. Bob, 75
Guerin, George, 61–2
Gwa'Sala-'Nakwada'xw Council, 91
Gwa'Sala-'Nakwada'xw people, 91, 137–8

Hall, Lizabeth, 13, 104–5, 107–10
Halq'emeylem language, 5, 23, 26, 27, 135
Hardesty, Marcel, 167
Harper, Elijah, 214
Harris, Cole, 21
Healing, and traditional practices, 44, 45–6, 46, 59, 72, 75, 76, 79–80, 135, 141, 163, 164, 167–8, 194, 203, 212
Health care, 208–9
Health and Welfare Canada, 84
Henderson, Staff Sgt. Doug, 74
Henry, Gaylene, 220, 221, 223–5, 227
Henry, Mavis, 153–4
Henry, Nelson, 102, 103
Hey'Way'Noqu Healing Circle for Addictions Society, 89, 124, 154
Hill, Daisy, 89–90
History of the Canadian Peoples, 52
Hobbema, 110, 111, 113, 114
Hodgson, Maggie, 137, 168, 193
Hogarth, Douglas, 72
Hollow Water, 118, 164–8
Homosexuality, 122

Howard, Lillian, 123–4, 135
Hudson, Pete, 84
Hyde, Naida, 15

Incest. See Sexual abuse
Indian Act, 24, 54, 55, 76, 82, 83, 114, 216
Indian Affairs, 54, 87, 106, 169; and residential schools, 49, 55–6, 57–8, 61, 64, 76–7, 78, 86
Indian agents, 24, 54, 56, 82, 94, 95
Indian Child Welfare Act, 89, 92
Indian Givers, 173
Indian policies (colonial), 24, 53–4
Indian policies (federal), 9–10, 17, 18, 24–5, 30, 39, 84, 108, 109, 208, 215–16, 218, 219; and child welfare, 83, 84; and family reunification, 107, 108–9; and residential schools, 49–50, 54, 55–7, 82;
Indian policies (provincial), and child welfare, 83, 107, 139; and family reunification, 109
Indian Shaker church, 44, 79
Infant mortality, 209
Institute for Indigenous Education, 222
Irwin, Ron, 77, 78, 217

Jack, Jarry, 75
Jack, Pam, 144, 148, 151, 163
Jackson, Michael, 146
Jacob, Eva, 117
James, Randy, 79–80
Japanese-Canadian redress, 76
Jesuit Relations, 51
Jesuits, 11, 17, 50–1
Joe, Felix (family), 5
Joe, Peter, 155–62
John, Ed, 73, 74–5, 78
Johnson, Gilbert, 62, 64
Johnson, Patrick, 88
Joseph, Beverley, 79
Joseph, Carolyn, 79
Julian, Bev, 15

Katz reserve, 128
Kimelman, Edwin, 88
Kinsmen's Children's Centre, 178
Klassen, Ernie, 87
Koczapska, Pam, 33, 36, 37, 230
Ktunaxa-Kinbasket people, 176, 193–6, 204
Ktunaxa-Kinbasket Tribal Council, 193
Kuper Island residential school, 47–8, 58–62, 77, 79–80, 121
Kurtz, Father, 48
Kwakiutl people, 105–6

Pedophiles. *See* Sex offenders, Sexual abuse
Penelakut people, 59, 79
Pennier, Nancy, 136
Penton, James, 145
Peterson, K., 153
Petitot, Father Emile, 119
Phillips, Florence, 194, 196
Pierre, Sophie, 184, 193–4
Plint, Arthur Henry, 64, 66–8, 70, 71, 72, 73, 75
Poggemoeller, Mary, 87
Point, Gwendolyn (Shoyshqelwhet), 5, 7–9, 19, 44
Police. *See* R.C.M.P.
Pornography. *See* Sexual abuse
Port Alberni, 64, 71, 75
Post-Traumatic Stress Disorder, 63, 64
Poundmaker's Lodge and Treatment Centre, 116, 137, 181
Poverty, 30, 39–40, 54, 85–6, 108, 208–9
Pratt, Lt. Richard Henry, 55
Price, James Ernest, 112, 113
Priddy, Penny, 234
Prince, Lynda, 142
Prince Albert penitentiary, 90
Prisoners, 90, 145–7, 162–3, 180–1. *See also* Sex offenders
Prostitution, 122

R.C.M.P., 38, 56, 58, 133, 139–40; and residential schools, 71, 74, 75–6, 124, 141
Recollets, 50
Repatriation. *See* Child apprehension, Family reunification
Reserve system, 55
The Resettlement of British Columbia, 21
Residential School Project, 74–5, 124, 141
Residential schools, 10, 22–4, 47–80, 81, 113; abuse at, 57, 59–60, 102, 129, 157; and civil suits, 64, 71, 72, 73, 77–8; and criminal charges, 64, 71–2, 73–5, 77, 140–1; education at, 49, 56–7, 61, 62; and government policies, 50, 54, 55–7, 76–7, 78, 82; history of, 50–61; illness and death at, 49, 57–9, 60; impact of, on communities, 62–3, 82, 83, 103, 143–4, 169; protests against, 49, 57, 58, 67, 70–1, 72, 73, 83; and restitution, 63–4, 71, 73, 76–8; sexual abuse at, 47–8, 66–9, 71–80, 119–21, 129–30, 140–1, 156
Restitution. *See* Residential schools
Restorative justice, 151–4, 166–71; difficulties with, 153–4, 168, 171
Rice, Emily, 47–8, 58, 77

Rice, Rose (Rose Marie Mitchell), 47–8, 77
Rich, Katie, 116
Richardson, Faith, 93, 94, 100, 101, 102–04
Robinson, Geoffrey, 178, 179
Rodgers, Richard, 76
Roman Catholic Church. *See* Catholic Church
Round Lake Treatment Centre, 87
Royal Commission on Aboriginal Peoples, 61, 217; and alcohol abuse, 174; and justice, 154; and residential schools, 49, 61, 76, 77, 83; and social services, 183; and suicide, 210; and youth, 207, 213
Rupert's Land Industrial School, 57

Salvation Army, 78
Sand, Amy, 181
Sarcee residential school, 58
Saskatchewan, 58, 77
Saturday Night, 49
Scott, Duncan Campbell, 58
Seabird Island Community School, 135–6
Secwepemc people, 10, 14, 21, 76, 78. *See also* Shuswap people
Selkirk, 57
Sentencing circles, 152, 159–60, 160
Separation, 85
Settee, Frank, 163, 164
Sex offenders, 143–72; and prisons, 145–6, 147, 148–51, 155, 160–4, 167; and restorative justice, 151–4, 166–71; roots of, 144–5, 146, 147; treatments for, 149, 150–1, 162–71
Sexual abuse, 32, 115–42. and criminal charges, 139–41; extent of, 116–19, 121–2; in foster care, 37–8; healing from, 116, 124, 132–3, 134, 135, 136–7, 138–9, 141–2, 149; and missionaries, 118–19; in pre-contact societies, 117, 144, 161; prevention of, 136, 137, 138; within families, 108, 122–4, 126–9, 144–5, 146, 147, 151. *See also* Child apprehension, Healing, Residential schools, Sex offenders
Shingwauk's Vision, 119
Shipmaker, Earl, 87
Shuswap people, 73, 74, 86–7, 140–1, 192–3. *See also* Canim Lake, Secwepemc people
Siddon, Tom, 76–7
Sir William Macdonald Elementary School, 198–9
Sisters of St. Ann, 77, 121
Sixties' Scoop, 9–10, 30, 88, 121
Sliammon reserve, 89
Snow, Agnes, 141